WITHDRAWN

Encountering Chinese Networks

Encountering Chinese Networks

Western, Japanese, and
Chinese Corporations in China,
1880–1937

Sherman Cochran

UNIVERSITY OF CALIFORNIA PRESS
Berkeley • *Los Angeles* • *London*

University of California Press
Berkeley and Los Angeles, California

University of California Press, Ltd.
London, England

© 2000 by the Regents of the University of
California

Library of Congress Cataloging-in-Publication Data

Cochran, Sherman, 1940–.
    Encountering Chinese networks : western,
Japanese, and Chinese corporations in China,
1880–1937 / Sherman Cochran.
        p.   cm.
    Includes bibliographical references and index.
    ISBN 0-520-21625-3 (alk. paper)
    1. Business networks—China—History.
2. Industrial management—China—History.
3. Corporations—China—History.
4. Corporations, American—China Case
studies.   5. Corporations, British—China Case
studies.   6. Corporations, Japanese—China
Case studies.   I. Title.
HD69.S8C63   2000
338.7′0951—dc21   99-38446
                                                          CIP

Manufactured in the United States of America

09 08 07 06 05 04 03 02 01 00
10 9 8 7 6 5 4 3 2 1

The paper used in this publication meets the
minimum requirements of ANSI/NISO Z39.48-1992
(R 1997) (*Permanence of Paper*).

To the memory of my father
and
our native place

Contents

List of Tables

Acknowledgments

The Chinese saying, "I have given you bricks, and you have returned them as jade" (*paozhuang yingyu*), aptly conveys what friends and colleagues have done for me as I have researched and written this book. I am grateful to them all and especially to Thomas Lyons, Kenneth Pomeranz, Thomas Rawski, William Rowe, and Jonathan Spence, who have each commented on more than one draft of the manuscript. I would also like to thank Beatrice Bartlett, Cheng Linsun, Parks Coble, Hamashita Takeshi, Michael Hunt, Walter LaFeber, Robert J. Smith, Sugimoto Takashi, and Ezra Vogel for their comments. These and others who have discussed parts of the manuscript with me deserve credit for whatever jade has found its way into the following pages. I take the blame for the bricks.

My research for this book has spanned a period of growing contact between scholars in the United States and China, and thanks to fellowships from the Committee for Scholarly Communication with the People's Republic of China and the Luce Foundation for Asian Studies I have been able to benefit from this cooperation. On research trips to China, I have received sustained and learned guidance from Chen Jiang, Chen Zengnian, Ding Richu, Du Xuncheng, Feng Shoucai, Han Weizhi, Lu Xinglong, Huang Hanmin, Ma Bohuang, Ma Changlin, Pan Junxiang, Shen Zuwei, Tien Ju-Kang, Wang Qingcheng, Wang Xi, Xu Dingxin, Xu Xinwu, Zhang Xianwen, Zhang Zhongli, Zhang Zhongmin, and Zhu Hong.

I am grateful for the opportunity to have consulted unpublished documents in several different archives: in China, at the Center for Research on Chinese Business History in the Shanghai Academy of Social Sciences, Shanghai Municipal Archives, and Second National Archives (Nanjing); in England, at the British-American Tobacco Company Archives, Public Records Office, and Unilever Historical Archives; in Japan, at the Business Archives Association and Mitsui Bunko (both in Tokyo); in Sweden, at the Regional Archives (Vadstena); and in the United States, at the Cornell University Wason Collection and Manuscripts and Archives, Duke University Library Manuscript Department, Harvard-Yenching Institute Archives, Hoover Institution and Archives, and New Haven Colony Historical Society.

As a member of Cornell's History Department and East Asia Program, I have had the privilege of research assistance from several graduate students: Jiang Ningkang, Kawai Toyoko, Lu Yan, Brett McCormick, Jennifer Robertson, Tsuji Yohko, Wang Shaoguang, and Zheng Liren. They have all made stimulating suggestions and given vital help with source materials. Several staff members in Cornell's History Department have helped to put the manuscript in proper form, and Jennifer Evangelista has done the most word processing of all. Kathryn Torgeson did a professional job on the index. Sheila Levine, Rose Anne White, and Sheila Berg efficiently managed the editing and production of the book.

My greatest debt is to my family and friends. On the recent death of my beloved wife, Jan, I found myself in need of their support as never before, and I wish I had a way to repay them for rushing to my rescue. It is because of them that I have been able to finish this book.

CHAPTER I

Introduction

Corporations versus Networks

When I landed in China, I felt that someone had taken me by the heels and thrown me into the Pacific Ocean. I had to swim out. The thing was overwhelming. Here was a country of four hundred million people extraordinarily true to their civilization. . . . Their ways, unlike though they were to mine, were worthy of my respect.

My conviction, therefore, was that I ought to trade with these people as nearly as possible according to their ideas. . . . I knew that not in my lifetime could I educate a handful to my ways; I must adapt myself to theirs.

That is the word in either cigarettes or civilization—adaptability.

James A. Thomas, "Selling and Civilization"

James A. Thomas wrote these words after presiding over British-American Tobacco Company's operations in China for almost twenty years, and he expressed here a dilemma that many managers have faced on entering China's market in the present as well as the past: how to retain control over a large corporation while adapting its "ways" to Chinese "civilization." By his "ways," Thomas seems to have meant his corporation's organization and practices, and within his concept of "civilization," he seems to have included networks of Chinese merchants and workers that his company encountered in China. The relationship between these two subjects, corporations (with their "ways") and networks (in Chinese "civilization") is the subject of this book. Have Western, Japanese, and Chinese corporations in China imposed new organizations and practices and transformed existing Chinese networks? Or have Chinese networks resisted corporations' organizations and practices, causing corporations to assign or delegate authority to networks?

This book explores these questions historically by focusing on Western, Japanese, and Chinese corporations' relations with networks of Chinese merchants and factory workers during the late nineteenth and early twentieth century. Each of the chapters traces the history of one of six companies—two Western owned, two Japanese owned, and two Chinese owned. John D. Rockefeller's Standard Oil Company and James B. Duke's British-American Tobacco Company originated in the West and dominated worldwide markets to such an extent that they became known as "the Oil Trust" and "the Tobacco Trust." Mitsui Trading Company and Naigai Cotton Company also distinguished themselves—Mitsui as Japan's biggest overseas trading company and Naigai as Japan's biggest overseas manufacturer of cotton textiles. And Shenxin Cotton Mills and China Match Company became China's biggest enterprises in their industries.

In all of these cases, it is argued here, corporations encountered and interacted with networks. In theory, a corporation may be clearly distinguished from a network because one is hierarchical and the other is not. According to Walter W. Powell's theoretical distinction, hierarchical structures have "clear departmental boundaries, clean lines of authority, detailed reporting mechanisms, and formal reporting procedures"; and, networks, by contrast, emphasize "lateral forms of communication and mutual obligation."[1] But in practice, as shown in the following chapters, corporations and networks were not entirely distinct from each other. On the contrary, in every case corporations and networks crossed the boundary drawn in this theoretical distinction and readily interacted with each other in a variety of dynamic relationships that changed over time.

Before describing these interactions between corporations and networks in Chinese history, it is worth considering whether corporations and networks have followed a similar historical pattern outside China. Have Western corporations in Western history, Japanese corporations in Japanese history, and Chinese corporations in the history of the overseas Chinese all interacted with social networks? According to leading authorities on these subjects, the answer seems to be no.

ISSUES IN HISTORY OUTSIDE CHINA

Specialists on the history of Western, Japanese, and Chinese corporations outside China have all made the distinction between corporate hierarchies and social networks, and they have not viewed these hierarchies and networks as mutually interdependent. In fact, they have argued that successful corporations have developed distinctive Western,

Japanese, or Chinese ways of doing business precisely by relying on hierarchies to the exclusion of networks (in the cases of Western and Japanese corporations) or networks to the exclusion of hierarchies (in the case of Chinese businesses).

The Western path to success for corporations has been most fully staked out by the historian Alfred D. Chandler, Jr. In amply documented books on Western corporations in Western history during the late nineteenth and early twentieth century, he has argued that the successful ones proceeded from personal capitalism (based on networks) to managerial capitalism (operating through hierarchies). In a recent comparison of American, German, and British corporations, for example, Chandler has concluded that American and German firms surpassed British firms because they made this transition, abandoning "personal (nonhierarchical) management" (which British firms retained) and replacing it with impersonal "managerial hierarchies" to achieve tighter bureaucratic control over the major functions of industrial enterprises —purchasing, production, and distribution.[2] Between the 1880s and 1910s, the Western corporations that moved down this path thus acquired new "organizational capabilities" that allowed them to carry out nothing less than a "managerial revolution" in Western history.[3]

The Japanese path to success for corporations has also been discussed by historians. Several specialists on Japanese business history have noted that Japanese corporations constructed managerial hierarchies that exercised control over distribution in the market and production in the factories in Japan more closely than American corporations did in the United States during the nineteenth and early twentieth century. William D. Wray has replied to Chandler's characterization of American corporations by observing that Japanese "managerial hierarchies operated at levels lower than those in American companies. . . . By contrast [with corporate hierarchies in America], in Japan the hierarchies extended *downward into* the operating units where salaried managers served first as members and then as heads of the section within the units."[4] Kawabe Nobuo has cited examples of Japanese firms' successes at reorganizing local Japanese wholesalers into sales companies known as "distribution *keiretsu*" that acquired the "power to control wholesalers," and Yui Tsunehiko has concluded that the typical American firm kept its "managerial hierarchy . . . concentrated in the corporate head office. . . . In contrast, Japanese enterprises tended to allocate their expertise and personnel heavily to the factories."[5]

A third path has been marked out to describe how overseas Chinese businesses have achieved success. Up to now, historians of the overseas Chinese have not traced this path clearly outside China through the late nineteenth and early twentieth century (the period covered by Chandler and the Japan specialists cited above), but sociologists have done so with reference to Chinese businesses outside China in Taiwan, Hong Kong, and Southeast Asia since World War II, and they have concluded that Chinese businesses have matched Western and Japanese businesses in efficiency by depending on social networks rather than corporate hierarchies. "In the Chinese case," according to one sociologist, Wong Siu-lun, "entrepreneurs tend to dominate the market by activating particularistic ties such as regional networks rather than by building up large, impersonal corporations."[6] Other sociologists, Edward Chen and Gary G. Hamilton, have described the difference between the Chinese way and the Western way by contrasting "the network characteristics of the Chinese economy [that] are rooted in such local institutions as kinship and regionality" and the "firm autonomy in the West [that] rests upon strong states and legal institutions."[7] Under Hamilton's leadership, several scholars have participated in an ambitious comparative study of "network capitalism," and they have made a point of distinguishing between Western corporations with hierarchical organizations, on the one hand, and Chinese businesses with social networks, on the other. This distinction has been concisely summarized by S. Gordon Redding: "In many Western economies, the main efficiencies in coordination derive from large-scale organization. In the case of the Overseas Chinese, the equivalent efficiencies derive from networking."[8]

These studies of Western, Japanese, and Chinese businesses outside China, as summarized here, might seem to resolve the issue of how Western, Japanese, and Chinese businesses have differed historically from each other. Outside China, one might infer from these interpretations, businesses have succeeded in the Western way by replacing social networks with corporate hierarchies; they have succeeded in the Japanese way by doing the same with even deeper hierarchies; and they have succeeded in the Chinese way by rejecting corporate hierarchies in favor of social networks. These categorizations are neat, but they raise questions about the interpretations on which they are based. Have Western and Japanese corporations achieved success historically by using hierarchies without networks, and have Chinese businesses done so by relying on networks without hierarchies? Or have the specialists cited here adopted approaches that have caused them to underestimate the interactions between corporate hierarchies and social networks over the course of time?

In his portraits of Western corporations in Western history, Chandler has convincingly pictured them as dynamic historical actors constructing hierarchies, but he has left the impression that they have moved through time unopposed. In his descriptions of hierarchical corporations and their takeovers of family firms, he has virtually ignored resistance from family networks to these takeovers. Similarly, in his account of corporations extending direct control over marketing and manufacturing, he has chosen not to investigate social networks of local merchants and factory workers even though other scholars have questioned whether local merchants willingly acquiesced to corporations' direct control over the marketing of goods[9] and have argued that factory foremen jealously guarded their autonomy and tenaciously resisted corporations' attempts to achieve direct control over the hiring and firing of workers in the United States and Britain between the 1910s and the 1930s.[10] Chandler's numerous and well-documented examples leave no doubt that Western corporations in Western history made use of corporate hierarchies, but his interpretation also leaves open the unexplored possibility that these corporations encountered and interacted with social networks that have received little attention in his books.

Like Chandler, historians of Japanese business have concentrated on the construction of corporations' managerial hierarchies and have minimized or omitted encounters with social networks of merchants and workers. In descriptions of Japanese corporations' direct marketing in Japanese history, for example, Yui has said these corporations engaged in "piggy backing . . . on the well-used sales channels for traditional products"; Kawabe has claimed that corporations "reorganized existing wholesale systems"; and W. Mark Fruin has suggested that they "labored to establish sales channels."[11] But these historians have not characterized the social networks of merchants in the "sales channels" and "wholesale systems" or discussed the interactions between Japanese corporations and merchant networks. Among Japanese business historians, Fruin has perhaps made the strongest case for corporations' effects on workers—"the importance of enterprise policies for promoting social change in work structures and meanings"—and he has shown awareness of Japanese corporations' efforts to bring previously autonomous Japanese factory foremen and workers under managerial control.[12] Nonetheless, like other business historians, he has paid little attention to the activism of foremen and networks of workers who, according to labor historians, aggressively resisted the corporations' impositions of authority in Japan until the first years of the twentieth century.[13]

While Chandler and Japanese business historians have left the impression that Western and Japanese corporations moved unopposed through time, Hamilton and other sociologists writing about contemporary East Asia discuss businesses as though they are fixed in time. By drawing a seemingly timeless distinction between Western businesses with hierarchies and Chinese businesses with networks, they have run the risk of essentializing Western and Chinese businesses (not to mention Japanese ones). Their Western/Chinese dichotomy might easily be construed to mean that each business has been stuck with an immutable approach either as a Western firm using hierarchies or as a Chinese firm relying on networks. This distinction helps to heighten awareness of companies' predispositions toward their respective Western, Japanese, or Chinese business cultures, but it does not allow for the possibility that a corporation (regardless of whether it was owned by Westerners, Japanese, or Chinese) learned to deal with and make use of both hierarchies and networks.

In short, these interpretations of business history outside China are valuable but should not be accepted uncritically. On the one hand, they provide a convenient point of departure for this book because they delineate three approaches—Western corporate hierarchies, Japanese corporate hierarchies, and Chinese social networks—that were all adopted by corporations in China during the later nineteenth and early twentieth century. On the other hand, their delineations along these lines should not be taken to mean that businesses in China never deviated from three distinctive and unchanging ways of doing business—a Western way, a Japanese way, and a Chinese way. As shown in this book, Western, Japanese, and Chinese corporations all experimented with numerous "ways" of doing business in the course of their interactions with social networks in Chinese history.

ISSUES IN CHINESE HISTORY

Like specialists on businesses outside China, specialists on businesses in China have also distinguished sharply between corporate hierarchies and social networks. In each China specialist's choice of topic, he or she has almost invariably investigated either a corporate hierarchy or a social network, not both. Perhaps for this reason, scholars writing on this subject have produced conflicting interpretations of how hierarchies and networks affected each other in China during the late nineteenth and early twentieth century. In nearly every case, those researching corporate hierarchies have concluded that these hierarchies successfully imposed their authority on networks, and those researching networks have concluded that the networks successfully resisted hierarchies' attempts to impose authority.

In studies of Western corporations and Chinese networks, scholars have differed over the issue of who controlled the marketing of Western-made goods in China. On one side, Western scholars researching the worldwide operations of Western-based multinational corporations and Chinese scholars concerned with the effects of economic imperialism have argued that during the late nineteenth and early twentieth century Western corporations successfully introduced hierarchies to exercise control over marketing in China no differently than in other countries. Mira Wilkins, a leading specialist on the history of American multinational corporations, has advanced this argument and has cited several examples, including Standard Oil Company and British-American Tobacco Company, which are the subjects of chapters 2 and 3. "Just as in Europe, so in China," she has remarked about American businesses' adoption of direct marketing, "companies with new products took the lead." [14] While Wilkins has investigated Western managers' marketing strategies in Chinese history, the Chinese historians Wang Jingyu, Huang Yifeng, and Nie Baozhang have conducted research on how these strategies were carried out by Western corporations' Chinese compradors, and they have reinforced Wilkins's conclusions by characterizing Chinese compradors as compliant subordinates who remained under Western managers' full control (*kongzhi*) in corporations' managerial hierarchies.[15]

On the other side of this issue, several specialists on Chinese economic history have reached exactly the opposite conclusion. Never, they have maintained, did Western (and other non-Chinese) corporations in China wrest control over marketing from Chinese merchants at any time during this period. Rhoads Murphey has noted that Western businesses faced a series of formidable obstacles such as the language barrier, which they "never significantly dented," and he has concluded that on Chinese merchants' "home ground [Westerners] never . . . replaced [Chinese] as the commercial manager of the domestic market either for imports or for exports." [16] In line with this interpretation, Hao Yen-p'ing has called attention to Western corporations' limitations because

of another set of barriers—this one deriving from Chinese loyalty to social networks based on the values of "familism and regionalism." Lacking Chinese family and regional ties, Western firms could not establish
a relationship based on trust between Chinese and themselves. So, according to Hao, they delegated authority to Chinese compradors who—
far from being compliant subordinates—remained independent merchants and by no means slavishly conformed to all of the dictates of their
Western superiors in Western corporations' managerial hierarchies.[17] As
summarized by Dwight H. Perkins, the consensus among these China
specialists is as follows: "Foreign merchants . . . were never able to compete successfully with Chinese merchants on the Chinese domestic market. . . . As Chinese merchants increased their knowledge of the requirements of foreign markets and sources of supply, even foreign trade
gradually passed into Chinese hands." [18] Perkins's use of the word *never*
(which also was used by Murphey in two of the quotations cited above)
allows for no exceptions throughout the late nineteenth and early twentieth century.

On Japanese corporations in China, specialists have recently started
another debate—this one on the history of relations between Japanese management and Chinese labor. On one side of the argument, Peter
Duus has done research on Japanese management of cotton mills in
early-twentieth-century China, and he has concluded that Japanese corporations successfully reorganized and reformed Chinese workers. Using corporate hierarchies, these firms replaced a Chinese system of indirect labor recruitment (which had been carried out by Chinese labor
contractors) with a Japanese system of direct employment and training,
according to Duus. As a result, Japanese corporations were able "to
transform [Chinese] labor recruits who came illiterate, uneducated, and
'ignorant of the elements of cleanliness and sanitation' into a disciplined
work force." [19]

On the other side of the argument, Emily Honig has used documen-
tary sources and oral interviews to learn about Chinese women working
in the same cotton mills during the same period as described by Duus,
and she has concluded that the Chinese system of recruiting and training workers was emphatically not transformed by Japanese corporations. "In form, at least," Honig has acknowledged, "the Japanese had
the ingredients of a rational hiring procedure" for direct employment of
Chinese workers in Japanese-owned mills in China, but in practice the
Japanese failed to carry out this procedure. When attempting to assert
their authority, Japanese mill owners found that Chinese workers were

bound to their Chinese foremen's social networks, which were based on real or fictive kinship relations and native-place ties, and Japanese managers further discovered that Chinese foremen were connected with powerful gangs that "could mobilize the forces of a massive network" against any corporation's attempt at direct managerial control over workers. "Some mills," Honig has concluded, "tried to institute such a system [for directly recruiting and training Chinese workers] in the mid-1920's and early 1930's, but when they were not defeated by the objections of [Chinese] foremen who resented this intrusion on their power to hire workers, the [Chinese] gangs often usurped this power." [20]

In writing about Chinese businesses in China, historians have contradicted each other no less flatly. For the adversaries in this debate, the issue is whether corporate hierarchies or social networks prevailed within Chinese businesses (rather than between Chinese businesses and Chinese merchants or workers). On one side, William T. Rowe has argued in an influential history of the city of Hankou during the eighteenth and nineteenth centuries that Chinese guilds developed corporate structures that closely resembled Western ones. Citing examples of their joint-stock business partnerships and other sophisticated institutional arrangements and financial techniques, he has described these guilds as "internally constituted along increasingly nonparticularistic lines [so that they] tended to become proto-capitalist corporations." He has gone so far as to say that these Chinese guilds possessed functional equivalents of all the elements of Western-style capitalist enterprises except one, industrial production, and he has hypothesized that in the twentieth century they could easily have added it. In his words, "The 'modern' element missing from this system was, of course, industrial production. There appears to be little reason, however, to think that investment in industry could not have been subsequently incorporated into the complex financial machinery at guilds' disposal." [21]

On the other side of this debate, William C. Kirby has called into question Rowe's interpretation: "Although Rowe argues that some Chinese business organizations would have passed Max Weber's test of 'economic rationality,' this has not been the dominant view of scholarship." Identifying his own interpretation with the dominant view, Kirby has documented successive Chinese governments' legal efforts to induce Chinese businesses to adopt Western-style impersonal corporate structures during the early twentieth century, and he has concluded that Chinese businesses ignored or rejected these laws and remained committed to Chinese social networks. "With its own organizational structures and values rooted in networks of family and regional ties, what we may call a 'capitalism with Chinese characteristics' resisted the corporate structure."[22]

Each of these three issues poses a question that is addressed in this book. The question of whether Western (and Japanese) businesses ever directly marketed their goods through their own hierarchical distributing systems or always delegated authority for marketing to networks of Chinese merchants is taken up in chapters 2 through 4. The debate over whether Japanese management used its corporate hierarchies to recruit, train, and transform Chinese factory workers or deferred to networks of Chinese foremen and gangs is discussed in chapter 5. And the dispute over whether Chinese businesses adopted Western-style corporate structures or retained Chinese social networks is explored in chapters 6 and 7.

PROSPECTS FOR DOING BUSINESS

Chinese history during the late nineteenth and early twentieth century provides abundant opportunities for addressing the issues swirling around the relationship between corporate hierarchies and social networks even though Chinese society was not as technologically developed as Western society was at the time. In analyzing Western corporations in Western history, Chandler has emphasized the importance of the technological context in which these firms made the transition from personal to managerial capitalism. As first movers, they took advantage of inventions of continuous-process machinery for oil drilling, cigarette making, and other industrial purposes, and as beneficiaries of the diffusion of technology, they capitalized on new systems of transportation such as nationwide railways. Similarly, the Japan specialists cited above have either explicitly or implicitly acknowledged that Japan rapidly closed its technological gap with the West during the later nineteenth and early twentieth century, and the specialists on Chinese businesses abroad have stated or assumed that Taiwan, Hong Kong, and Southeast Asia have done the same since World War II.

Compared to these other societies, Chinese society as a whole undeniably lacked technological sophistication during the late nineteenth and early twentieth century. China did not have a nationwide railway system that would have enhanced possibilities for long-distance trade among China's nine "macroregions"—the Northeast, North, Northwest; Lower, Middle, and Upper Yangzi; and Southeast, South (Lingnan), and Southwest (Yun-Gui)—as delineated by G. William Skinner.[23] For that matter, China also lacked several other institutions often associated with the process of modern economic growth: a stable central government, a unified banking system, a standardized currency, and effective laws for registering and regulating businesses.

Nonetheless, despite China's lack of technological sophistication compared to that of the West and Japan at the time, all of the businesses described here, regardless of their national origins, operated in approximately the same technological environment in China. None of them was a first mover that benefited from technological breakthroughs in China, and all of them had access to up-to-date technology imported from abroad. Similarly, they all were affected by the absence of a nationwide railway system, the instability of governments, the complexities of multiple currencies, and the limitations of the legal system.

In this setting, Western, Japanese, and Chinese businesses all learned about new technology and incorporated it into their operations, but they did not reorganize their corporate hierarchies and deal with social networks solely on the basis of what they learned about technology. They also were motivated to restructure their businesses by the challenge that they faced on encountering Chinese society—the challenge that Thomas described in the epigraph at the beginning of this chapter. As they set up their headquarters for China in Shanghai, all found themselves in an unfamiliar business environment. Western and Japanese corporations had to adjust to a foreign setting, and even Chinese businesses were not fully at home in Shanghai, because their owners and managers, like most people in this immigrant city, were "Shanghai sojourners" whose native places were located elsewhere in China.[24] Once established in China, none of the corporations described here simply proceeded to do business as usual. These firms grew to be large, efficient, and profitable in China not only because each one conducted its business in the Western way, the Japanese way, or the Chinese way but also because they all learned to do business in other ways.

CHAPTER 2

Standard Oil Company

On January 22, 1882, John D. Rockefeller formed the Standard Oil Trust and led Western businesses down the path from personal capitalism to managerial capitalism. As characterized by Chandler, Standard Oil was "the first of the great industrial consolidations" in America and the world.[1] As early as the mid-1880s, from its headquarters at 26 Broadway in New York City, Standard Oil's "extensive managerial hierarchy began to coordinate, monitor, and plan for this global industrial empire." Its "interrelated three-pronged investment in production, distribution, and management . . . made it a first mover on a global scale."[2] In the vanguard of businesses blazing a new trail, Standard Oil adopted a policy of extending its managerial hierarchies abroad as well as at home, and it thus might well seem, in retrospect, to have set the stage for a dramatic encounter between Western and Chinese business practices in China during the late nineteenth century.

In the event, Standard Oil postponed this dramatic encounter until the early twentieth century. Although the company carried out its policy of establishing foreign affiliates in all of the world's other major markets by 1891, it did not do so in China until more than a decade later.[3] In the meantime, in China it surrendered almost all control over the marketing of its kerosene to a sole Chinese agent between 1883 and 1893, and it then took at most indirect control over marketing by delegating authority to Chinese compradors between 1893 and 1903. For these twenty years, 1883–1903, it withheld its corporate hierarchy from China and delegated authority for the distribution of its goods to Chinese social networks.

MARKETING THROUGH A CHINESE AGENT, 1883–1893

After forming a trust in 1882, Standard Oil appointed a Chinese merchant, Ye Chengzhong, to be its sole agent in China from 1883 to 1893 and left kerosene distribution for China entirely in his hands. Before 1883 Standard Oil had relied on Western trading companies to market its kerosene, which was virtually all burned in lamps for illumination in East Asia, and in the 1870s and early 1880s it had made a very sluggish start in China compared to Japan and the Dutch East Indies. As shown in table 1, by 1880 U.S. exports of kerosene (nearly 100 percent of which came from Standard Oil) included only 97,000 barrels delivered to China compared to 3.3 times more to Japan and 5.5 times more to the Dutch East Indies. By contrast, in 1885, two years after Standard Oil transferred its account to Ye, exports to China shot up to 551,000 barrels—5.7 times more than in 1880—and surpassed the amount shipped to either Japan or the Dutch East Indies. Thereafter, in the early 1890s, exports to China grew steadily, if less spectacularly.

Ye was more successful than Standard Oil's distributors in other countries because of the nature of his control over marketing in China. In analyzing the roles played by Ye and other Chinese distributors of foreign goods, it is tempting to characterize them as mere "compradors"—in-house middlemen between East and West—who were marginal figures in China's economy and society, and historians have attached this label to Ye.[4] But between 1883 and 1893 Ye reached far beyond the confines of Standard Oil's Shanghai office and managed the marketing of its kerosene every step of the way throughout at least three of China's regions—the Lower and Middle Yangzi and North China. As the historian Hao Yen-p'ing has perceptively observed, figures like Ye should be considered as at least "comprador-merchants," because "the comprador was not only a commercial middleman but also usually an independent merchant in one way or another."[5] Even this designation is not adequate as a description of Ye because it does not convey the large scale of his operation.

TABLE I.   U.S. EXPORTS OF KEROSENE
ILLUMINATING OIL TO EAST ASIA, 1870–1905
(in thousands of 42-gallon barrels)

Year	China*	Japan	Netherlands East Indies	Total
1870	11	—	6	17
1875	56	62	116	234
1880	97	323	532	952
1885	551	470	494	1,515
1890	577	902	439	1,918
1895	681	579	361	1,621
1900	1,237	1,221	267	2,725
1905	2,616	639	233	3,488

SOURCE: Anderson, "Petroleum as a Strategic Commodity in American–East Asian Relations," 13, table VI.
   * Including Hong Kong.

YE CHENGZHONG'S INTERREGIONAL TRADE

Before landing Standard Oil's account in 1883, Ye Chengzhong at age forty-three had already created a flourishing interregional chain of shops. Although wealthy at this relatively young age, he had not been heir to a family fortune. On the contrary, his family had been impoverished for several generations, and in his youth his own generation at first seemed equally ill-fated. Born in Zhenhai County, Ningbo prefecture, in 1840, he was only five when his father died, and at eight he received less than six months of formal education in a village school before going to work to help support his mother and his four sisters and brothers. Certainly no scion of an elite family, he acquired his wealth in a remarkable mid-nineteenth-century rise from rags to riches.

Like many others suffering from Ningbo prefecture's economic decline in the mid-nineteenth century, Ye set out as a sojourner to seek his fortune in Shanghai, 150 kilometers northwest of his native place. In 1853, at age thirteen, with the help of an old family friend, he became an apprentice at a grocery store in Shanghai's French Concession and began making deliveries on the Huangpu River in his employer's sampan. Within three years, he raised enough capital to open his first store, a small shop in the Hongkou district of Shanghai, and six years later, in 1862, he was able to start a larger store called Shunji Imports (Shunji yanghuo hao), which specialized in hardware (*wu jin*).[6]

From this base, Ye proceeded to build up an interregional chain of eighteen stores, all specializing in the import and export of hardware.

Figure 1. Ye Chengzhong, Standard Oil's sole agent in China, 1883–93. Reprinted from Wright, ed., *Twentieth-Century Impressions*, 565.

He identified these as chain stores by giving them names that contained "Shunji" (the name of his original store) plus a character representing the store's location; for example, his store in Hankou was known as Han Shunji, the one in Tianjin was named Jin Shunji, and the one in Nanshi, the southern district of Shanghai, was called Nan Shunji (South Shunji). In the Lower Yangzi he introduced eleven such stores, six in Shanghai and one each in Ningbo, Wenzhou, Nanjing, Wuhu, and Zhenjiang. In the Middle Yangzi he owned three, two at Hankou and one at Jiujiang. In South China he opened one at Guangzhou. In North China he had two more, one each at Tianjin and Yantai. And in Northeast China he had yet another, at Yingkou. To supply these stores, he gradually acquired a fleet of ten large junks that were seaworthy for coastal as well as riverine shipping.[7] By the time of his death in 1899, his assets were valued at between six and eight million ounces of silver (taels).[8]

Thus, despite his humble origins, Ye Chengzhong developed one of China's biggest businesses and used his stores as wholesalers and retailers to distribute Standard Oil's kerosene. He built up this chain of stores and exercised his authority over and beyond it by taking advantage of strong connections with associates from his native place.

YE'S NATIVE-PLACE TIES

If Ye's ancestors did not bequeath wealth to him, they did give him a native place that was famous for its members' financial success and subethnic solidarity. Since the tenth century his birthplace, Ningbo prefecture, had been known for producing merchants with commercial acumen and fierce loyalty to their native place, and in the nineteenth century, after Shanghai eclipsed Ningbo as a port, Ningbo merchants created an extensive network of native-place associations that dominated finance in Shanghai and managed trade between the Lower Yangzi and other regions.[9] The members of these and other native-place associations preferred to confine their dealings to fellow natives from their home localities because they spoke each other's local dialect and expected eventually to return home where the reputations of their families, lineages, and native places were at stake.[10] As an heir to Ningbo's long tradition and as a participant in Ningbo merchants' nineteenth-century networking, Ye took full advantage of his native-place connections to manage interregional distribution of Standard Oil's goods.

At the highest managerial level of his operation, Ye entrusted fellow Ningbo men with responsibility for distribution of Standard Oil's kerosene. In the Middle and Upper Yangzi regions, his Ningbo associate was Ding Shen'an. Based at one of Ye's Hankou shops, Ding took responsibility for marketing goods delivered to Yangzi River ports west of Jiujiang (leaving Yangzi ports east of Jiujiang under Ye's own supervision from Shanghai). In North China Ye assigned comparable responsibilities to another trusted Ningbo associate, Wang Minghuai. Before sending Wang north, Ye had employed Wang in Shanghai at his first import-export shop, Old Shunji (Lao Shunji), and in 1880, on opening his branch in North China at Tianjin, he sent Wang to manage it.[11]

While delegating responsibility to Ningbo men such as Ding and Wang, Ye kept their operations strictly subordinate to his own. Ye retained absolute authority in Shanghai to place all orders with Standard Oil (including those for the Middle and Upper Yangzi, North China, and other regions) and made all decisions about allocations of available supplies to every distributing point in China. He settled accounts with Ding, Wang, and other regional distributors on a monthly basis and paid them sales commissions of 2 to 3 percent. On these terms, Ye distributed Standard Oil's kerosene through his subordinates as long as he served as Standard Oil's agent, and subsequently the company retained Ding as a comprador until 1915.[12]

Ye was also inclined to recruit Ningbo men for lower-level staff positions. Favoring people from one's native place was typical of nineteenth-century Ningbo traders who, in the words of the historian Susan Mann, relied on "a close-knit and carefully controlled system for recruiting Ningpo [Ningbo] youths into trade in Shanghai."[13] In fact, even by the standards of Ningbo chauvinists, Ye ranked above the rest. Within Shanghai he aligned himself with Ningbo people by becoming a leader of Shanghai's Ningbo guild (Siming gongsuo) and by making major donations to several of Shanghai's Ningbo charities: 200,000 taels to establish an elementary school, Chengzhong Xuetang (named after himself); 20,000 taels to set up a charitable hall, Huai De Tang, to care for widows and children of deceased members of his staff; 30,000 taels for a Shanghai cemetery reserved for burials of Ningbo people; plus annual contributions to these and other charities that provided food, clothes, medicine, and coffins for Shanghai's poor.[14]

Meanwhile Ye contributed directly to his native place by building several schools and vaccination clinics, buying 400 mou of land for his ancestral temple, and donating 30,000 taels to establish a charitable hall, Zhong Xiao Tang, for housing and feeding destitute members of his own lineage. As noted by one of Ye's eulogists after his death in 1899, "His intense love for his fellow provincials of Chekiang [Zhejiang province, home of Ningbo prefecture], among whom no one ever appealed to him in vain, has made his name idolized by them."[15]

YE'S RELATIONS WITH WESTERNERS

Ye made an effort from an early age to cultivate relationships with Westerners. Before arriving in Shanghai at age thirteen in 1853, he had no preparation for dealing with Westerners, but thereafter he consciously trained himself for the task. On his first job delivering groceries in the French Concession, he began to learn pidgin English, and ten years later, in the early 1860s, after opening his first small shop, he hired instructors to teach him and his staff English, commercial law, and customs regulations at night.[16] Through this self-training, Ye learned to deal with foreigners in person and in English, and after becoming Standard Oil's agent in 1883, he regularly used his learning to protect and enhance his position, especially in holding his own against Jardine, Matheson and Company, China's leading British trading firm, which coveted the kerosene trade in general and Ye's account with Standard Oil in particular.

Although enthusiastic about selling kerosene, Jardine's was reluctant to commit itself to major oil schemes in China without Ye's cooperation. Jardine's was optimistic about the future of the kerosene trade because it was impressed by China's rising imports, especially after 1882, when a cheap kerosene-burning lamp was produced by Chinese manufacturers in Guangzhou (Canton) and sold widely in China. In a report prepared by Jardine's in 1884, its managers could barely contain their excitement over the prospects for imported kerosene:

> The chief portion . . . is due to provincial demand, 511,770 gallons having been sent into the interior under transit pass (1/2 of import duty), of which 380,780 were sent by Chinese. The above facts are remarkable as showing no prejudice against the foreign origin of any article will prevent a ready sale, provided its price, quality and general utility show it is adapted to the wants and purses of the most numerous class of consumer.[17]

Eager to make this "ready sale," Jardine's presented a series of proposals to Ye.

Ye commanded deference from Jardine's such that his endorsements confirmed some proposals and his opposition killed others. In the mid-1880s, for example, as soon as he consented to a joint account with Jardine's, it was used to import as much as 380,000 gallons of kerosene per annum. Then, early in 1890, when he vetoed a plan by John Macgregor of Jardine's to import refined oil from the United States, it was promptly dropped. By the same token, later in the year when he agreed to buy stock in the proposed London & Pacific Petroleum Company through which Jardine's intended to develop oil-bearing property in Peru, this new firm was established and put into operation, albeit only briefly, until 1894.[18]

In each of these cases, Ye demonstrated his capacity to prevail over the foreign managers of the most powerful Western trading company in China. In addition, this evidence points to the conclusion, as Edward LeFevour has observed in his study of Jardine's, that Ye's "hold on the kerosene market in China was usually unchallenged in the eighties and nineties."[19] During these two decades, Ye's net profits from the sale of Standard Oil's kerosene amounted to more than 100,000 yuan per year.[20]

YE'S DISMISSAL AND LEGACY

Despite Ye's iron grip on China's kerosene market during his ten years as Standard Oil's sole agent, the company finally fired him. It dismissed him on the grounds that he and his Chinese associates had abused their credit privileges and had committed fraud.

Since becoming an agent for Standard Oil, Ye had perennially violated the company's rules. For example, he had regularly taken advantage of its policies to gain more access to liquid capital than the company allowed. Whereas he was given a grace period of 90 to 100 days between his acceptance of goods and his payment for them, he gave his agents a grace period of only 25 to 30 days and used the credit during the interim to finance his own investments.[21]

After repeatedly complaining about Ye's financial manipulations, the company was prompted to act in 1893. In this instance Ye hoarded kerosene while the company's price was low, sold it at a higher price after market demand had risen, and pocketed the difference between the company's specified retail price and the actual sales price. Exasperated with Ye and determined to widen its Chinese sales force beyond his network, Standard Oil refused to renew his appointment.[22]

As soon as Ye was fired, Jardine's jumped at the chance to take his place as Standard Oil's agent. "The [Jardine] firm's interest in kerosene is now quite a full one," one of Jardine's executives wrote privately to another in 1893,[23] and in the same year Jardine's presented to Standard Oil a comprehensive plan that would have made it the sole agent throughout Asia for both Standard Oil and one of Standard Oil's affiliates, American Tidewater Company. But once Standard Oil ceased to rely on Ye, it finally began to consider extending its own worldwide marketing system to China. After negotiating for nine months, it declined Jardine's offer.[24]

MARKETING THROUGH CHINESE COMPRADORS, 1894–1903

Between 1894 and 1903 Standard Oil faced its first serious competition in China, but it responded to the challenge by creating only a small-scale marketing system there. In 1893 it belatedly extended its administration for worldwide marketing into China, assigning responsibility for China (and the rest of Asia) to Standard Oil of New York, and this subsidiary, in turn, set up the company's first offices and appointed its first Western salaried sales representatives in China. But these Western sales representatives did little more than transfer responsibility for marketing from Ye Chengzhong to Chinese compradors. The superficiality of this change was evident in the contrast between Standard Oil's approach and the more aggressive tactics of its new rivals for China's market.

STANDARD OIL'S MARKETING SYSTEM

Between 1894 and 1903 Standard Oil continued to rely on no more than a handful of Western salaried representatives in China. In 1893, on dismissing Ye Chengzhong, it hired British merchants in Shanghai and Hong Kong, provided them with minimal logistical support, and found that they, in turn, delegated authority to Chinese compradors in those two cities and to a foreign trading company in Hankou.

In Shanghai Standard Oil chose as general manager of its China head-quarters an Englishman named Henry J. Everall. In residence at Shanghai since the 1880s, Everall had studied the Chinese language and had worked in Shanghai for the American Trading Company—a firm later characterized by Standard Oil's in-house magazine as the "repository from which so many of the Company's North China pioneers were drawn."[25] Like other foreign general managers of trading companies, Everall hired a Chinese comprador as a salaried employee to recruit other Chinese employees for the firm and to guarantee their personal integrity and business transactions.

Perhaps in reaction against Ye, Everall did not recruit compradors from Ye's native Ningbo. Instead he turned to Shanghai's other leading merchant group, the Cantonese from Xiangshan (later known as Zhongshan), a coastal county that contained Macao and was near Hong Kong and Guangzhou in South China. If Everall expected to avoid the kind of favoritism that Ye had shown toward family and native place, then he was mistaken to choose the Cantonese from Xiangshan.

Between the 1860s and the 1890s, they had come to dominate the ranks of Shanghai's compradors by recommending family members and native-place associates to foreign firms, and, on their retirement, they had regularly bequeathed their own positions to relatives and other Xiangshan men. In fact, they had become so dominant that the very term "Xiangshan men" was used in the late nineteenth century to designate "the comprador class."[26]

Whether or not Everall was aware of the Cantonese compradors' network of family members and native-place connections, he enmeshed Standard Oil in it by seeking advice from Wei Wenpu, a leading Xiangshan man who by the 1890s had long served as comprador for one of Shanghai's oldest Western-owned financial institutions, the Chartered Bank of India, Australia, and China. Predictably, Wei recommended Chen Yichi, who was Wei's own son-in-law and the son of another well-connected Xiangshan comprador, Chen Shutang (a.k.a. Asong). In 1894, although Chen was only twenty-four years old at the time, Everall accepted Wei's recommendation, appointed Chen comprador, retained him throughout the late 1890s and early 1900s, and thus made Standard Oil's Shanghai office as dependent on a social network of Xiangshan compradors and distributors as it had previously been on Ye's social network of Ningbo merchants.[27]

Outside Shanghai Standard Oil's marketing system for China had only one other office before the early twentieth century. Located in Hong Kong, it, like the one in Shanghai, was opened in 1894 as a regional office (qu hang) with a Western general manager who depended for marketing on a Chinese comprador, Huang Zhaotang. Known as the Hong Kong and South China Branch, this office was responsible for sales in Southeast, South, and Southwest China, whereas the Shanghai office, known as the Shanghai and North China Branch, covered all of the rest of the country except the Middle and Upper Yangzi.[28]

In the Middle and Upper Yangzi regions, Standard Oil had no office of its own, entrusting its distribution there to the Hankou office of C. Melchers and Company. This firm was well positioned to market Standard Oil's product because it had opened offices in Hong Kong in 1866, in Shanghai in 1877, and in Hankou in 1884 and had become the biggest German-owned trading firm in China during the late nineteenth century.[29] Like other German trading companies, Melchers specialized in opening China's market to newly introduced products,[30] and in Hankou it promoted kerosene by taking daring measures not tried by Standard Oil's own offices. For example, after evaluating Chinese commercial houses and designating sales territories for them, it confirmed their appointments as distributing stores (*jingxiao dian*) by boldly allowing each to take a certain amount of kerosene without making a security deposit. Besides granting credit, it protected the sales stores against price fluctuations between the time of kerosene delivery and the settlement of accounts. If prices rose in the interim, Melchers allowed distributing stores to pay the original (lower) price for the goods, and if the price fell, it allowed them to pay the current (also lower) price. Melchers' commissions to these Chinese distributing stores varied according to each one's volume of business and location and ranged between 2 and 5 percent.

To enhance the Chinese stores' appeal to customers, Melchers advertised widely, putting up posters, painting walls, handing out colored cards, and selling cheap German-made wall lamps (*chiang deng*). In Melchers' territory it identified Standard Oil's kerosene with its home country of Germany by labeling the product "German" and thus implied (misleadingly) that it produced as well as distributed the goods. As a Chinese former employee of Standard Oil later recalled, Melchers' sales techniques "stimulated great interest at Standard Oil," and it retained this German trading company as its agent in the Middle and Upper Yangzi until 1912.[31]

Although Melchers' Hankou office was more innovative than Standard Oil's offices at Shanghai and Hong Kong, the combined efforts of all three did not increase the company's sales in Hong Kong and China as fast as its sales were rising worldwide. As shown in table 2, between 1884 and 1894, under Ye's agency, Standard Oil's sales in China as a percentage of its worldwide exports had jumped from 3.5 to 11.3 percent and had risen in Hong Kong from 3.2 to 7.8 percent. Between 1894 and 1903, by contrast, despite its investments in marketing, the company's worldwide exports to China and Hong Kong between 1899 and 1903 slipped downward to an average of 8.8 and 6.6 percent respectively. Meanwhile, as the share for China of Standard Oil's worldwide sales diminished, the American company faced a challenge there from European oil companies.

EUROPEAN OIL COMPANIES AND THE INTRODUCTION OF BULK DISTRIBUTION

In the late 1890s, compared to American-owned Standard Oil, European oil companies introduced new and more effective techniques for

Year Ending June 30	Hong Kong		China		Hong Kong's and China's Combined Share of U.S. Worldwide Exports	
	Million Gallons	Thousand Dollars	Million Gallons	Thousand Dollars	% of Gallons	% of Dollars
1874	0.0001	0.1	0.83	196	.4	.5
1875	0.25	47	2.12	411		
1876	0.27	52	0.94	177		
1877	0.22	54	1.34	318		
1878	0.58	98	3.67	597		
1879	0.39	46	5.44	690	1.7	2.0
1880	0.49	57	3.58	366		
1881	1.67	205	4.55	555		
1882	3.71	412	9.68	1,064		
1883	4.22	460	6.09	639		
1884	4.86	505	8.38	836	3.2	3.5
1885	7.73	714	15.42	1,455		
1886	6.82	614	26.27	2,417		
1887	2.81	240	7.26	635		
1888	4.47	421	10.73	1,046		
1889	6.72	641	9.85	907	3.3	4.0
1890	11.15	1,137	13.07	1,251		
1891	10.81	1,040	27.16	2,586		
1892	16.53	1,304	17.37	1,249		
1893	12.76	804	27.87	1,808		
1894	16.89	1,020	40.38	2,436	7.8	11.3
1895	10.56	819	18.02	1,175		
1896	10.50	876	25.69	2,159		
1897	14.98	1,146	42.52	3,353		
1898	15.64	967	44.32	2,839		
1899	*18.20	*1,399	22.68	1,791	5.6	7.8
1900	*19.44	*1,985	32.78	3,266	7.2	9.4
1901	*18.93	*1,698	27.42	2,388	5.9	7.9
1902	*18.47	*1,586	56.70	4,759	8.9	11.9
1903	*17.44	*1,622	19.32	1,776	5.3	7.2
1904	*22.69	*2,566	*41.09	*4,729	8.6	10.6
1905	18.66	1,741	89.47	8,187	13.1	17.7
1906	5.56	526	54.38	4,181	6.9	8.7
1907	12.05	1,169	77.91	5,843	10.1	12.5
1908	11.11	979	103.74	8,499	11.0	13.4
1909	10.37	889	87.01	7,112	9.0	11.2

(continued)

TABLE 2   (*continued*)

Year Ending June 30	Hong Kong		China		Hong Kong's and China's Combined Share of U.S. Worldwide Exports	
	Million Gallons	Thousand Dollars	Million Gallons	Thousand Dollars	% of Gallons	% of Dollars
1910	12.69	933	65.82	5,015	7.8	9.5
1911	12.07	911	107.17	6,644	11.7	13.1
1912	14.79	1,094	78.16	4,824	7.9	9.9
1913	7.77	740	79.02	5,762	8.3	9.8
1914	20.09	1,322	86.01	6,349	9.2	10.3
1915	24.66	1,296	86.91	5,178	12.6	12.1
1916	16.86	1,218	90.79	5,737	13.1	13.3
1917	21.01	1,276	80.62	4,925	12.2	11.3
1918	8.05	588	40.64	2,882	9.2	7.3
1919	16.33	1,518	92.24	8,221	15.0	12.0
1920	26.36	3,736	164.64	19,078	20.9	18.1

SOURCES: U.S. Department of Commerce and Labor, Bureau of Statistics, *Monthly Summary of Commerce and Finance of the United States* (title varies), May 1896, 1459, 1474; 1904, 2432–33; June 1904, 4896; June 1907, 2532–33; June 1910, 2194; June 1913, 1360–61; June 1916, 41; June 1919, 53; June 1920, 50; Williamson and Daum, *The American Petroleum Industry*, vol. 1, 742, 752; Hitchcock, *Our Trade with Japan, China, and Hong Kong, 1889–1899*, 121, 166; Rosenthal, "The China Market, Myth or Reality?" 8–9.

Note: Until the turn of the century Standard Oil contributed about 90 percent of total American kerosene exports; thereafter its share declined. But nearly 100 percent of U.S. kerosene exports to Hong Kong and China were made by Standard. Therefore, the percentages given in this table understate the Chinese proportion of Standard Oil's export business. Moreover, from about 1910 on the amount of American (Standard) kerosene imported into China exceeded declared exports to China by a wide margin. Some of the oil that Standard sold in China was originally invoiced for other destinations such as Singapore and Japan.

* Includes small quantity of lubricating oil.

supplying kerosene to China. As shown in table 3, in 1889, with the arrival of the first imported kerosene from Russia, the United States had ceased to be China's sole supplier of kerosene, but before the company's dismissal of Ye Chengzhong and its installation of its own marketing system in 1893, the American share had still amounted to a full three-fourths of the market. Between 1895 and 1904, by contrast, as kerosene began reaching China from Sumatra as well as Russia, the American share dropped from 75 percent to an average of 45.8 percent per annum.

Since Standard Oil supplied almost 100 percent of the kerosene exported from the United States to China throughout the period, this decline in the American share deeply concerned the company's management. In 1897 W. H. Libby, Standard Oil's well-traveled troubleshooter for overseas operations, suggested trying "almost anything that would foreshadow and advertise some new and aggressive Eastern policy." [32] In the same year one of his colleagues, F. Q. Barstow, grumbled, "Every day makes the situation more serious and dangerous to handle," and he predicted, pessimistically, "If we don't get control of the situation soon, the Russians, Rothschilds [a Paris-based combine that dominated oil production in Russia], or some other party may." [33] In fact, by 1897 two of Standard Oil's rivals had already begun to "get control of the situation" in China.

One of these rivals, Marcus Samuel of the English trading firm M. Samuel and Company, was the first to introduce bulk distribution of kerosene into China. In the early 1890s Samuel had cut the costs of handling and transportation in Asia by shipping kerosene in tank steamers, railroad tank cars, and horse-drawn tank wagons and by storing it in tanks installed in Asian cities. In 1891 he had won from the Rothschilds a ten-year contract that had allowed him to distribute their Russian oil as long as he sold it east of Suez. The next year, 1892, he had convinced operators of the Suez Canal to lift the ban on the shipping of bulk oil through the canal, and by the end of 1894, this Russian bulk oil had been carried to China by tank steamers and pumped into newly built storage tanks in the coastal ports of Shanghai, Xiamen, Shantou, and Hong Kong. Under the management of Samuel's affiliate, Arnhold, Karlberg and Company, this Russian bulk oil became available on arrival in China at two-thirds the price of Standard Oil's kerosene. [34]

Samuel gained this price advantage over Standard Oil in China because in the nineteenth century the American company shipped bulk oil in tank steamers only to Europe. In the 1890s (as in the 1870s and 1880s) it continued to transport all of its exports to Asia in wooden cases that each contained two five-gallon tins of kerosene. Although Samuel was initially surprised to discover that Chinese wholesalers greatly valued Standard Oil's wooden cases and tin cans and refused to supply their own containers, he overcame this problem by building canneries in several Chinese ports where Chinese workers had the task of transferring kerosene from large tanks to small tins. [35]

Immediately after Standard Oil's kerosene monopoly in China was broken by this English trading company, the American firm was also challenged by a Dutch firm, Royal Dutch (an English translation of Koninklijke, an abbreviation of Naamlooze Vennootschap Koninklijke

TABLE 3.   CHINESE IMPORTS OF KEROSENE ILLUMINATING OIL, 1886–1920

Year	United States Million Gallons	United States % of Total	Russia Million Gallons	Russia % of Total	Sumatra Million Gallons	Sumatra % of Total	Borneo Million Gallons	Borneo % of Total	Japan Million Gallons	Japan % of Total	Total Million Gallons
1886	23.0	100.0									23.0
1887	12.0	100.0									12.0
1888	16.6	100.0									16.6
1889	13.0	72.5	5.7	27.5							20.7
1890	23.6	76.6	7.2	23.4							30.8
1891	39.3	79.7	10.0	20.3							49.3
1892	31.9	78.8	8.6	21.2							40.5
1893	36.7	73.4	13.3	26.6							50.0
1894	51.7	73.7	18.0	25.6	0.5	0.7					70.2
1895	23.1	44.3	26.6	51.1	2.4	4.6					52.1
1896	33.5	50.0	28.3	92.2	5.2	7.8					67.0
1897	48.2	48.5	36.9	37.2	14.2	14.3					99.3
1898	50.1	51.7	19.9	20.5	26.9	27.8					96.9
1899	40.7	46.0	35.7	40.4	12.0	13.6					88.4
1900	34.4	41.2	32.7	39.2	16.4	19.6					83.5
1901	57.8	47.7	22.5	18.6	40.6	33.5	0.2	0.2			121.1
1902	43.3	49.3	10.1	11.5	33.8	38.4	0.7	0.8			87.9

Year											
1903	31.1	36.5	13.5	15.9	39.9	46.9	0.6	0.7			85.1
1904	67.1	43.0	32.6	20.9	55.9	35.9	0.3	0.2			155.9
1905	80.0	52.5	12.7	8.3	48.5	31.9	11.1	7.3			152.3
1906	62.9	48.9	0.0	0.0	38.8	30.2	26.9	20.9			128.6
1907	95.6	59.3	0.7	0.4	39.1	24.2	25.9	16.1			161.3
1908	121.7	65.4	2.8	1.5	43.5	23.4	18.0	9.7			186.0
1909	84.0	47.6	3.6	2.3	43.4	29.8	14.7	10.1			145.7
1910	96.1	60.0	2.2	1.4	42.8	26.7	19.0	11.9			160.1
1911	157.5	66.8	2.8	1.2	49.5	21.0	26.0	11.0			235.8
1912	123.4	62.6	4.0	2.0	47.3	24.0	22.4	11.4	0.02 insig.		197.1
1913	112.5	61.1	6.0	3.3	41.9	22.8	23.6	12.8	0.03 insig.		184.0
1914	162.4	70.6	7.2	3.1	37.5	16.3	22.6	9.8	0.5	0.2	230.2
1915	128.9	69.7	0.9	0.5	30.1	16.3	23.9	12.9	1.2	0.6	185.0
1916	108.8	74.6	1.0	0.7	19.2	13.2	10.4	7.1	6.4	4.4	145.8
1917	107.4	68.6	0.3	0.2	33.6	21.5	9.8	6.2	5.4	3.5	156.5
1918	48.2	43.7	0.0	0.0	8.5	44.0	11.7	10.6	1.9	1.7	110.3
1919	157.3	79.5	0.0	0.0	33.6	17.0	6.4	3.2	0.6	0.3	197.9
1920	140.7	74.5	0.9	0.5	37.3	19.8	9.5	5.0	0.4	0.2	188.8

SOURCE: Rosenthal, "The China Market, Myth or Reality?" 17–18.

Nederlandsche Maatschappij tot Exploitatie van Petrleumbronnen in Nederlandsch-Indie). Like Samuel, Royal Dutch transported oil in bulk using tank steamers, and it added an organizational innovation by operating these steamers within a comprehensive wholly owned industrial consolidation. Hence, from the oil's point of origin in Sumatra to the kerosene's distributing points in China (and other countries), Royal Dutch kept procurement, refinement, transportation, and distribution under its ownership. Reducing transportation costs to China was easier for Royal Dutch than for Standard Oil, because, as noted by Henri Deterding, Royal Dutch's sales manager in the late 1890s, "compared with Pennsylvania, Sumatra and Java was 'just around the block' from Shanghai and Hong Kong." [36]

More difficult, Deterding recognized, was the task of lowering the cost of local distribution within Asia, and he gave it top priority. "The first step I want to take," the thirty-year-old Deterding announced on assuming his position with Royal Dutch in 1896, "is replacing the [Singapore] Straits agents by private employees. . . . I am thinking of a larger and better-regulated sale." [37] In China, as in the Straits settlement, he assigned salaried employees to replace trading companies as managers of kerosene transactions, and by the end of 1897 he established offices in several Chinese cities—not only Shanghai and Hong Kong but also Hankou, Zhenjiang, Tianjin, Fuzhou, Xiamen, and Shantou.

Under Deterding's management, Chinese imports from Sumatra doubled in 1897 and again in 1898, bringing Royal Dutch no less than one-third of China's kerosene trade by 1901. This meteoric rise prompted Standard Oil to dispatch two of its top executives to Asia to investigate, and from them the American company received confirmation of Royal Dutch's remarkable record. "In the whole history of the oil business," the awed Americans reported to their superiors at Standard Oil's headquarters in New York, "there has never been anything more phenomenal than the success and rapid growth of the R. D. Co." [38]

If Standard Oil was troubled by Royal Dutch and Marcus Samuel as separate threats in the late nineteenth century, it felt still greater competitive pressure when its two rivals joined forces in the first years of the twentieth century. Between 1900 and 1902, while they were still separate, Standard Oil tried to drive them out of the market by cutting prices. As C. M. Pratt of Standard Oil bluntly stated the company's strategy, "We want to keep and enlarge the gallonage rather than increase profits." [39] But this strategy backfired. Not only did it bring down Standard Oil's own profits (resulting in book losses for the company in China and other Asian markets during 1901 and 1902), it also caused Samuel (by then head of Shell Transport and Trading Company) and Royal Dutch to band together with each other and with Rothschilds to form a joint marketing company, the Asiatic Petroleum Company (APC), which was responsible for distributing all three oil companies' kerosene in competition with Standard Oil throughout Asia.[40]

ASIATIC PETROLEUM COMPANY'S DISTRIBUTION

On June 27, 1902, APC was formally established. It immediately made a bid for control of China's market by recruiting Chinese distributing agents who operated on a grander scale than those carrying Standard Oil's kerosene. In its new marketing system for China, APC invested at least three million British pounds sterling—two million through its China headquarters, which were set up at Shanghai, plus another million through its office in Hong Kong.[41] APC drew on this financial backing to recruit Chinese compradors and agents who resembled Standard Oil's earlier sole agent, Ye Chengzhong. Just as Standard Oil had left distribution first in Ye's hands and subsequently in compradors' hands, so too did APC distribute through a combination of Chinese compradors and agents.

In APC's headquarters at Shanghai, it hired a comprador, Tao Bingjun, who was strikingly similar to Ye. Like Ye, Tao took advantage of ties to family and native place. Tao hailed from Ningbo, Ye's home, and hired two of his sons and several of his other relatives as staff members in APC's Shanghai headquarters. When he retired, he bequeathed his job to his son, Tao Tingyao.[42]

Outside Shanghai, APC similarly allowed its Chinese sales agents (*daili chu*) to rely on their own social networks. Its single biggest agent, Fu Shaoting, for example, was permitted to recruit other sales agents and set the boundaries of his sales territory according to his own specifications. Like Tao in Shanghai, Fu assigned APC positions to family members—brothers, cousins, and other relatives—and extended his marketing throughout all of Jiangxi province and half of Hunan province, with distributing centers in the cities of Zhangshu and Ji'an.[43]

In China's other regions, merchants held sales territories of comparable size.[44] According to a Chinese former APC employee, these merchants typified APC's sales agents: "APC usually recruited commercial

agents [*daili shang*] who were Chinese merchants [*xing shang*] running
big commercial firms [*banzhuang*]. For them, selling kerosene was only
a sideline. APC took advantage of their preexisting economic status."[45]
Taking APC's kerosene as a mere "sideline," these Chinese merchants
distributed it along with a variety of other consumer goods: hardware
(as Ye had done earlier in distributing Standard Oil's kerosene), groceries (*za huo*), grain, soy sauce, pickles (*da jiang yuan*), imported yarn
(*yang sha*), or imported flour (*yang fen*). Not until later did Chinese
agents begin to specialize in kerosene, and even then they generally carried four additional products—cigarettes, matches, candles, and soap
—which caused their firms to be known as the Five Foreign Goods
Shops (*wu yang zi hao*).[46]

To win cooperation from the Chinese merchants, APC offered a range
of benefits. It paid commissions on sales of 2 to 4 percent, and it covered
all expenses in each merchant's locality for the salaries of APC's employees, the rentals of local offices and storage tanks, and the administrative expenses for clerical supplies and postage. In addition, APC lent
prestige, which, according to one Chinese observer, served as an important attraction to some of APC's early agents: "These merchants did not
benefit much from their work for APC. But they thought they got face
[*you mianzi*] when they landed an account with the big foreign company."[47] APC also attracted Chinese agents by requiring them to abide
by no rules except that they make cash deposits, which varied in amount
according to the volume of each agent's business. Otherwise APC left
its Chinese agents free to rely exclusively on social networks of family
members and native-place associates and to expand their sales territories however they wished even at the expense of other APC agencies.

By offering this combination of high material incentives and minimal
supervisory restrictions, APC quickly enlisted many of China's leading
merchants as agents and captured a large share of the country's kerosene
market. Pleased with these initial results, APC thereafter routinely re-
newed the contracts of its Chinese sales agent and consistently retained
the policy of nonintervention in their business practices.[48]

APC and the European oil companies that owned it thus posed a direct challenge to Standard Oil in China at the turn of the century. Their
investment in bulk distribution in Chinese cities and their recruitment of
Chinese sales agents throughout the country gave them greater market
access than Standard Oil enjoyed at the time. In light of this record and
Standard Oil's shrinking market share, it is hardly surprising that Ralph

W. Hidy and Muriel E. Hidy, in their history of Standard Oil's worldwide operations, have assessed the company's efforts to market goods in
China between 1894 and 1904 as "relatively ineffectual."[49]

MARKETING THROUGH A CHINESE "NATIVE STAFF," 1903–1914

Shortly after the turn of the century, Standard Oil rebounded from its
failures in China and made an aggressive bid to regain predominance
there. Between 1903 and 1914, as Standard Oil's vice president, W. E.
Bemis, noted at the time, it created a new marketing system in China by
investing no less than U.S. $20 million—as much as it spent in all the
rest of Asia combined.[50] Not only did it build a physical plant for bulk
distribution on a far grander scale than Samuel, Royal Dutch, and APC
had done. It also set out to transform its Chinese agents' social networks
by imposing rules that were to be enforced by newly recruited Western
and Chinese salaried employees. In other words, it tried to overcome its
European rivals by extending its corporate hierarchy deeply into China's
market for the first time.

BULK DISTRIBUTION NATIONWIDE

To establish an infrastructure for its Western and Chinese employees,
Standard Oil installed in China a physical plant consisting primarily of
storage tanks, canneries, and tankers. The company built the tanks and
canneries and sailed the tankers in all of China's nine regions, and it concentrated them most heavily in cities at the cores of the country's richest
and most populous regions.[51]

For its storage tanks outside treaty ports, Standard Oil had no legal means of acquiring property because China's treaties with Western
countries barred foreigners from buying Chinese land except in designated "concessions" within treaty ports. To circumvent this provision,
the company used senior Chinese staff members or commission agents
(*jingli*) as dummy fronts. Outside foreign concessions, it had a Chinese
buy land in his own name, submit the deed to the company's legal department in Shanghai, and sign a "lien form" saying that as a debtor he
had mortgaged the land to the company, his creditor. By these means the
company documented its claim to property outside treaty ports where it
built storage tanks, warehouses, offices, and other buildings. In areas

where it had not yet established contacts with Chinese agents, it persuaded Western consuls and missionaries to recruit Chinese to buy land on its behalf.[52]

To supply and draw on this network of storage tanks, Standard Oil launched its own fleet and constructed its own canneries. From the United States, it exported kerosene to China in large steel tank steamers capable of docking in coastal and riverine deep-water ports. To reach tanks in less accessible Chinese cities, it transferred the kerosene onto its own low-draft steamers, iron and wooden barges, railway tank cars, and motor tank trucks. Of all these vehicles, perhaps the most famous were its riverine vessels, which numbered in the hundreds—several times more than those of the leading Chinese shipping firm, China Merchants' Steam and Navigation Company. Like Standard Oil itself, these ships had Chinese names that began with the Chinese character for "beautiful" (*mei*), which can also mean "American": the *Meifu, Mei'an,* and *Meiping* on the lower reaches of the Yangzi River; the *Meichuan, Meitan, Meixia,* and *Meilu* on the Chuan River in the Upper Yangzi region; the *Meiyun* and *Meiying* on smaller waterways.[53] From the tanks, Standard Oil's canneries in China drew kerosene that was poured into five-gallon cans and then packed into wooden cases, two cans per case. To reach cities lacking canneries, Standard Oil loaded cases onto ships, junks, sampans, pack animals, and other forms of conveyance.

With the benefit of this logistical infrastructure, Standard Oil gained access to all parts of China. To manage distribution wherever its tanks were located, it recruited Western—mainly American—sales representatives.

RECRUITING WESTERNERS FOR CHINA

When asked by American newspaper reporters in 1913 what had been the key to Standard Oil's marketing strategy in Asia, one of the company's American executives in New York replied, "Superior manufacturing and distributing methods. But most important—superior men!"[54] By "superior men," he meant the Americans who had been recruited and trained to serve the company as salaried sales representatives.

To attract promising recruits, Standard Oil offered its representatives more lavish salaries and benefits than were available at any company or other organization of any kind in China. It paid a starting salary of $2,000 gold per year, compared to starting salaries of $1,200 for a representative of British-American Tobacco Company and $1,000 for a Chinese-speaking American foreign service officer. It led its recruits to believe that at the end of their first three years each of them would return home for a six-month furlough with a salary of $5,000, and to entice a successful man back to China for a second tour, it more than fulfilled this promise.[55] In China, it covered all of the costs of its Westerners' housing and medical needs—with care supplied by its own physicians—and subsidized the cost of their board and insurance, up to $3 per day for board and 3 percent of their salaries for insurance. To ease fears about the future, it guaranteed that on retirement each representative would receive a pension amounting to 60 percent of his average salary during the last five years of his employment.[56]

The company's new American recruits found life luxurious on this budget. "Frankly speaking," wrote one, Harold Sheridan, to his mother on arriving in Shanghai in 1913, "we are living like princes out here, . . . and the East has 'got it' over any other place in the world for excessive luxury at comparatively no expense."[57] At age twenty-two, he reveled in his new privileged position.

> We lead a very easy and extremely luxurious life. Our servants do everything for us, from cleaning our guns, boots, helmets, etc.; keep our rooms immaculate at all times; serve tea or a light lunch in our room at any time; keep our clothes aired and pressed; our huge daily pile of sweaty clothes are taken every day to the laundry by them. . . . I tell you, I can easily understand the fascination of the Far East where living is cheap, and a white man need never lift his little finger unless he cares to.[58]

Sheridan's salary far exceeded not only his Chinese servant's pay but also his Chinese translator's wages, which annually amounted to $144 gold, a mere 7 percent of his wages.[59] Excited by his sudden financial elevation above the Chinese people around him, he took pride in what he perceived to be his racial superiority. He exulted to his mother six months after his arrival, "400,000,000 yellow people look up to you and respect you as a superior being because you are white, and are pleased to render you services of any description befitting what they consider your fitting position. It's great out here."[60]

Besides providing high salaries and benefits, Standard Oil also gave its Western salaried representatives a limited amount of training. In the first years of the twentieth century, the American company began encouraging its representatives in China to take language lessons by offering to cover their tuition costs. In addition, it gave them on-the-job training in the Chinese language as well as technical subjects—accounting, transportation, management. On the theory that firsthand exposure was the best teacher, it sent them as observers to travel with experienced Western sales representatives and their Chinese assistants.[61]

By requiring their salaried representatives to study and use Chinese on the job, the company expected them to achieve command of the language, and to prevent backsliding, it employed a language specialist, based in Beijing, to travel around the country conducting impromptu tests and placing those who failed in remedial courses. One Dr. Kerr (Ke'er Boshi) held this position as language specialist before World War I, and on his retirement he was succeeded by a Dr. Mann (Man Boshi). In 1912 Standard Oil opened a school at its New York headquarters for training new recruits, but its three-month course gave little attention to foreign languages and none at all to Asian ones.[62]

By the standards of Western companies in China at the time, Standard Oil's training program seems to have been relatively sophisticated, but it was far too superficial to produce American China specialists capable of replacing Chinese compradors and sales agents. From outside its training program, Standard Oil acquired some expertise on China by recruiting resident Westerners: missionaries such as V. G. Lyman, R. J. Corbett, and S. S. Corbett; diplomats such as a former British consul named Newman; and students such as the Yanjing (Yenching) University graduate H. S. Hopkins.[63] Still, it could not extend its corps of specialists much beyond this handful without a longer and more rigorous language training program. As Harold Sheridan joked in a letter to his mother during his first year in China, "I'm taking two Chinese lessons a week now—in a short time I will write you a letter in Chinese. (About 15 years equals a short time.)"[64] His jocular attitude toward learning the language, his limited success along these lines, and his heavy dependence on Chinese translators seem to have typified the experiences of Standard Oil's Western representatives in China. At best, their feelings toward language study were mixed, as reflected in this flippant comment in the company's in-house organ, the *Mei Foo Shield:* "To the Soconyite, [the study of Chinese has been a] perennial source of woe—did we hear somebody say, joy?"[65]

By paying high wages and giving recruits some language training, Standard Oil assembled a staff of Western salaried representatives that was qualified to supervise marketing at its distributing centers in China. But for the purpose of widely recruiting and closely monitoring Chinese commission agents, the company depended on a Western-trained "native staff."

TRAINING A "NATIVE STAFF" [66]

In the first years of the twentieth century, as Standard Oil assigned more Westerners to China, it added a large number of English-speaking Chinese staff members to work with them.[67] It treated these Chinese staff members differently than it had treated its Chinese compradors and agents. Rather than deal with them on the basis of personal guarantees and give them full latitude to market goods through their own social networks, Standard Oil recruited them in open competitions and trained them to prevent Chinese agents from violating the company's marketing policies.

Standard Oil's open competitions took the form of publicly announced examinations. On this basis it selected young English-speaking Chinese men for admission to a school that it opened at its Shanghai headquarters. After giving each class a six-month training course, the company then assigned those who graduated to its offices in all parts of China.[68]

By offering new recruits relatively high salaries, Standard Oil induced Chinese staff members to join the company and begin their climb up its corporate hierarchy. Compared to its salaries for American representatives, Standard Oil's salaries for Chinese were low, but compared to salaries available to Chinese in other companies at the time, its starting salaries were high: 70 yuan per month for a university graduate, 45 yuan per month for a senior high school graduate (*gaozhongsheng*), and 40 yuan per month for a junior high school graduate (*chuzhongsheng*).[69]

The company also offered a new recruit prospects for advancement in one of two specialties, either sales or accounting. In the sales department, a Chinese could rise as high as assistant manager (*fu li*), responsible for supervising Chinese salesmen (*yingye yuan*), Chinese interpreters for Western sales representatives, Chinese stock checkers, and Chinese inspectors. In the accounting department, a Chinese could climb as high as chief Chinese accountant and itinerant checker, who earned 300 to 400 yuan per month and had authority over Chinese accountants, Chinese statisticians, Chinese cashiers, Chinese bookkeepers, and other Chinese clerks. Although Standard Oil granted Chinese employees no insurance coverage, no furloughs, and few of the other benefits that it gave to Westerners, it did reward them for long-term service by paying pensions amounting to 30 to 40 percent of each Chinese employee's last annual salary.[70]

Once Standard Oil signed up its new Chinese recruits, it sent them away from their home localities to offices in its far-flung marketing organization. From its national headquarters in Shanghai, the company's Western management assigned salaried representatives at several levels: to regional offices (*qu hang*) in large metropolises (*da chengshi*) at the cores of China's regions; divisional offices (*fen hang*) in middle-sized and small cities (*zhong xiao chengshi*); and suboffices (*zhi hang*) in county seats (*xian cheng*).

Throughout this elaborate administrative organization, Standard Oil's Western managers retained ultimate authority over their Chinese staff members. Every year Western supervisors set raises for their Chinese subordinates whether they served in offices at the national, regional, divisional, or local level. Every three years the parent company sent a team from its New York headquarters to audit the accounts of its China offices at all of these levels.[71]

In conducting daily business, Standard Oil's Western managers were able to monitor the Chinese staff's work because of the company's policy that all internal documents had to be written in or translated into English. Under this policy Western managers took the quality of an employee's English into account when granting raises and promotions. As a result, its Chinese senior staff members spoke and wrote English as fluently as their Western colleagues. Its Chinese clerks kept accounts in English and were able to speak English haltingly. Even its Chinese manual laborers could speak with Westerners in pidgin English.[72]

To prevent Chinese employees from diverting or peddling information, Standard Oil maintained a policy of strict security on prices, salaries, transfers, and other decisions within the company. It swore each employee to secrecy on the subject of his salary, and it authorized transfers at the level of the regional office without permitting any say in the decision for lower offices at the divisional and local levels. Standard Oil's ban on the exchange of this information seemed extreme to Chinese employees who customarily gossiped more than Westerners did about such matters, and even Western employees commented privately and repeatedly on the company's determination to maintain secrecy.[73]

By maintaining secrecy and deploying its Chinese staff members outside their home localities, Standard Oil sought to limit their reliance on family members, native-place connections, and other social ties in their dealings with Chinese commission agents. Under its Western-style marketing system, the company instructed its staff to recruit these commission agents on a fundamentally different basis than had been previously attempted by itself, APC, or any other Western company in China.

RECRUITING CHINESE COMMISSION AGENTS AND SUBAGENTS

Under its new marketing system, Standard Oil's goal was to have its salaried staff recruit as many Chinese commission agents as possible. Whereas in the past it, like APC, had left marketing exclusively in the hands of compradors and prominent merchants, now its new salaried staff also approached other Chinese merchants outside the compradors' and merchants' social networks.[74] Casting its net more widely than ever before, the company offered small as well as large Chinese merchants a variety of incentives to carry its product.

As in the past, Standard Oil required that its agents post cash deposits before accepting goods and paid them 2 percent sales commissions for what they sold. In addition, it began to offer them a wide array of other financial services that its compradors and other Chinese intermediaries had previously offered only to members of their own social networks. For example, it granted credit, releasing goods on consignment and allowing 15 to 30 days before payment was due. On a Chinese commission agent's cash deposit, it paid interest at an annual rate of 5 to 8 percent, and in 1913 it introduced other options—conversion of the deposit into gold or U.S. dollars or investment in Standard Oil's stock. When an agent's sales rose high enough, the company allowed him to take goods whose value exceeded his cash deposit by an ever greater margin. For sales high above usual quotas, it presented an agent with a special gift such as a gold watch. To cover agents' losses, it gave compensation for leakage, provided insurance in case of natural disasters, and supplied legal assistance following robberies. At the annual holiday celebrating Chinese New Year, it hosted banquets for its agents and covered their expenses for round-trip travel to regional offices and for meals and small gifts (such as American-made candy).[75]

Besides material incentives, Standard Oil also supplied promotional assistance in the form of advertising. According to one of its former long-term Chinese employees, the company organized a team of more than twenty painters to travel around China's cities and countryside painting walls and billboards, even in "all the impoverished villages and out of the way places" (*qiong xiang pi rang*).[76] The company's most widely disseminated sign read, in Chinese, "Burn Standard Oil's Old 'Eagle Brand' of Kerosene [its cheapest brand] and Use Its Candles and Lamps." In 1907 it introduced kerosene lamps with glass chimneys, and thereafter it exported to China two million per year. It touted the safety and efficiency of the lamp, which at one filling could produce bright and clean light for eleven hours and by burning one gallon of kerosene could give illumination for 240 hours.[77] Using this lamp as a promotional device, it sold each one for only a few cents and gave away many other premiums—home furnishings such as mirrors, hammers, and pliers and home decorations such as Chinese New Year's pictures (*nian hua*), scrolls that served as wall hangings (*gua hua*), and miniature cards depicting series of Chinese figures and scenes to entice collectors. Needless to say, Standard Oil stamped on each of these devices its own trademark, "Meifu" in Chinese and "Mei Foo" in Roman letters, which means "beautiful and trustworthy."[78]

Standard Oil's distribution of kerosene in five-gallon tin cans placed another promotional device in its agents' hands: they became extremely popular in China. As a Western observer noted, Chinese consumers imaginatively modified the cans and used them for a wide variety of purposes: "Five gallon Socony kerosene cans are used as water buckets; cut across diagonally and used as dust pans; knocked down and with wooden wheels added used for a baby carriage!"[79] In fact, these cans were so popular that Standard Oil's local agents profited from selling them separately from the kerosene that they contained.

ENFORCING COMPANY POLICIES

While using material and promotional inducements to recruit Chinese commission agents and promote high sales, Standard Oil depended on its salaried staff to monitor these agents' business practices and prevent violations of the company's policies. To recruit as many agents as possible, the company set limits on the size of each agent's sales territory. Unlike APC (and like the Chinese government at the time under the Qing dynasty), the company had a law of "avoidance" (*huibi*).[80] The aim of this law was to "avoid" formation of powerful social networks based on family ties and native-place connections. Under Standard Oil's version of the law, a Chinese commission agent was permitted to preside over only one sales territory at a time and was forbidden to employ his sons, brothers, and other relatives as distributors of the company's product.[81]

To enforce this policy, Standard Oil carefully recorded who handled its goods all the way to their ultimate destination. It required its commission agents to register (*dengji*) subagents with its salaried staff members, and it technically retained control over goods until transactions were made with consumers, even in small rural stores (*xiangzhen shang dian*). In rural areas, its subagents were canvassers or drummers (*tuixiao yuan*) at periodic markets (*pao xiang jian*) in small towns where generally kerosene shops furnished the only permanent facilities except for teahouses, wine shops, and eating places. The salaried staff had intermittent contact with these rural canvassers, distributing goods to them on consignment, granting them loans, and reserving part of the company's annual bonus fund specifically for them.[82]

According to contemporary observers, Standard Oil made more sales in the countryside than in the cities. A survey done in 1935 found that 54 percent of Chinese farm families regularly bought kerosene.[83] This figure suggests that the historian John King Fairbank did not exaggerate when he characterized kerosene as "the most widespread product of modernity since it gave the peasantry better illumination than candles or a wick in wood oil." [84] Meanwhile, in China's cities, Standard Oil's sales staff kept track of goods even to the level of retailing. As noted by Hidy and Hidy, who had privileged access to Standard Oil's restricted archives, "In some places, as in Wuhu, for example, the hand of the New York company extended into street peddling." [85]

While Standard Oil's sales staff was responsible for scrutinizing its Chinese commission agents' marketing practices, its accounting staff had the task of evaluating their credit ratings. Every morning at ten o'clock the Chinese chief accountant in each branch recorded the ratio of security deposits to value of stocks held by all agents in his jurisdiction. He labeled any agent holding kerosene valued at more than twice his security deposit as a "bad risk"; any agent whose goods ranged from equal to double the value of his security deposit, a "fair risk"; and any agent whose goods were valued at less than his security deposit, a "good risk." Every month the Chinese chief accountant summarized these credit ratings for review by his Western superior. As a Chinese former accountant with thirty-three years of service to Standard Oil later recalled, a mistake on this form "was considered unforgivable" because "the most dreadful thing to a [Western] head man [*daban*] was bad

Figure 2. Hauling five-gallon cans of kerosene into the North China countryside, Shanxi province, 1919. From Record Group 151, FC, Box 25, National Archives of the United States, Washington, D.C.

Figure 3. Loading kerosene on a boat in the Middle Yangzi region at Xiangtan in Hunan province, 1930. From Record Group 151, FC, Box 25, National Archives of the United States, Washington, D.C.

debts [*dao zhang*] . . . [which left] bills unpaid for a long time and piled up official correspondence from all sides."[86] To avoid this outcome, the company rewarded consistently punctual agents with annual bonuses of between 1 and 1.5 percent.

ACHIEVING RESULTS

To a remarkable extent, Standard Oil's expensive new marketing system achieved its avowed goals of raising sales and recruiting more agents and subagents. The exact number of Standard Oil's Chinese commission agents in the early twentieth century is difficult to calculate for lack of nationwide data, but the statistics available on three of China's nine regions provide some basis for estimating the total. In North China, one of China's oldest regional economies and most populous areas, the company had 120 to 170 Chinese commission agents. In Northeast China, a developing frontier economy, it had 40 agents. In Jiangxi province, an area low in population and wealth, it had 19 agents. By extension, if North China was representative of China's three largest regions, if the Northeast was representative of the three medium-sized ones, and if Jiangxi was representative of the three smallest, then Standard Oil's total number of Chinese commission agents was at least 500.[87]

The number of Standard Oil's subagents is more difficult to estimate because they are less well documented. The few available figures suggest that at least 5 subagents served under each agent. For example, the poor region of Jiangxi had about one hundred subagencies operating under its 19 agents, and the richer region of Northeast China had "several hundred" subagents under its 40 agents. If it is valid to assume that at least 5 subagents worked under the average agent, then the company's subagents numbered at least 2,500.[88] Whatever the exact number, it seems likely that one of the company's former Chinese employees was not exaggerating when he recently observed that the Chinese agents' and subagents' shops formed "the major channel [for kerosene]to penetrate into China's urban and rural markets [because] these shops had extensive contacts with local people, had their own sales networks, were reliable, and enjoyed good reputations."[89]

Once Standard Oil's new recruits were in place, the company compiled an enviable record of eliminating bad debts and increasing sales. Between 1906 and 1914 Standard Oil's total transactions in China were valued at U.S. $100 million, and on all of this business, it wrote off bad debts amounting to a mere U.S. $440 (634 taels).[90] At the same time,

Standard Oil's sales swiftly surpassed those of APC and its other competitors. Engaging in repeated price wars, Standard Oil raised its share of China's market from 42 percent in 1900 to 67 percent in 1911, 77 percent in 1921, and 88 percent in 1928.[91] As of 1910 Standard Oil sold more kerosene in China than in any other Asian country, and by the late 1920s its marketing system was valued at U.S. $43 million.[92]

The introduction of Standard Oil's Western-style managerial hierarchy was critical to its success. In general, it retained the same kind of Chinese commission agents in the twentieth century as it had in the nineteenth, but now it empowered its salaried salesmen and accountants to punish a Chinese commission agent for violating the company's policies. For example, it disciplined one Chinese agent by reducing his sales territory from the whole of Zhejiang province to one city within the province, Hangzhou; and it punished another by trimming his sales territory from the whole of Shanghai to one district within the city, Nanshi.[93] Once Standard Oil had its newly trained young staff members in place, it kept them there, retaining the same people for decades until the company was forced to withdraw from China in the late 1940s and early 1950s.[94]

CONCLUSION

In retrospect, Standard Oil's decisive installation of its own marketing system between 1903 and 1914 marked the key turning point for it in China, and its success along these lines bears on the debate (summarized in chapter 1) over whether Western and other non-Chinese businesses ever wrested from Chinese merchants control over the marketing of goods in Chinese history. This case shows that at least one non-Chinese firm did impose its marketing organization on China and, therefore, that Western and other non-Chinese businesses did not always leave their distribution to Chinese networks. To be sure, Standard Oil's experience in the 1880s and 1890s indicates that it distributed through local networks longer in China than in any other major market, and the company's decision not to institute a Western-style system of direct distribution any sooner suggests that it found local networks in China to be the most resilient and tenacious ones in the world. Nonetheless, once the company installed its marketing system in China between 1903 and 1914, it made effective use of its direct control over kerosene distribution, widening its market, defeating its rivals, and dominating China's market throughout the first half of the twentieth century.

Standard Oil unquestionably imposed a Western-style business organization and used direct marketing to achieve the desired results during the early twentieth century, but was it representative of big Western businesses (not to mention small ones) in China? It spent more to install its direct marketing system in China than in all other Asian countries combined, and other Western businesses could not afford to make such large investments without giving the matter careful consideration. Even British-American Tobacco Company, a business with operations in China comparable in scale to those of Standard Oil, paused to compare its Western bureaucratic organization to its Chinese social networks before it decided whether to follow Standard Oil's example.

CHAPTER 3

British-American Tobacco Company

Like Standard Oil, British-American Tobacco Company (BAT) is a classic example of a Western-owned company that made the transition from personal to managerial capitalism and extended its corporate hierarchies overseas. In 1902, two decades after the founding of the Standard Oil Trust, BAT was established with headquarters in New York and London, and by the outbreak of World War I in 1914, it created foreign affiliates that extended its reach to six continents, including Asia. As a result, in Chandler's words, BAT had "a worldwide, integrated organization [with a] managerial hierarchy," and it "intensified efforts to replace independent sales jobbers or agents with salaried managers." [1]

In China, again like Standard Oil, BAT faced the dilemma of whether to delegate authority to Chinese networks or institute its own Western-style corporate hierarchy, but BAT dealt with the dilemma differently than Standard Oil did. Instead of first delegating authority and later taking authority into its own hands, BAT experimented during its first eighteen years (1902–20) with two approaches, simultaneously marketing its goods both directly through autonomous Chinese commission agents and directly through its salaried managers and staff members. Only then, after comparing the results, did its management decide which approach was preferable. In the meantime, it broadened its operations into purchasing and manufacturing—functions that Standard Oil did not perform in China. Whereas Standard Oil did not build derricks to extract crude oil or set up refineries to process it in China,[2] BAT installed purchasing stations to buy raw tobacco in China's countryside and constructed factories to manufacture cigarettes in China's cities. As a result, BAT faced the issue of how closely to exercise managerial control over not only Chinese merchants but also Chinese factory workers and tobacco growers.

DISTRIBUTING TWO WAYS, 1902–1912

During BAT's first decade in China, it created a rivalry within the company by distributing its goods through both a Western-style managerial hierarchy and Chinese social networks. On the one hand, BAT's top-ranking Westerner, James A. Thomas, and his handpicked English-speaking assistant, Wu Tingsheng, tried to recruit and build up their Sino-Western salaried staff so that it would take full responsibility for marketing at BAT (as a Sino-Western salaried staff did at Standard Oil during the first decade of the twentieth century). On the other hand, BAT's Chinese commission agents, led by a Cantonese merchant named Zheng Bozhao, set out to boost BAT's sales faster and higher than Thomas's and Wu's corporate hierarchy was able to do. In the competition, each of these men shaped BAT's approach to marketing.

JAMES A. THOMAS AND
BAT'S WESTERN-STYLE MARKETING SYSTEM

The founder of BAT and chairman of its board of directors was James B. Duke, an American originally from North Carolina. In 1905 he chose a fellow North Carolinian, James A. Thomas, to serve as head of BAT's China branch. Thomas had represented Duke's American Tobacco Company overseas as early as 1888, and in his position with BAT in China he wasted no time introducing each component of a Western-style marketing system: a large-scale infrastructure, Western salaried representatives, and English-speaking Chinese salaried representatives, all organized in an administrative hierarchy.

To create an infrastructure for marketing, BAT invested in warehouses on a national scale. By 1912, according to the British minister to China, Sir John Jordan, there was "probably not a city of any size in the eighteen provinces where such warehouses [had] not been established by the British-American Tobacco Company." BAT's own records for the early 1920s show that by then the company had no less than 246 warehouses spread throughout all of China's nine regions: 55 in the Northeast, 49 in the North and Northwest, 69 in the Lower Yangzi, 48 in the Middle and Upper Yangzi, 19 in the South and Southeast, and 6 in the Southwest.[3]

To manage distribution from these warehouses, Thomas recruited Westerners, especially American Southerners with whom he had a kind of American-style native-place tie. As Thomas later recalled, "Most of the Far Eastern representatives of the company in the early days were recruited from North Carolina and Virginia. From infancy [they] had cultivated, cured, and manufactured tobacco, so that it was second nature to them. In addition, these farm-bred boys were healthy, well-reared, and had a background of good character and good habits."[4]

Thomas hired only bachelors under the age of twenty-five and paid them $1,200 per year plus living expenses—a starting salary for new recruits in China second only to the one paid by Standard Oil. Although BAT, like Standard Oil, had a company policy of keeping salaries secret, Thomas made clear that ambitious Western employees might eventually live in sumptuous mansions after rising to much better paying positions, including division head at a salary of 3,000 yuan per month, Shanghai manager at 5,000 to 6,000 yuan per month, or general manager, Thomas's position, at more than 10,000 yuan per month, which was equivalent to $60,000 to $100,000 per year, the highest salary paid to any businessman in Asia at the time. Thomas offered a $500 bonus to new recruits for passing the company's language examinations, which were held once every six months, and both Chinese and Westerners observed that some of BAT's Western representatives became fluent in more than one dialect of Chinese.[5]

Whether fluent in Chinese or not, Western salaried representatives still relied heavily on BAT's Chinese salaried employees. As one Chinese-speaking American recalled after serving as a BAT representative in North and Northwest China between 1911 and 1914, "We were called salesmen. But actually we did no selling. The large majority of foreigners in the company spoke no Chinese; [Chinese] interpreters and dealers took care of that end. The foreigners were really inspectors, overseers, advisors. More than anything else, it seemed to me, our job reduced itself to advertising."[6] Another American who served as a BAT representative in Northeast China in the 1910s made the same point more bluntly. "I was simply window dressing for our [BAT] Company," he recalled. His Chinese assistant, however, made him seem to be much more than that: "Being a good Chinese, he always kept the Foreigner puffed up and believing himself [to be] a man of great affairs." But the perceptive American was well aware that it was the Chinese assistant who handled all the "business affairs."[7]

To conduct business affairs and make sales for Westerners, BAT recruited and trained English-speaking Chinese comparable to the ones who worked for Standard Oil in China. Its candidates included young graduates of Shanghai's missionary colleges where English was the medium of instruction, and it supplemented their educations by giving them a six-month training course. According to a Chinese who completed the course at age twenty-one in 1916, his Western teachers at BAT exhorted him and other Chinese trainees to attack their prospective posts aggressively and to jar local Chinese commission agents out of complacent attitudes toward selling. When this young man took up his first assignment in Henan province at Zhengzhou—a North China city far from Shanghai—he noted that he was set apart from local Chinese commission agents not only because he received a salary (1,200 yuan per year) rather than commissions but also because he enjoyed other perquisites: housing, furniture, servants, and a cook.[8]

BAT assigned its Western and Chinese salaried representatives to positions in a five-level administrative hierarchy that reached throughout China. Presiding at the top was a small group of Western executives known as the Administrative Committee (xingzheng weiyuanhui) that met in the company's Shanghai headquarters. At the next level were five regional "departments" (bu), one each in the Northeast, North, Lower Yangzi, Middle Yangzi, and South. At the third level were seventeen "divisions" (qu), each located in a different province. At the fourth level were ninety subprovincial "territories" (duan). And at the lowest level were county and subcounty "districts" (qu). The total number of units at this lowest level is not known, but local observers scattered across all regions of China recorded the presence of BAT's salaried employees— drummers and inspectors (diaocha yuan)—in markets at all levels of the urban hierarchy down to and including standard market towns.[9]

Through this formal administrative organization, BAT sought to recruit Chinese commission agents on a highly selective basis. Before assigning a Chinese the title "sales merchant" (jingxiao shang), it insisted that his trading firm be capitalized at tens of thousands of yuan, possess a shop or warehouse that would be devoted exclusively to handling

BAT's cigarettes, and supply two letters from Chinese guarantors (*pu bao*) promising to cover the candidate's debts. To be sure that all requirements were fully met, the company printed standardized forms that served as contracts and had to be completed by Chinese applicants and their guarantors.[10] As implied by these strict requirements, BAT originally conceived of its candidates as wealthy and prominent Chinese, and it set out to recruit them through Thomas's first close Chinese associate, Wu Tingsheng.

WU TINGSHENG'S CONTACTS WITH OFFICIAL ELITES

In 1898, four years before the founding of BAT, Thomas made contact with Wu Tingsheng (1876–1935), a twenty-two-year-old recent graduate of a missionary college and a fluent speaker of English with no experience in business. Wu had been born and raised in Ningbo prefecture, the place renowned for producing Standard Oil's Ye Chengzhong and many other prominent Chinese merchants; but Wu's father, Wu Caiqin, had been a Christian minister since 1876 and had given Wu a religious education—not a commercial one—first at the Ningbo Mission School and then at the Shanghai Anglo-Chinese College, a school founded in 1882 by the American Southern Methodist Mission and known for its heavy emphasis on English-language instruction.[11]

Wu was introduced to Thomas by a Dr. Whitney, an American who had worked with Wu's father as a medical missionary in Ningbo and had taught Wu English in exchange for lessons in Chinese. According to Thomas's later recollections, Wu struck him from the first as "ambitious . . . and . . . of fine address and pleasing personality. He understood also how to approach a Chinese merchant and gentleman."[12]

Lacking experience in commerce, Wu preferred to promote BAT's sales by winning support from officials and local political elites rather than from merchants. Because he had not earned an imperial academic degree (which was the hallmark of officials under the Qing dynasty until the abolition of the imperial examination system in 1905), he convinced BAT to finance the purchase for him of an official title, "expectant prefect" (*houbu dao*). He also received from BAT a large salary —1,500 yuan per month, the most paid to any Chinese employee of a foreign firm in China at the time—plus an annual expense account of several thousand yuan to cover the costs of gifts, banquets, mahjong games, and other social occasions that he hosted.[13] By these means, according to the recent recollections of Wu's son, Wu became "a bureau-

Figure 4.   Wu Tingsheng, BAT's top
English-speaking Chinese salaried
manager. Reprinted from *Who's Who
in China*, 869.

crat as well as a merchant" and took advantage of his "official capacity"
to build up his social network.[14]

With this orientation, Wu approached local elites in previously un-
tapped markets as though he were an official on tour. In Wu's son's
words, Wu "inspected nearby towns [in] a tug towing two or three small
boats. On the stern of the tugboat a big flag with the word 'Wu' was
hoisted. Four men in soldier's uniforms stood behind. They struck gongs
and blew long horns as the boats were arriving at the destination. Local
officers and gentries came out to welcome them respectfully."[15] Whether
Wu made contacts who should be characterized in his son's words as
"officers and gentries" or in the words of other Chinese observers as
"local bullies and evil gentry" (*tuhao lieshen*),[16] all available Chinese
sources agree that Wu preferred to deal with local political elites and
officials rather than merchants.

In his negotiations with officials under the Qing imperial government,
Wu struck numerous deals. As BAT spread its web of offices and warehouses throughout China during its early years, he enabled the company
to extend its reach outside treaty ports to nontreaty ports where property laws prohibited foreigners from buying land. As a dummy front for

BAT, he bought property in Beijing, Suzhou, Hangzhou, and Jiaxing—all nontreaty ports.[17]

By the fall of the Qing dynasty in 1912, Wu had developed a thick network of official connections at the capital in Beijing, in the provinces, and in selected localities, especially around Shanghai. At BAT his title was top manager (*da xie*), not comprador, and he distinguished himself from other compradors by specializing in relations with officials. By the same token, he distinguished himself from merchants who served the company as distributors and operated through a different set of contacts.

ZHENG BOZHAO'S NATIVE-PLACE ASSOCIATION

By contrast with Wu Tingsheng, BAT's other major Chinese distributor, Zheng Bozhao, was not able to converse with James Thomas. Unlike Wu, Zheng had received no Western-style education and, despite an early attempt at language study, had learned to speak no more than a few words of pidgin English. Throughout Zheng's long life (1861–1951), he always claimed to feel uncomfortable around Westerners and never adopted Western customs, preferring to wear Chinese long robes rather than Western business suits, live in a modest Shanghai-style attached house (*lilong*) rather than a Western-style freestanding mansion, and work in a small cramped portion of a low-slung building at the corner of Henan and Hankou roads in Shanghai rather than in one of the city's numerous skyscrapers with a view of the river along the bund.[18] Having little in common with Thomas, Zheng came to Thomas's attention only because of his Chinese trading company, Yongtaizhan, which swiftly emerged as BAT's leading distributor first in Shanghai and then throughout China.

Yongtaizhan trading company had a preexisting social network consisting of experienced tobacco merchants who were bound together by native-place ties. Zheng's own work with Yongtaizhan dated back to 1891 when, at the age of thirty, he had first joined the firm as a low-level clerk. Like all of Yongtaizhan's other shareholders (*gudong*), Zheng was a Cantonese from Guangdong province, hailing from Xiangshan County,[19] which had been the leading producer of Chinese compradors in the nineteenth century and had been the native place of the compradors who had succeeded Ye Chengzhong at Standard Oil in China during the 1890s. Like Ye, Zheng has been labeled a "comprador,"[20] and, again like Ye, his independence and large-scale operation made him

Figure 5.   Zheng Bozhao, BAT's leading
Chinese commission agent (known as an
"independent seller" in BAT's terminol-
ogy). Reprinted from Thomas, *A Pioneer
Tobacco Merchant in the Orient,* opposite 108.

far more than an in-house middleman between a Western company and
Chinese merchants.

Zheng became head of Yongtaizhan by the turn of the century, and
even after it began to distribute BAT's cigarettes, he did not alter its
fundamental character as a native-place network. For his Shanghai-
based firm, he recruited staff members almost exclusively from his native place in South China (nearly a thousand miles away), with his son
and brother-in-law holding positions as his immediate subordinates and
another two hundred fellow Cantonese serving beneath them. Zheng referred to himself as the firm's "family head" (*jiazhang*), but his paternalistic attitude toward his fellow Cantonese by no means implied generosity toward them. He ordered Yongtaizhan's workers to keep secret
their wages, which ranged from as little as 20 to 30 yuan per month for
a "small" clerk up to 100 yuan for other nonmanagerial staff members,
and he offered virtually no health care, pensions, or other benefits.[21]

At an early age Zheng's miserliness earned him the unflattering nickname "the Pockmarked Man from Chaoyang" (Chaoyang mazi),[22] and
later, even after amassing an immense fortune worth between U.S.

$3 million and $5 million,[23] he was known to be niggardly toward his workers and unwilling to make donations to philanthropic causes. Eventually Zheng became "about the richest man in Shanghai," in the estimation of the industrialist Liu Hongsheng, who at the time was himself one of the richest men in Shanghai (see chap. 7). Despite Zheng's great wealth, he "is not making himself known here [in Shanghai] in any philanthropic way," Liu complained in private correspondence with family members, and even in his native Xiangshan, Zheng made relatively small donations, such as 50,000 yuan for establishing schools, which according to Liu represented a tiny fraction of Zheng's wealth and showed his consistent lack of generosity.[24]

Zheng and his Yongtaizhan trading company enjoyed immediate success with BAT. Zheng's firm had distributed cigarettes for other Western-owned cigarette companies before BAT was founded in 1902,[25] and it first came into contact with James Thomas when it joined the Shanghai Tobacco Trade Association that Wu Tingsheng had formed on Thomas's behalf between 1898 and 1901. As early as 1904, just before Thomas's appointment as BAT's general manager in China, the Western company retained Yongtaizhan. "[W]e are entirely reorganizing this [Shanghai Tobacco Trade] Association," BAT's management in Shanghai wrote to the company's New York headquarters in 1904. "We are taking out the dummies and dead men, we are also cutting off the bonus on outport business, and we are putting in Wing Tai [Yongtaizhan] and some more new blood."[26] Once "put in," Zheng was authorized to distribute cigarettes outside Shanghai as well as within it.

Between 1905 and 1912 Zheng seized on this authorization from BAT to take advantage of his long-standing and carefully cultivated contacts outside Shanghai. He had developed some of these contacts directly with shippers (*chuan hu*) who had carried cigars between the Philippines and Chinese ports along the Yangzi River for Zheng's firm before he began to distribute cigarettes for BAT. For other contacts, Zheng depended on a local man, Feng Xifan, who became head of Yongtaizhen's "transportation department" (*yunshu bu*). Zheng had never previously granted authority to any other non-Cantonese at Yongtaizhen, but he made an exception in Feng's case because he needed Feng as a native of Zhenjiang in the Lower Yangzi Valley to broaden his contacts with merchants in this region so that he could take full advantage of the opportunity to sell BAT's cigarettes on an interregional basis. While thus loosening the usual requirements for leaders in his native-place association, Zheng did not waive these requirements altogether, for he insisted that Feng must do a full apprenticeship and learn to speak fluent Cantonese.[27]

With Feng as his intermediary, Zheng began distributing through commercial shippers (*yunshu shangren*) who carried locally made products to Shanghai from their native places in Lower Yangzi cities—Hangzhou, Wuxi, Jiaxing, Wenzhou—and hauled loads of BAT's cigarettes home with them on the return trip. Through Feng, Zheng linked his social network with other social networks, and his Yongtaizhen surpassed BAT's other Chinese distributors. Of the Eight Great Guilds (*ba datong hang*) serving BAT, it alone exceeded the company's sales quotas every year before 1912.[28]

By 1912, with this successful record, Zheng Bozhao fully captured the attention of James Thomas who invited him and Wu Tingsheng to take a tour of BAT's operations in the United States and Europe. Thrilled by the invitation, both of the company's two leading Chinese accepted it, and on the trip each cut a different figure: Wu seemed urbane and cosmopolitan, speaking fluent English; Zheng appeared to be narrowly parochial, never speaking any language other than Cantonese. On the face of it, their hosts had more reasons to feel at ease with Wu than with Zheng, and when the two Chinese returned to Shanghai, it was Wu who received the more attractive offer.

FINANCING TWO KINDS OF CHINESE NETWORKS, 1912–1919

Between 1912 and 1919 BAT expanded its marketing in China mainly by investing in two separate operations, one under Wu Tingsheng and the other under Zheng Bozhao. In 1912, at the end of Wu and Zheng's trip to the West, BAT immediately offered financial backing to Wu and later did the same for Zheng. The company thus pitted Wu and Zheng against each other in the 1910s before deciding which of the two would be the chief distributor in its marketing operation throughout the 1920s and 1930s.

WU TINGSHENG AND UNION COMMERCIAL TOBACCO COMPANY

In 1912 BAT founded Union Commercial Tobacco Company (Xiehe maoyi gongsi) as a wholly owned subsidiary with Wu Tingsheng as general manager and one million yuan for initial capital. BAT provided all of the goods to be sold by Union, and it allowed Union to take all goods on consignment, requiring no deposit or payment until after the goods were sold.[29]

Between 1912 and 1919 Wu characteristically concentrated on building up his network of official contacts. In 1912 he moved to Beijing, the capital of the newly founded Republic of China, where he became BAT's resident lobbyist. A year later he improved his political position by becoming an adviser (*ziyi*) to the State Council (Guowuyuan) and special commissioner for the investigation of the tobacco tariff in the Beijing government's Ministry of Finance. From these posts he supplied BAT with timely intelligence reports on frequent changes in the Beijing government to help the company negotiate new official agreements even before each new Chinese political leader had publicly announced his abrogation of old ones.[30]

While claiming these and other successes with officials at Beijing and with regional warlords such as Zhang Zuolin in Northeast China and Lu Yongxiang in the Lower Yangzi, Wu fell short of winning approval for his grandest scheme: an official monopoly for BAT over the production and distribution of all cigarettes sold in China. Despite Wu's three years of lobbying for this monopoly, he reached no agreement with officials before the talks were terminated in 1915.[31]

Without official endorsement for his proposed tobacco monopoly, Wu proved unable to build up sales through Union. Wu's failure seems to have been attributable to his neglect of local Chinese distributors. With BAT's financial backing, he established branches for Union in the core cities of China's regions—at Shanghai and Nanjing in the Lower Yangzi region, Hankou in the Middle Yangzi region, Tianjin in North China, and elsewhere—and he tried to use advertising to achieve a popular appeal. For example, he declined when BAT offered to give him the exclusive right to distribute its Ruby Queen brand because the cigarette's Chinese brand name, Great England (Da Ying pai), sounded proforeign and unpatriotic to him, and he instead took exclusive rights to the Purple Mountain brand (Zijin shan), which was named after a well-known sacred site near the city of Nanjing. Wu also arranged for Chinese celebrities to endorse Union's brands.

Despite all of his efforts—cultivation of official contacts, creation of branch offices, and use of BAT's advertising—Wu was not able to make Union competitive as long as his sales organization failed to solidify linkages with local Chinese wholesalers and retailers. In the words of a Chinese specialist on commercial history, Wu failed at Union for lack of "connections with middle- and low-level sales agents" (*zhong xia ceng tuixiao shang*).[32]

In 1919, when Thomas resigned as BAT's general manager in China, Wu almost immediately lost his position with the company. Wu's last assignment in 1919 was to collect debts in North China, and after he returned to Shanghai six months later empty-handed (having collected a fraction of the debts and having spent what little he had collected on parties with officials), he took a tongue-lashing from Thomas's successor and promptly resigned. Wu had failed BAT, according to Thomas's successor, because he had lavished money and attention on members of the Chinese official elite and had ignored Chinese small-scale commercial distributors and other merchants.[33]

Once rid of Wu, BAT ceased to distribute its goods through Chinese who depended heavily on official connections, employing such people only for purposes other than marketing. In 1924 it recruited as Wu's replacement Shen Kunshan, a grandson of the prominent nineteenth-century Chinese official Shen Baozhen and a graduate of Cambridge University. As BAT's Arnold Rose in Shanghai wrote to his superiors in London, "It seemed absolutely essential to have someone who could get really in touch with what is going on in the Official world. It is too difficult for a foreigner, or any of the Chinese of the class that we usually employ, to find out what is going on, and I fear that we may wake some morning and find that things have gone a bit too far unless we keep very much on the qui vive."[34] But BAT did not ask Shen or any other Chinese with strong official connections to form a company like Wu's Union Commercial Tobacco Company or to distribute its cigarettes. For marketing, it relied instead on Chinese who—despite their lack of influence with officials—had proven themselves as commercial agents.

ZHENG BOZHAO'S INTERREGIONAL NETWORK

In 1912, the same year that BAT inaugurated Union Commercial Tobacco Company under Wu Tingsheng, it showed that it regarded Zheng Bozhao as its second most promising Chinese distributor by offering him exclusive rights to distribute Ruby Queen as soon as Wu declined to handle this brand.[35] On granting this privilege, BAT released Zheng (as it had released Wu) from its usual restrictions: he was permitted to sell this brand anywhere in China without regard for the boundaries of BAT's specified sales territories, and he was allowed to recruit Chinese commission agents without regard for the rules and regulations that were used by the company's salaried representatives in their recruitment of Chinese commission agents. In 1912 BAT apparently expected less from Zheng than from Wu, because at that time it did not make direct investments in Zheng's trading company, Yongtaizhan, as it did in Wu's Union Commercial Tobacco Company. BAT only began to recognize Zheng's potential and invest in his company after he succeeded at tapping interregional markets by using techniques that had not been tried either by Wu or by BAT's corps of Western and Chinese salaried representatives.

Unlike Wu, Zheng concentrated on merchants rather than officials, and unlike BAT's salaried representatives, he recruited Chinese commission agents as members of his social network rather than on the basis of formal criteria. He was willing to appoint merchants and shippers as sales merchants for BAT on the basis of Cantonese native-place ties or previous experience in the tobacco trade, and because he trusted these recruits, he freely waived BAT's formal requirements that each sales merchant should own a trading company capitalized at tens of thousands of yuan, possess a shop or warehouse that would be devoted exclusively to handling BAT's cigarettes, and supply two letters from guarantors promising to cover all debts. Setting these requirements aside, Zheng asked for nothing more than one shop guarantee and assured prospective Chinese sales merchants that they would never be replaced as long as "there is no incident" (*wu teshu shigu*)—that is, as long as they were not caught committing a serious financial blunder or criminal offense. To make the offer still more enticing, Zheng allowed Chinese sales merchants to handle BAT's goods on consignment (*si xiao*). He waived security deposits for anyone who could not afford them, and he paid interest on the security deposits that were made. As Zheng's competitors pointed out, these lenient and flexible policies permitted some Chinese to become sales merchants for BAT without putting up any capital at all.[36]

As Zheng recruited more and more sales merchants and extended the boundaries of his interregional trading network in China, he elaborated his own informal hierarchy consisting of merchants within his social network. First he selected from among the country's commercial centers more than forty entry points (*zhudian*)—some large (*da zhudian*) and others small (*xiao zhudian*). Then at the large entry points, Zheng recruited large-scale dealers (*da jingli*) to whom the goods were supplied by BAT's salaried representatives (not by Zheng's own trading company), and at the small entry points, he recruited small-scale dealers (*xiao jingli*) who received goods from the large-scale dealers. The large-scale dealers distributed goods in sales territories smaller than provinces and larger than counties and earned a commission of 1 to 3 percent on sales. The small-scale dealers distributed goods in territories the size of one county or at most a few counties and received a commission of 2 to 3 percent. At both levels Chinese sales merchants served simultaneously as retailers and wholesalers, selling some goods directly to consumers and distributing the rest to the other sales merchants or retail merchants (*lingshou shang*) who each made sales in territories smaller than a county and earned a commission of 2 to 3 percent. To boost sales, Zheng offered Chinese commission agents incentives. He paid commissions on a sliding scale—the higher one's sales, the higher the percentage of one's commission.[37]

Through Zheng's network of merchants, he achieved extraordinary results. His sales of Ruby Queen far surpassed Wu's sales of Purple Mountain and BAT's sales of any other brand, making Ruby Queen the second most popular cigarette in the world.[38] Zheng was declared the winner in his competition with Wu Tingsheng, and Zheng's success caused BAT to revise its entire approach to marketing in China.

BAT'S ADOPTION OF THE "INDEPENDENT SELLER" SYSTEM

In light of ZhengBozhao's success, BAT shifted responsibility for marketing overwhelmingly into the hands of Chinese independent sellers (*du xiao*) like Zheng during the 1920s and 1930s. Rather than recruit Chinese agents through its administrative hierarchy of salaried Western and Chinese representatives, it gave this responsibility to Zheng and other Chinese merchants whose distributing networks resembled his.

BAT made major concessions to Zheng. In 1919 it authorized him to work with all twelve of the company's existing regional offices and any additional regional offices that it would establish in the future. In each region, he was permitted to select any Chinese regional dealer and to make this dealer directly responsible to Zheng himself; this dealer was, in turn, allowed to recruit one or more merchants (*shangren*) as subordinate distributors. As part of the deal, BAT agreed that if Zheng's territories turned out to be profitable, he would take a 2 percent commission on all sales, the Chinese regional dealer (*qu jingxiao shang*) would receive 1 percent, and all of the subordinate large-scale and small-scale dealers combined would earn another 4.5 percent. If it turned out that Zheng's territories were unprofitable, then BAT would absorb 75 percent of Zheng's losses.[39]

In 1921 BAT made a substantial investment in Zheng's operation and formed a partnership with him by legally establishing the Yongtaihe Tobacco Company, Ltd., capitalized at one million yuan, with BAT holding 51 percent of the stock. While BAT held a controlling interest, Zheng took the rest of the stock and served as general manager and chairman of the board of directors. The members of the board included Zheng's closest Cantonese associates and three of BAT's top Western executives in China: Zheng Guanzhu (Zheng's son), Huang Yicong (Zheng's brother-in-law), Arthur Bassett, Joseph Daniel, and William Morris.[40]

By holding controlling interest in Yongtaihe, BAT kept Zheng's independence as an "independent seller" legally circumscribed, but in practice it gave him broad latitude. For example, the company legally required Zheng to leave to BAT's salaried representatives all responsibility for setting prices, collecting revenue (through vouchers), and carrying out accounting procedures. Nonetheless, when one of BAT's Chinese salaried representatives secretly reported to his Western superiors that Zheng had violated the procedures, practiced nepotism, and falsified account books, BAT's Western management chose to ignore the offenses. According to Cheng Renjie, the Chinese employee who reported on Zheng, after he described Zheng's violations of BAT's policies to Arthur Bassett, BAT's American legal counsel, Bassett said he would overlook them as long as Zheng's business ran smoothly and turned a profit for BAT.[41]

BAT's decision in the early 1920s to shift marketing responsibility into the hands of Zheng and other Chinese independent sellers set the course for its future. Thereafter between 1921 and 1941, Zheng's Yongtaihe Tobacco Company alone made at least 29 percent of BAT's total sales in China and probably as much as 50 or 60 percent. By 1930 Zheng was so successful in the Lower Yangzi region that BAT disbanded its Western-style corporate hierarchy for its entire "Eastern Division," which had previously supplied Shanghai, Suzhou, and their hinterlands. More broadly, Zheng concentrated on five of China's nine regions, and other Chinese, also known as independent sellers, covered sales territories that overlapped with his and with each other's throughout the country. These independent sellers each worked through a native-place association in one or more of China's regions: Guo Yunge in the North-east; Cui Zunsan, Gong Hexuan, Zhao Zhongtao, and the Tongyi Company in the North and Northwest; Wang Guanshi, Zheng Zhong-wei, and Gu Haijian in the Middle and Upper Yangzi; Ge Zhuxuan in the Southeast; the Gongyi Hang in the South; and Xu Jinsen in the Southwest.[42]

It is difficult to measure the scale of these Chinese independent sell-ers' trading networks at all levels, but some inferences may be drawn from fragmentary evidence. In 1937 Zheng's Yongtaihe distributed BAT's cigarettes through warehouses in 169 counties, and other distrib-utors handled goods in another 378 counties, giving the company ware-houses in more than one-fourth of the 1,949 counties into which China (excluding Outer Mongolia and Tibet) was divided in 1937. Figures available for 1937 on one of BAT's Chinese independent sellers are sug-gestive of the density of the company's regional trading network. Based at Tianjin in North China, this seller presided over 321 large-scale deal-ers, about 2,000 small-scale dealers, and approximately 26,000 retail merchants.[43]

As BAT's Chinese independent sellers pushed up sales in the 1920s and 1930s, the company became more and more dependent on them without abandoning its formal administrative hierarchy of Western and Chinese salaried representatives. In fact, in the 1920s it increased the number of its offices in China at all levels: from 5 to 6 at the regional level, from 12 to 16 at the provincial level, and from 90 to 246 at the subprovincial level. BAT retained this nationwide administrative orga-nization to check on the performances of BAT's Chinese independent sellers at all levels of the market. At the top, BAT's Administrative Com-mittee met weekly or more often at Shanghai to assess incoming infor-mation on market conditions and to issue policies on prices, flow of goods, and personnel management. As policies came down from this committee to salaried representatives staffing its administrative organi-zation throughout China, the latter saw that the policies were followed by the Chinese independent sellers in their territories.[44]

In theory, BAT's administrative organization of Western and Chinese salaried representatives was kept separate from Chinese independent sellers' networks and was capable of punishing Chinese independent sellers for violating the company's policies. BAT prohibited anyone from working simultaneously as a salaried representative in the company's administrative organization and as a commission agent under one of its

Chinese independent sellers, and it officially instructed salaried representatives to report commission agents for selling below the company's
prices, failing to maintain a good credit rating, selling outside authorized sales territories, or handling brands made by BAT's competitors.
But only in very rare cases did the company go so far as to fire a commission agent on the basis of reports from its salaried representatives,
and, dating from 1919, if not earlier, BAT's formal administrative organization generally served to encourage and accommodate Chinese independent sellers' networks, not to limit or discipline them.[45]

By relying heavily on Chinese independent sellers and holding them
on a light rein, BAT captured a large share of China's market. Between
1902 and 1937 it secured as much as 80 percent and never less than
60 percent of China's cigarette market (not including the market for
handmade tobacco products), and it became dominant throughout
the country, making more than half the cigarette sales per year during
the 1930s in each of China's nine regions except one, South China.
Throughout most of this period, it was prevented from establishing
a complete monopoly by Chinese-owned rivals, but compared to any
other past enterprise in China, it achieved unprecedented dominance of
the tobacco market on a national scale.[46]

BAT'S RELATIONS WITH INDUSTRIAL WORKERS
AND TOBACCO GROWERS

Soon after its founding, BAT extended its operations in China beyond
marketing to encompass cigarette manufacturing and tobacco purchasing. As a result, it began to deal with Chinese factory workers and tobacco sellers. To manufacture cigarettes in China, it built factories in
six Chinese cities—large mills in Shanghai (1906, 1917) and Hankou
(1907) plus smaller ones in Shenyang (1909), Harbin (1914), Tianjin
(1922), and Qingdao (1925)—and by 1925 it employed in these factories a total of twenty-five thousand Chinese workers. As early as 1913
the company distributed seed (imported from the United States) and
procured China's first harvest of "bright" tobacco (the type used in cigarettes), and by the mid-1930s it operated six curing plants in three
provinces (Shandong, Henan, and Anhui), where a total of about three
hundred thousand Chinese families, or two million people, cultivated
the crop.[47] Just as BAT experimented with more than one strategy
in dealing with Chinese marketing agents, so too did it conduct experi-
ments with Chinese factory workers and tobacco growers.

BAT'S RELIANCE ON NUMBER ONES BEFORE 1927

In its factories BAT set up a corporate hierarchy and adopted a policy of direct managerial control over Chinese workers on the shop floor, but this policy was not carried out in practice. In 1920 BAT's managers explained their policy to a top executive from British-owned Lever Brothers, the world's biggest soap manufacturer, when he visited China to assess the country's possibilities for his own company. In his report to his superiors in London the executive from Lever Brothers pointed out the differences between "the more common means" of supervising Chinese workers and BAT's policy. The more common means was to leave authority in the hands of a foreman or forewoman (known in China as a Number One), who "recruits the labour for which he is responsible from his own home district [and] has a sort of clannish influence over them. This makes for more harmonious working and reduction of friction which sometimes exists between workmen from different localities." The other alternative, which BAT theoretically adopted, was to "dispense" with the Number One and "save the amount he charges them, but what is much more important, they save the 'squeeze' which [he] takes out of the workpeople. . . . By paying a higher rate of wages they [at BAT] get and retain a better type of worker." [48] Although BAT's management claimed to follow this policy of exercising direct managerial control over Chinese workers, in practice before 1927 its Number Ones had full control over all dealings with workers—hiring, training, paying of wages, and firing—and kept their recruits independent of BAT's central personnel office.

BAT's Chinese Number Ones recruited workers and retained authority over them on the basis of bribes, native-place ties, and fictive as well as real kinship relations. At its factory on Tong Bei Road in Shanghai, for example, the tobacco leaf department (*yanye bu*) had a Number One who was notorious for requiring bribes from her recruits and for pocketing parts of some workers' wages on the grounds that the withheld portions were "fines." In the factory's cigarette packing department (*baozhuang bu*), a male Number One instructed workers to call him "Great Uncle" and a female Number One became known as "Auntie," emphasizing that workers had filial obligations to show them deference and give them "presents." Meanwhile, in the factory's cigarette rolling department (*zhuanyan bu*), the head of the department's five Number Ones assigned status to workers as his "disciples" (*tudi*) and "small claws and teeth" (*xiao zhao ya*) in secret societies: the God of Justice Society (Guandi hui), the Great Society of Paradise (Du tian da hui), and the Society of Boxers (Quan she).[49] Similarly, in one of BAT's factories, the chief inspector, who was a high-ranking figure in the Green Gang, refused to hire workers unless they consented to become his disciples and give him gifts whenever there was a festival, a celebration, or a day of mourning in his home. In August 1921 the Chinese workers complained to Zhang Guotao (Chang Kuo-t'ao), a Communist labor leader who was trying to organize them, that this inspector used the rituals of brotherhood in the Green Gang to subordinate and exploit them. According to Zhang's account, "One man jumped up and said, 'This "old man" pays no attention to fraternal responsibilities. Not only does he constantly exploit us, but he even takes advantage of our wives and sisters if they are the least bit attractive.' . . . The others spontaneously nodded their heads and repeated, 'It is true. It is true.'"[50]

If BAT did not interfere with relations between Number Ones and workers on the job, it also left Number Ones with responsibility for meeting workers' most basic needs off the job, especially the need for housing. In the mid-1920s BAT provided workers with some services—clinics, baths, savings funds, and schools for workers' children[51]—but it did not provide housing. At the time Arnold Rose, a member of BAT's board of directors at Shanghai, urged the company to construct housing units for workers as Japanese-owned cotton mills had done in Shanghai. If it followed the Japanese example, Rose predicted, BAT would be spared strikes because Chinese workers would "understand us and be grateful to us."[52] But his proposal was not heeded, and, as he feared, BAT became the target of numerous strikes. In fact, of all the companies in presocialist China, it was subjected to the most strikes, a total of fifty-six between 1918 and 1940.[53]

Although BAT did not respond to these strikes by building housing for Chinese workers, the company did begin to try to oust Number Ones after an especially long and acrimonious strike in 1927 and 1928. According to Elizabeth Perry's detailed analysis, BAT's management confronted labor leaders who included Guomindang officials, Communist cadres, and Green Gang members, and at the end of a 109-day strike, the company agreed to remit higher taxes to the Guomindang government, recognize the BAT union, and improve workers' livelihood. In the course of the strike, the company found Chinese labor increasingly aggressive and confident, especially after two Green Gang leaders ousted a Communist leader and forged a close alliance with the Guomindang government.[54] Thereafter, apparently hoping to undercut these labor leaders and thereby weaken support for strikes, BAT began to crack down on Number Ones.

CAMPAIGNS AGAINST NUMBER ONES, 1927–1937

In May 1928, only a few months after settling the long strike, BAT posted regulations that directly prohibited its Number Ones' standard practices. "The factory administration [gongchang] has the full authority to determine which workers are hired and fired," the company's new regulations proclaimed. While BAT expressed in these regulations "no objection to any clubs [julebu], associations [huishe], or trade unions [gonghui]," it insisted that membership for workers in any such groups be entirely voluntary. In the most significant of the regulations, BAT declared that the "wages will be given to workers directly by the factory." It instructed workers not to give any money to "staff members [zhiyuan] in order to seek or keep jobs," and it announced that it had already fired several managers who were suspected of taking bribes.[55] Such regulations, if enforced, would have undercut Number Ones and given BAT's management direct control over workers.

BAT recruited enforcers to carry out these regulations. In the late 1920s it hired sixty-four policemen to patrol its factories. The police force's chief, Kan Angui, was an officer in the Shanghai Police Force (Da Shanghai gong'anju); the remaining members were all Chinese civilians. In 1936, still unable to discipline its workshop heads, BAT replaced them with twenty-five college graduates. The company gave these young Chinese a three-month training course and, after administering a final examination, stationed them on the shop floors in its factories.[56]

Despite BAT's promulgation of new regulations and deployment of police, college-trained supervisors, and other enforcers, it failed to achieve direct managerial control over its workers. On January 23, 1937, BAT acknowledged in a confidential letter to its factory managers that its workers were still being recruited by Number Ones, then known as "overseers" (guanli yuan). The company urged its factory managers to stop recruiting through these overseers and to rely instead on "workers with good reputations to introduce new workers" to its factories.[57] Thus, after ten years of campaigning, BAT was still not able to discipline Number Ones or break their control over workers before the Japanese military invasion of 1937.

While BAT's management never dealt directly with Chinese industrial workers in its factories, its salaried staff members did deal directly with Chinese tobacco growers at its leaf purchasing centers in Shandong province. BAT made this direct relationship possible not by eliminating all Chinese networks but by depending on one Chinese network to exclude the rest.

In 1913 BAT recruited Tian Junchuan, a local merchant, to set up its tobacco purchasing center in Shandong province at Weixian along a railway line that originated one hundred miles to the southeast in the coastal port of Qingdao. During the previous year, Tian had resigned from his job with the company that ran this railway and opened the Tongyihe General Store at Weixian. It was there that he and one of BAT's Shanghai compradors, Zhang Xiaofang, came to terms. Under Tian's arrangement with BAT, he was given no managerial position and was paid no salary. Instead, while working with BAT, he continued to operate his store and to pay his own staff, which consisted of some two hundred clerks. As compensation for his services, he received a 1 percent commission on all of BAT's purchases of tobacco leaf at Weixian.[58]

Through his local contacts Tian bought land and recruited staff members for BAT. After BAT's comprador Zhang made initial investments on behalf of the company, Tian completed the transactions, giving BAT sites at six railway stations where it built seven leaf purchasing centers, each with its own curing plant and its own up-to-date technology—a new Philadelphia Drying Machine imported from the United States. Because all of these purchasing centers were located outside treaty ports, where foreigners were legally prohibited from buying land, Tian paid for them in the name of his Tongyihe General Store using money supplied by BAT. At the principal site, Ershilibao, he built a guest house, also in the name of his general store, to accommodate the staff members who worked for BAT. There he interviewed local Chinese before making recommendations to BAT, which employed sixteen hundred hired hands in the busy season at Ershilibao alone, not to mention its workers at Weixian's other leaf purchasing centers. As anticipated by job applicants clamoring for appointments at Tian's guest house, his backing was decisive; at Weixian many members of BAT's staff, especially interpreters and secretaries, were recommended and guaranteed by him.[59]

Tian also recruited tobacco growers. He induced Chinese farmers to plant tobacco by offering them free tobacco seed (imported by BAT from the American South), access to credit, loans of equipment (such as thermometers and iron pipes for curing sheds), and payments in cash on delivery of crops. This promotional effort lasted only a few years and was discontinued in the late 1910s, by which time the cultivation of Weixian bright tobacco had spread widely—from 39 acres in 1913 to 23,210 acres in 1920.[60]

After relying on Tian to organize local staff members and peasants, BAT built purchasing centers where its Western and Chinese salaried representatives came face-to-face with the local Chinese at harvest time every year. BAT's Western managers were mainly Americans who had grown up in the tobacco belt of Virginia and North Carolina, and they personally inspected and graded samples of each Chinese grower's tobacco. They worked with BAT's Chinese staff members (including translators, secretaries, registrars, accountants, weighmen, and other clerks), but neither the Western nor the Chinese staff members bargained with the growers about the grading and pricing of tobacco leaf. To be sure, they required that each grower express agreement with the grade assigned to his crop before cash payment was made, but if a grower objected to the grade given, his only recourse was to try again by returning to the end of the line of waiting growers—a line that, according to contemporary observers, was commonly as much as two-thirds of a mile long. Despite BAT's refusal to bargain, Chinese tobacco growers continued to sell to BAT because they found other Chinese and Japanese tobacco buyers no more accommodating and because they valued BAT's willingness to pay in cash on the spot.[61]

In practice, if not in theory, Tian presided over BAT's tobacco buying at Weixian from his position as head Chinese cashier. In this capacity he supervised all payments to growers and calculated BAT's total expenditures, which, in turn, indicated his own commission at 1 percent on all BAT's leaf purchases. Annually he earned 80,000 yuan from this source plus another 20,000 to 30,000 yuan from selling BAT's cigarettes, and in the 1930s when he finally retired, he saw to it that his son replaced him as BAT's head cashier.[62]

Apart from the formal purchasing process, Tian had other extensive dealings with Chinese tobacco growers. In the 1920s and 1930s, after BAT no longer needed to recruit growers and ceased to hand out tobacco-related pieces of equipment free of charge, Tian's Tongyihe General Store sold these items to tobacco growers on a large scale. In fact, he came to dominate the local market for beancake fertilizer, iron pipes, coal, and other items needed by cultivators to grow and cure tobacco, and he expanded his local store into an interregional chain with branches in the big cities of Qingdao, Tianjin, and Shanghai. In Weixian, as a lender of beancake fertilizer, coal, and money, he annually took in about 100,000 yuan until 1926 when, under charges of usury, he stopped making loans. By then these profits and other income from BAT and the Tongyihe General Store had made him a millionaire.[63]

Like Number Ones in BAT's cigarette factories, Tian subordinated his recruits to himself and retained authority over them. He appointed himself arbiter of their disputes and claimed that they readily brought their problems to him because they preferred not to have the local heads of their rural townships (*xiangzhang*) and wards (*quzhang*) meddle in their relations with BAT. In cases in which Tian failed to prevent tobacco growers' complaints from escalating into violent protests, he and BAT had another line of defense behind the local militia, which received from BAT monthly payments of 600 yuan during the harvest and 400 yuan during the rest of the year. In fact, BAT housed a branch of Weixian's public security bureau within its own office, and the bureau's uniformed policemen stood guard at the company's gates and escorted its Western managers every day between their American-style houses (which were built by the company) and their jobs at the leaf purchasing centers.[64]

Thus Tian made it possible for BAT's salaried managers to buy tobacco directly from Chinese growers, and once in place, BAT's direct purchasing system set a precedent in Weixian. As Yip Hon-ming has shown in her richly detailed study of tobacco growing in Weixian, local Chinese merchants procured tobacco very differently than BAT did. They had an indirect purchasing system that involved "numerous and various intermediary dealers [who] tended to clog and thus complicate the circulating channels." BAT's "direct purchasing system . . . was . . . more simplified and rationalized [and] free from layer-upon-layer encumbrances and unnecessary divergences."[65] With these and other advantages, BAT and a few relatively large Chinese and Japanese cigarette firms squeezed out small local Chinese tobacco buyers at Weixian, especially during the depression of the 1930s.

BAT'S INDIRECT PURCHASING

In 1917, shortly after establishing its direct purchasing system at Weixian, BAT opened another tobacco purchasing center, at Xuchang in central Henan province 350 miles southwest of Weixian. But in Xuchang, unlike Weixian, it did not begin to buy tobacco directly from growers until the 1930s. At Xuchang, BAT tried to replace the existing system of indirect purchasing only after its buildings were deliberately destroyed in 1927.

In 1917 the company sent a comprador, Ren Bozhong, to buy land at Xuchang, which, like Weixian, was not a treaty port and was located along a railway, in this case the Beijing-Hankou Railway. In Xuchang, Ren bought several hundred mu of land for BAT in the name of a Chinese family estate, the Yong'an Tang, and he constructed a tall and massive building on this land. He persuaded farmers in the vicinity of Xuchang to grow bright tobacco by handing out free seed and curing equipment, and these farmers almost immediately produced the desired results: crops yielding 2.5 million pounds of bright tobacco in 1918, 16 million pounds in 1920, and 32 million pounds in 1924. In BAT's one big purchasing center at Xuchang, the company's salaried Western and Chinese staff members received tobacco from hundreds of independent Chinese merchants who collected it in surrounding villages and sold it through tobacco firms (*yan hang*) in the city. Between 1917 and 1926 BAT used this indirect purchasing system to procure each year an average of 10.5 million pounds valued at 20 million yuan, making Xuchang second only to Weixian as a producer of bright tobacco in China.[66]

In 1927 BAT's tobacco purchasing center at Xuchang was seized by General Feng Yuxiang and his troops at the height of the fighting during Chiang Kai-shek's Northern Expedition. BAT's Ren Bozhong was charged with illegally selling land to foreigners, and he fled to Hong Kong. BAT's inventory of tobacco leaf and its curing equipment were confiscated and auctioned off, and its prominent building was burned to the ground. Citing this and other losses, BAT pleaded with the British authorities to intervene militarily, but the British government declined, and the company's purchasing system in Xuchang was left in disarray. BAT's losses turned into its rivals' gains as Chinese cigarette companies, led by Nanyang Brothers Tobacco Company, began to purchase tobacco at Xuchang on a grander scale, and Chinese tobacco buying firms formed a guild that had more than a thousand members and procured more than 80 percent of the tobacco produced in the area.[67]

After 1927 BAT sought to regain prominence in Xuchang by turning to its original Chinese fixer, Wu Tingsheng. Since leaving BAT in 1919, Wu had held official positions, and on rejoining BAT, he took full advantage of his appointment in the Nationalist government's Ministry of Finance. In 1932 Wu formed a new firm called the Xuchang Leaf Tobacco Company, which bought the property formerly held by Ren Bo-

zhong's Yong'an Tang (a dummy front for BAT), and began to align local officials and other members of Xuchang's elite against the Xuchang
Tobacco Guild. In 1934 Wu linked his campaign in Xuchang with Chiang Kai-shek's government in Nanjing by forming the Committee for
the Improvement of American Seed Tobacco, which worked in cooperation with the Nationalist government's Ministry of Finance. In 1935,
after receiving these official sanctions, he rebuilt BAT's old purchasing
center in Xuchang and arranged for it to have the exclusive privilege of
transporting tobacco on freight trains operated by the Nationalist government's Ministry of Railways, leaving the Xuchang Tobacco Guild
with no comparably priced means of transporting goods to Shanghai.[68]

By the end of 1935 Wu ended the competitive threat that BAT's rivals
had posed at Xuchang. With official backing, he transported BAT's tobacco by rail at rates that could not be matched by the Xuchang Transportation Company, which had been carrying tobacco for the Xuchang
Tobacco Guild from Xuchang to Shanghai. Soon the guild began to
dissolve and hundreds of tobacco merchants withdrew from the trade.
Once Wu had disposed of this competition, he left tobacco growers little
alternative except to deliver their own crops to BAT's purchasing center
at the Xuchang Leaf Tobacco Company, and in 1935 large numbers of
them began to do so, traveling up to 70 or 80 miles for the purpose.[69]
Only then did BAT finally engage in direct purchasing of tobacco at
Xuchang.

Wu paid a heavy price for this victory on behalf of BAT. First he was
sued by the Xuchang Tobacco Guild and the Xuchang Transportation
Company for illegally buying land on behalf of foreigners and for engaging in corrupt dealings with officials. Then, after he won the case in
court, he was accused of bribing the judge. Finally, at the end of the year,
he suffered from an attack that he did not survive. On December 31,
1935, while walking home from the Xuchang Leaf Tobacco Company,
he was stopped by two men who pointed their guns at his left temple and
shot him to death.[70]

CONCLUSION

BAT's record in China contrasted sharply with that of Standard Oil.
During the first years of the twentieth century, both companies introduced Western-style corporate hierarchies that were transferred to
China from the West. But while Standard Oil continued to retain this
approach for half a century, BAT reconsidered it after less than twenty

years. In 1919, after comparing the company's Western bureaucratic approach with Chinese social networks, it shifted a large measure of responsibility from the hierarchy to the networks, as dramatized by its dismissal of its English-speaking manager Wu Tingsheng and its elevation of its Cantonese commission agent Zheng Bozhao. Thereafter, in the 1920s and 1930s, BAT did not abandon its Western-style corporate hierarchy, but it became much more dependent on Chinese commission agents, delegating authority to them, allowing them to retain their own business practices, and overlooking their violations of company regulations.[71] Meanwhile, in cigarette factories and tobacco fields, BAT exercised little direct managerial control over Chinese Number Ones who supervised its Chinese industrial workers and Chinese merchants who mediated with Chinese tobacco growers.

Despite BAT's decision to give less responsibility to its salaried staff and more to its commission agents and other Chinese intermediaries, it still probably retained more salaried staff members than did any other firm except Standard Oil in early-twentieth-century China. These two Western-owned businesses installed the deepest Western-style corporate hierarchies of all, and yet even they did not go so far as to give their hierarchies a fully Western character by staffing them at all levels with Westerners. Of all the foreign-owned firms in China, only the Japanese companies both established corporate hierarchies and staffed them at all levels with their own nationals.

CHAPTER 4

Mitsui Trading Company

During its first twenty-one years in China, 1877–98, the Japanese-owned Mitsui Trading Company (Mitsui Bussan kaisha) did not attempt to adopt a distinctively Japanese approach to the market. It had been founded in 1876, the year before it entered China's market, by the House of Mitsui, a leading Japanese merchant house dating from the seventeenth century, and after setting up its first overseas office at Shanghai in 1877, it initially followed the example of Western trading companies in China, delegating authority to Chinese compradors in much the same way that Standard Oil did during these years.

In 1898 Mitsui Trading Company's enterprising fifty-year-old president, Masuda Takashi, decisively departed from these past practices in China and began to introduce a new Japanese approach. Grumbling that Chinese compradors cost as much as 1 percent of Mitsui's total transactions in China, Masuda decided to rid the company of them, and he began pensioning them off. In their place, he declared, Japanese China specialists were to market Mitsui's goods in China.[1]

JAPANESE CHINA SPECIALISTS IN COMPETITION WITH THE WEST

In 1898, at the same time that Masuda proposed to replace Chinese compradors with Japanese China specialists, he also assigned top priority to his firm's sales of cotton textiles in China and began to compete directly with Western businesses for the market.[2] Masuda probably chose to concentrate more on cotton textiles than on any of Mitsui's other numerous exports because of China's potential as a consumer of cotton yarn and cloth. As he anticipated, within the next fifteen years China realized this potential by becoming the world's leading importer of cotton yarn and second-leading importer of cotton cloth (India was the leading importer of cotton cloth).[3]

When Masuda called his company's attention to this market in 1898, Japan's chances for overtaking Western rivals seemed slight as it did not have superior technology (having imported machinery from the West) or special access to raw cotton (having ceased to use Japanese-grown cotton in exported yarn and cloth when Japan's tariff on imported cotton was abolished in 1896). Moreover, before 1897 Japan had imported more cotton textiles than it had exported and had barely touched China's market for these goods.

And yet in 1913, only fifteen years after Masuda had set his sights on China's market for imported cotton textiles, he had achieved his goal. Within this time Japan's share had jumped from about 24 percent to 50 percent of China's market for imported yarn and from virtually zero to 20 percent of China's market for imported cloth (see tables 4 and 5). Leading the way in China, Mitsui Trading Company had quadrupled the value of its yarn sales (from 3,968,000 yen in 1898 to 20,199,000 yen in 1913) and had multiplied the value of its cloth sales by a factor of 63 (from 166,000 yen in 1897 to 10,530,000 yen in 1913). (See tables 6 and 7).

If, as characterized by the prominent Chinese economic historian Chao Kang, this Japanese victory was "a miracle in modern commercial history,"[4] then how was the miracle performed? Part of the explanation lies in Mitsui's introduction of a Japanese corporate hierarchy staffed by Japanese nationals—salaried employees who were trained by the company as China specialists.

TRAINING JAPANESE CHINA SPECIALISTS

Under the first of Mitsui's two China training programs, which lasted from April 1898 to October 1915, the company annually sent recent Japanese graduates of junior and senior high schools to Shanghai, Niuzhuang (Yingkou), Tianjin, Taipei, and Hong Kong for three years of full-time study. Age fifteen to twenty, these Japanese were known as "apprentices in Chinese commerce" (*shinkoku shogyo minaraisei*) and were

TABLE 4. COTTON YARN, BY COUNTRY OF ORIGIN, IMPORTED INTO CHINA, 1885–1913

(by % and million pounds of total imported cotton yarn)

Year	United Kingdom %	India %	Japan %	United States %	Total Million Pounds
1885	89	11	—	—	41
1891	52	48	—	—	161
1898	5	71	24	—	261
1906	—	77	23	—	339
1913	—	50	50	—	358
1926	—	24	75	—	77
1927	2	9	89	0.4	60
1928	—	2	98	—	38

SOURCE: Reynolds, "The East Asian 'Textile Cluster' Trade," 143.

TABLE 5. SHARES OF COTTON CLOTH, BY COUNTRY OF ORIGIN, IMPORTED INTO CHINA, 1902–1930

(by % of total imported cotton cloth)

Year	United Kingdom %	United States %	Japan %	Other %
1902	55.3	26.8	2.7	15.2
1905	49.2	35.5	2.5	12.8
1907	72.2	5.7	4.7	17.4
1909	54.7	18.1	8.3	18.9
1911	61.3	9.5	13.8	15.4
1913	53.3	7.9	20.2	18.6
1916	43.3	2.4	39.7	14.6
1917	32.6	0.4	55.0	12.0
1918	32.0	0.6	56.0	11.4
1919	25.6	1.4	60.8	12.2
1920	43.1	1.2	45.3	10.4
1921	43.1	2.1	42.6	12.2
1922	40.2	1.4	46.0	12.4
1923	34.8	0.2	51.7	13.3
1924	34.7	0.1	50.0	15.2
1925	23.9	0.7	65.5	9.9
1926	23.6	0.2	57.3	8.9
1927	16.6	0.2	68.1	15.1
1928	21.5	0.2	66.6	11.7
1929	22.1	0.3	65.4	12.2
1930	13.2	0.1	72.2	14.5

SOURCE: Chao, "The Chinese-American Cotton-Textile Trade," 121, table 21.

groomed to become China "traders" (*boekijin*). Although Mitsui expected the Japanese apprentices to commit themselves to long-term language study and employment in China, it permitted precocious students to move through its language school's curriculum at an accelerated pace. Perhaps the most precocious of them all, Mori Kaku (1883–1932), entered the company's school for apprentices in its Shanghai branch at the age of nineteen, completed the three-year course in only two years, and on graduation in 1904 moved swiftly up the company's hierarchy in China, becoming head of its Tianjin branch in 1914 at the age of thirty-one. Mori's meteoric rise was by no means typical, but it showed other employees and prospective employees that the company was willing to reward talented young China specialists with rapid promotions and high salaries.[5]

When first introduced, the apprentice program drew complaints from Mitsui's Japanese branch managers who doubted the value of investing in such inexperienced young people. In response, President Masuda made an inspection tour to observe firsthand the company's branches at Shanghai, Taipei, and Hong Kong in October 1898, and at his urging, the company's board of directors in Tokyo introduced a second program in December 1898. This second training program was for older and more experienced employees designated as "China trainees" (*Shina shugyosei*). Candidates were chosen on the basis not of age but of education (with a junior high school diploma as the minimum requirement), willingness to participate, and "indomitability of spirit" (*fukutsu no toshi*). Beginning in 1899, Mitsui annually selected ten employees, released them from their usual jobs, and sent them to China for three years of full-time study. The company arranged for them to study at branches in several cities, including Shanghai, Nanjing, Guangzhou, and Hong Kong.[6]

According to Mitsui's Shanghai branch manager at the time, Yamamoto Jotaro, Japanese in the company's training programs became familiar with China's customs as well as its language. By his account, all Japanese apprentices and trainees had to dress in the clothes of common Chinese "coolies," wear their hair "Chinese" style (which, before the overthrow of the Manchu monarchy in 1911, was actually Manchu style with a bald pate and a queue down the back), and live with Chinese families. To encourage even more intimate contact, Mitsui offered Japanese apprentices and trainees bonuses if they would marry Chinese women, but reportedly no one took advantage of the offer. Through these activities, Masuda noted, Mitsui taught Japanese apprentices and trainees

Figure 6.   Japanese members of Mitsui's Shanghai staff, 1893. Yamamoto
Jotaro, a young trainee at the time, is in the third row, third from the right.
Reprinted from *Yamamoto Jotaro,* following 62.

about "the mentality of the Chinese people, the basis for trust among
Chinese merchants, and the flows of commercial goods [in China] in full
detail."[7]

Unlike Japan's best-known language institute in China at the time,
Toa Dobun Shoin, Mitsui's received no support from the Japanese government. Operating on strictly private funds, it produced superior results, according to Yamamoto. He proudly reported at a meeting of the
company's branch managers in 1904 that its apprentices and trainees
were learning to speak and read Chinese better than the graduates
of Toa Dobun Shoin or any other foreign-language school in China.[8]
Yamamoto's claims have been confirmed by Chinese observers. For example, a Chinese from Xiamen in Southeast China recalled that Japanese staff members stationed there spoke not only Mandarin but also
the local dialects around the cities of Xiamen (Xiamen hua), Fuzhou
(Fuzhou hua), and Shantou (Shantou hua). They acquired this language
competence either by taking courses at Mitsui's language school or
by growing up in Southeast China and becoming educated in Chinese

Figure 7. Japanese members of Mitsui's much larger Shanghai staff, 1907. Yamamoto Jotaro, by then the manager of this office, is in the second row, seventh from the left. Reprinted from *Yamamoto Jotaro,* following 152.

schools before joining Mitsui. Dressing and speaking like local businessmen, they were able to pass for Xiamen natives.[9]

REPLACING CHINESE

Between 1898 and 1904, as Japanese graduated from Mitsui's training program, the company assigned them to replace Chinese compradors and other intermediaries in all departments of their business. It reserved all positions as staff members for Japanese, leaving only low-paying jobs as office workers for Chinese.[10] With these appointments, Mitsui began introducing its own Japanese salaried managers for marketing cotton textiles and buying raw cotton in China.

In marketing Mitsui became the first foreign firm to abolish the post of comprador and cut off relations with Chinese interregional wholesalers. In 1899 it pensioned off its comprador Jin Yangsheng and its eight other Chinese staff members in Shanghai and subsequently dismissed compradors at Tianjin in 1900, Taipei in 1901, and Hong Kong in 1902. Before 1902 the Japanese company had relied on two Chinese merchant houses, Gong Xin Hao and Yuan Sheng Hao, to arrange all of its shipments of cotton cloth from Shanghai to other parts of China, but thereafter it obviated the need for Chinese interregional wholesalers by posting Japanese representatives at metropolitan cities in six of China's nine major regions: at Niuzhuang in the Northeast; at Tianjin, Beijing, and Zhefu in the North; at Shanghai in the Lower Yangzi; at Hankou in the Middle Yangzi; at Taipei and Xiamen in the Southeast; and at Hong Kong and Guangzhou in the South.[11]

In purchasing as in marketing Mitsui used Japanese salaried representatives rather than Chinese compradors to manage the Sino-Japanese raw cotton trade, and it thereby gained control over this trade for the first time at the turn of the century. Before this time Mitsui had encountered much stronger resistance to its bids for control over cotton purchasing in China than in India, Asia's other leading cotton-growing country. After entering the Indian cotton market in the 1880s, Mitsui had almost immediately taken command of the Indo-Japanese cotton trade, but despite its entrance into China's cotton market as early as 1877, it had failed to gain control over the Sino-Japanese cotton trade as long as it retained Chinese compradors. Only at the turn of the century, after Mitsui dispatched Japanese salaried representatives to make upcountry purchases, did it begin to exercise managerial control over the Sino-Japanese cotton trade.[12]

INITIAL SALES OF COTTON TEXTILES

As a result of its organizational innovations, Mitsui ousted its Chinese compradors and used its Japanese China specialists to deal directly with local Chinese merchants, but this strategy did not increase its sales of cotton textiles as rapidly as its sales of other goods. As early as 1902, only four years after Masuda's call for the abolition of compradors, Mitsui's profits on trade in China tripled (from 114,381,000 yen for 1897–99 to 353,623,000 yen for 1900–1902), and its profit rate doubled (from 10.0 percent to 20.3 percent in the same three-year periods).[13] By contrast, the company's sales of cotton textiles in China did not keep pace: the value of its yarn sales less than doubled (from 3,968,000 yen in 1897 to 6,410,000 yen in 1902), and the value of its cloth sales more than doubled but on a much smaller scale, totaling only 8 percent of the value of its yarn sales. (See tables 6 and 7).

So, despite Masuda's determination to give cotton textiles top priority and his willingness to train and deploy Japanese sales representatives in China, he initially achieved comparatively modest results in this market. At the time his company could not compete directly with American rivals, because Japanese-made cloth was inferior. As one of Masuda's investigators reported after a trip to Northeast China in 1905, "Japanese-made cotton cloth has not become a substitute for American-made cloth. . . . Japanese manufacturers urgently need to improve the quality

TABLE 6. MITSUI'S SHARE OF JAPAN'S COTTON YARN EXPORTS, 1897–1919

(in 000 yen and % of Japan's total exports)

Year	Value of Japan's Yarn Exports (000 yen)	Value of Mitsui's Yarn Exports (000 yen)	Mitsui's share of Japan's Yarn Exports (%)
1897	13,490	3,968	29.4
1898	20,117	4,420	22.0
1899	28,521	8,498	29.8
1900	20,589	6,580	32.0
1901	21,466	4,556	21.2
1902	19,902	6,410	32.2
1903	31,419	8,896	28.3
1904	29,268	10,386	35.5
1905	33,246	10,716	32.2
1906	35,304	18,508	52.4
1907	30,343	8,862	29.2
1908	20,724	7,521	36.3
1909	31,657	10,532	33.3
1910	46,696	15,447	33.1
1911	43,238	16,202	37.5
1912	56,634	18,887	33.3
1913	73,089	20,199	27.6
1914	80,851	16,847	20.8
1915	69,004	17,480	25.8
1916	80,906	32,312	40.0
1917	113,782	28,133	24.8
1918	162,789	33,738	16.8
1919	121,636	27,107	22.2

SOURCE: *KMBK,* 239, table 14; 361, table 20.

of it." [14] Mitsui's sales of Japanese-made cloth did not begin to make significant headway against American-made cloth until the company began to receive direct aid in China from the Japanese government.

MITSUI'S COOPERATION WITH THE JAPANESE GOVERNMENT IN NORTHEAST CHINA, 1905–1907

Before 1905 Mitsui had tried to penetrate China's market for cotton textiles without direct aid from the Japanese government. To be sure, Mitsui had gained access to China's markets partly because of Japan's military victory in the Sino-Japanese War of 1894–95 and the subsequent Treaty of Shimonoseki, which had established Japanese concession areas in ten Chinese cities and had opened several Chinese ports for

TABLE 7.   MITSUI'S SHARE OF JAPAN'S COTTON
CLOTH EXPORTS, 1897–1919
(in 000 yen and % of Japan's total exports)

Year	Value of Japan's Cloth Exports (000 yen)	Value of Mitsui's Cloth Exports (000 yen)	Mitsui's share of Japan's Cloth Exports (%)
1897	2,512	166	6.6
1898	2,598	140	5.4
1899	3,910	293	7.5
1900	5,724	297	5.2
1901	5,462	371	6.8
1902	5,998	513	8.6
1903	6,875	787	11.4
1904	7,743	1,899	24.5
1905	11,492	1,028	8.9
1906	15,619	3,109	19.9
1907	16,345	6,687	40.9
1908	14,611	6,823	46.7
1903	17,673	7,442	42.1
1910	20,462	10,509	51.4
1911	28,684	9,801	34.2
1912	36,953	9,780	26.5
1913	43,105	10,530	24.2
1914	43,403	10,813	24.9
1915	48,494	12,288	25.3
1916	73,173	19,983	27.3
1917	148,108	33,980	22.9
1918	268,640	59,244	22.1
1919	351,195	69,240	19.7

SOURCE: *KMBK,* 245, table 17; 361, table 20.

foreign trade. But this indirect aid had not given Japanese companies trading advantages over Western companies; Western governments had immediately secured equally advantageous trading privileges by signing most-favored-nation agreements with the Qing government. Not until after the Russo-Japanese War of 1904–5 did Mitsui's new marketing system benefit from Japanese political intervention that was directly advantageous to itself and distinctly disadvantageous to its Western rivals.

A PROPOSAL FOR SECRET
BUSINESS-GOVERNMENT COOPERATION

At the end of the Russo-Japanese War the Japanese government secretly offered Mitsui direct aid in its quest for China's cloth market. The government made the proposal in exchange for Mitsui's help in reclaiming bank notes in postwar Northeast China (Manchuria) where the war had been fought. During the war the Japanese military had issued about 140 million yen worth of wartime currency for its soldiers' use in Northeast China, and after the war the Japanese government needed to withdraw currently circulating notes valued at about 50 million yen. Rather than redeem the notes for silver, Japan's Ministry of Finance and Ministry of Agriculture and Commerce proposed to Mitsui that it help the Japanese government to carry out a cheaper plan. Under this plan the government offered Mitsui the exclusive right to convert wartime notes into yen as long as Mitsui would accept these notes only in exchange for Japanese-made cotton textiles and would take no commission during its first two years of marketing the goods and no more than a 1 percent commission for as long as the war notes remained in circulation.[15]

In February 1906 Mitsui responded to the proposal by recruiting as its potential suppliers five of Japan's largest cotton cloth manufacturers: Osaka, Mie, Tenman, Kanekin, and Okayama. Mitsui proposed that it would be the head and sole distributor for the group, which became known as the Japan Cotton Cloth Export Association (Nihon menpu yushutsu kumiai). In addition, Mitsui continued to distribute in China for Japan's largest cotton textiles manufacturer, Kanegafuchi, which did not join the association but channeled the lion's share of its goods through Mitsui. Two months later, in April 1906, Mitsui's Fujino Kamenosuke led a delegation of Japanese cotton textile manufacturers on a tour of China where they laid plans for a Japanese cartel designed to oust American textiles from Northeast China. On the basis of this investigation, Mitsui formulated a strategy whereby the five Japanese mills in the association would make cloth as uniformly as possible and would ship it to Northeast China under a single trademark, Two Crabs, which belonged to Mitsui.[16]

To finance the plan Mitsui sent its Osaka branch manager, Fukui Kikusaburo, to appeal for special interest rates from the Yokohama Specie Bank in Tokyo. "The Japanese government has asked Mitsui to find a way to collect army wartime currency," Fukui told Takahashi Korekiyo, president of the Yokohama Specie Bank, but "we cannot really compete with the United States unless our interest rates are lower." In reply Takahashi said, "I understand, and I'll do my best."[17] Within four months, thanks to Takahashi's efforts, Mitsui began taking out loans at 4 percent rather than the higher 7 to 8 percent then being charged in Japan. This preferential lending rate was approximately the same or slightly lower than the interest rate available to the leading cotton textiles companies in the United States at the time.[18]

Once all parties agreed to the plan, Mitsui was given official permission to enter the Northeast China market within a few months after the Russian and Japanese governments reached an armistice and signed the Treaty of Portsmouth in November 1905, and it was allowed to export to the port of Dalian in Northeast China without paying any tariff. Not until almost two years after the armistice did the Japanese military authorities occupying Northeast China allow Western firms to resume trade in this region.[19]

CAPITALIZING ON OFFICIAL SUPPORT

Mitsui took advantage of the preferential treatment by reorganizing and enlarging its regional distribution system. During the war it had already spent 100,000 yen on marketing in Northeast China, and in the post-war period it invested on a much grander scale. First it upgraded its office at Niuzhuang and shifted the office's emphasis from buying Chinese-grown agricultural products to selling Japanese-made cotton cloth. Next Mitsui received official permission to use about four hundred miles of railway from Changchun to Dalian that had formerly been part of the Chinese Eastern Railway under Russian control and had recently been ceded to Japan and named the South Manchuria Railway. Then it shifted its head regional office for Northeast China from Niuzhuang to Dalian, the southern terminus of the South Manchuria Railway, and extended its distribution network to all the region's other major cities, adding branch offices in 1906 at Fengtian, Tieling, and Andong and in 1907 at Jilin, Changchun, Harbin, and Vladivostok.[20]

Between 1906 and 1907 Mitsui began to operate this distributing system with the avowed aim of eliminating American-made cloth piece goods from the markets of Northeast China and barring their reentry there. During the preceding fifteen years the market for American-made coarse cotton cloth in Northeast China had been steadily growing because of the region's cold climate, rapid population growth as a frontier economy, and relative lack of handicraft production compared to China's other regions; and during the Russo-Japanese War the market had boomed because of the wartime demand for tents and uniforms and because of local prosperity generated by Russian and Japanese spending in the region. But after the war Mitsui undercut the demand for the re-

maining American-made cloth by underpricing it. Disciplining manufacturers through the Japan Cotton Cloth Export Association and taking no commission for itself, Mitsui drove the price of Japanese-made
sheetings 20 to 30 percent below American-made goods of comparable
quality. Between 1906 and 1907 it enforced this pricing policy widely
and strictly—even forcing out of the association the smallest two of the
five Japanese manufacturers, Kanekin (which was absorbed by another
member of the association, Osaka) and Okayama.[21]

By the time American-made cotton textiles were officially allowed
back into Northeast China between 1907 and 1909, Mitsui had a virtual monopoly on the region's market. As the company's branch manager at Niuzhuang, Inoue Taizo, proudly reported to his superiors in
Tokyo in August 1908: "In two years, 1906 and 1907, about 40,000
bales [hyo] of cotton cloth have been sold, and their trademark and
goodwill have become known all over Manchuria. As a result, American cotton cloth has been entirely expelled, which means that we have
reached our original goal."[22] Although statistics are not available on
Northeast China specifically, those on China as a whole suggest that Inoue was scarcely exaggerating when he said American cotton cloth was
"entirely expelled." As shown in table 5, the American share of China's
market for imported cotton cloth plunged from 35.5 percent in 1905 to
5.7 percent in 1907.

THE BREVITY OF DIRECT OFFICIAL AID

Mitsui only briefly enjoyed the benefits of direct official aid in China's
cotton cloth market. It undoubtedly received long-term indirect and
informal aid of the kind given to it by the Yokohama Specie Bank and
the South Manchuria Railway Company; but its cloth sales benefited
from direct and formal official policies—including the Tokyo government's authorization to convert wartime currency into yen and the Japanese military authorities' permission to trade in Northeast China before Western companies were allowed to do so—for just two years,
1906 and 1907.

When Japan's direct political intervention ceased in 1907, Mitsui
had no official guarantee that it would retain a secure grip on the cotton
cloth market of Northeast China. In China's market for imported cotton cloth, Japan's share rose steadily but at a relatively low level, from
2.5 percent in 1905 to 8.3 percent in 1909, and America's share contin-

ued to be higher as it rebounded from a low of 5.7 percent in 1907 to 18.1 percent in 1909 (while the British continued to hold the lion's share). (See table 5.) In Northeast China Mitsui had achieved an advantage over its American competitors with official help between 1906 and 1907, but thereafter the outcome of this Japanese-American rivalry was determined by commercial competition in which neither side benefited from direct official aid.

JAPANESE-AMERICAN COMMERCIAL RIVALRY IN NORTHEAST CHINA, 1907–1913

In 1907, after the Japanese government ceased to intervene on Mitsui's behalf, the company put its marketing system to the test in direct competition with American rivals for the cotton cloth market of Northeast China. By focusing on this one fiercely fought battle, it is possible to see the basic elements of the American approach, the basic elements of the Japanese approach, and the reasons why one prevailed over the other.

AMERICAN DEPENDENCE ON CHINESE COMPRADORS

Manufacturers of cotton cloth in the American South relied on American firms in New York to export their goods to China, and these American export firms, on delivering the goods to Shanghai, depended on Chinese compradors to carry out long-distance trade through Chinese commission agents in other cities and regions of the country. To reach these Chinese commission agents, compradors operated through social neworks that supervised trade over long distances such as the five-hundred-mile trip from Shanghai to Dalian, the southernmost port in Northeast China.

In general, compradors in Shanghai conducted long-distance trade through an interlocked chain of contacts. Their first link was with Chinese brokers (*qianke*) or specialized wholesalers (such as cloth merchants, *bu hao*) who prepared orders and arranged credit with native banks (*qianzhuang*) for goods to be shipped outside Shanghai; their second link was with Chinese "guest merchants" (*ke shang*) who conveyed the goods from Shanghai to metropolises at the cores of their home regions; and their third link was with Chinese trading companies that distributed goods to wholesalers and retailers at the regional and local levels.[23] In the case of Northeast China, the last link in the chain consisted of a small number of large Chinese trading companies. As Robert H. G. Lee has pointed out, in the frontier economy of Northeast China, "only large trading firms could supply their agents with credit and goods as they fanned out into tribal territories to establish collecting and distributing networks." By the early twentieth century, according to Lee, these firms "were often very old establishments" that had a "near monopoly . . . over the regional trade."[24]

Despite the dangers of soaring transaction costs, American exporters of cotton cloth continued to depend on compradors and other Chinese intermediaries to guide their goods from Shanghai to Northeast China during the years after the Russo-Japanese War. As an American official on the scene reported at the time, "The [American] goods, from the time they leave the importer in Shanghai, are in Chinese hands. The dealer in Shanghai sells to the dealer in Newchwang [Niuzhuang], who in turn sells to the merchants in other cities or in the interior of Manchuria. The shipment and the sale throughout is controlled by Chinese."[25]

The rationale for leaving control in Chinese hands was expressed at the time by an American partner in the largest New York-based firm exporting American-made cotton textiles to China. His statement is worth quoting at length because it spells out the basic premises underlying the American approach.

> You know the existence of the merchant guilds at Shanghai and other ports and their value as distributing factors, far greater than anything that could be devised or established by any foreign enterprise. And you know the narrow margin of profit upon which native merchants operate, compelled by a fierce competition among themselves, adding a very small percentage to the cost of the goods after they leave foreign hands. The contention has been made and can be sustained that, leaving out transportation charges, the distribution of American goods between New York, where they come into the hands of the exporter, and the consumer in China is at a smaller cost of commissions and profits than that in any other direction at home or abroad.[26]

This American asserted that Chinese merchants operated on a "narrow margin of profit" without supplying figures, but other contemporary observers estimated that the cost of handling goods between cotton mills in the American South and consumers in China ranged from a low of 8.5 percent to a high of 17 percent of the value of the goods.[27] Whatever the precise figure, this New York-based exporter's claims remained convincing as long as no foreign trading company could find a way to do better.

MITSUI'S USE OF JAPANESE REPRESENTATIVES

By contrast with its American rivals, Mitsui distributed cotton cloth in Northeast China by relying on neither Shanghai-based Chinese compradors and wholesaling firms nor Chinese interregional guest merchants and regional trading companies. By eliminating these Chinese middlemen and replacing them with Japanese salaried representatives, Mitsui tried to cut costs so that it could afford to underprice its American competition.

According to both American and Japanese observers, Mitsui's direct marketing was the key to its success at lowering costs and promoting sales. The most informed and perceptive American assessment was made by Ralph Odell, a cotton textiles expert sent by the U.S. Department of Commerce to spend six months investigating China's market in 1914. On the basis of numerous interviews with Chinese, American, and Japanese cloth traders in Shanghai, Dalian, and other cities, he produced an impressive 242-page report (frequently cited in the notes to this chapter) that reached this conclusion:

> The most important factor in the development of Japanese trade has been the large and important firm of Mitsui Bussan Kaisha. . . . This firm, like other Japanese firms handling cloth and yarn, has, in many instances, cut out one or two of the middlemen between the manufacturer and the consumer and eliminated transshipment and other charges which English and American goods must bear. . . . Since the Japanese have entered the field, . . . with their aggressive and systematic methods, . . . they get in closer touch with the consumers.[28]

Getting "in closer touch with the consumers" did not mean that Mitsui retailed goods directly to Chinese consumers, but the phrase aptly summarized Mitsui's capacity to extend its foreign marketing organization much farther down China's urban hierarchy than its American rivals were able to do.

Another American contemporary observer, the consular official George Anderson, also singled out Mitsui's direct marketing as the critical ingredient to the victory of Japanese products over American ones. According to Anderson, it achieved an advantage in the first step of marketing by supplying information on local conditions faster than their rivals did. In his words, Mitsui's Japanese representatives in China "are so closely in touch with the field that a demand for any particular line of goods can be anticipated and the goods prepared and placed on sale be-

fore those of competitors."[29] Reporting up Mitsui's managerial hierarchy, these local representatives gave Japan the crucial advantage of
speed.

Japanese observers attributed Mitsui success to its direct marketing
too, and they emphasized the dedication of the company's Japanese salaried representatives in China. On a trip to survey marketing in Northeast China, Fukui Kikusaburo, Mitsui's branch manager at Osaka, met
one young Japanese employee who seemed to him to epitomize the spirit
of these representatives. When Fukui saw that the young man lived in a
tiny room that was owned by a Chinese native bank and overlooked
a courtyard full of horse dung, he said that he felt like bowing down
and paying homage to this young man's self-sacrifice, his ability to speak
Chinese, and his success at selling cotton cloth at the local level directly
to Chinese customers.[30] Later Fukui drew a sharp contrast between this
Japanese approach and the American one:

> American merchants used Chinese representatives to send their goods from
> Shanghai to Chinese wholesalers in Niuzhuang and other cities. So it took
> time and money. But [Japanese] people from Mitsui sold Japanese cotton
> goods directly to Chinese, put up with loneliness, slept on horse dung, and
> made such [inspired] efforts that it brings tears to your eyes. This was the rea-
> son that Japan could expel the American power.[31]

Fukui's emotional tribute might have exaggerated the dedication of Mitsui's Japanese salaried salesmen, but their commitment to the company's ideals, their willingness to serve in low-level hardship posts, and
their usefulness in marketing should not be overlooked. As Fukui noted,
by living in local residences outside company compounds, Mitsui's Japanese salesmen were better situated than their Western counterparts to
reach Chinese local wholesalers and make deals face-to-face on a regular basis. Moreover, judging by Fukui's presence rather than by his
words, it seems safe to infer that Mitsui's central management moni-
tored the performance of its salesmen at all levels—even down to the
lowliest employee sleeping on horse dung—and checked to see whether
the company's Japanese China specialists effectively took advantage of
their newly acquired training in China's language and customs by building up contacts and making sales.

These American and Japanese observers all agreed that direct marketing was necessary and crucial for Mitsui's victory over its American
competition. It was not, however, the only element in the company's
overall marketing strategy.

MITSUI'S ECONOMIC APPEAL

To make inferior Japanese-made cloth competitive with superior American-made cloth, Mitsui did more than train, deploy, and monitor Japanese employees. It also instructed these employees to offer Chinese customers financial advantages: low prices, unsecured credit, and other services.

Between 1908 and 1914, as during the Japanese military occupation of 1905–7, Mitsui continued to keep the price for Japanese-made cotton cloth a full 20 to 30 percent below the price for American-made cloth. Mitsui needed to maintain this large price differential, according to local Chinese wholesalers interviewed in Northeast China in 1914, because the local wholesalers would have carried American-made cloth if it had been priced 10 or 15 percent higher than its Japanese counterpart but not 20 to 30 percent higher.[32] In other words, Mitsui gave local Chinese wholesalers a premium of 5 to 20 percent to tempt them into rejecting American-made cloth and selling Japanese-made cloth exclusively.

Mitsui offered local Chinese wholesalers other financial inducements by granting credit and accepting payment in kind. Like other trading companies, it offered to sell cotton cloth outright (in gold yen or sometimes silver yen, not local currency) to local Chinese wholesalers, and, unlike others, it also gave them the option of taking goods on credit—usually for 30 to 45 days and occasionally up to 60 to 90 days—and selling for a 2 percent commission. As payment from the Chinese wholesalers, it accepted either cash or agricultural goods such as raw cotton, raw silk, and soybeans in place of cash.[33] As an American consular official noted in 1909, "In much of the Manchurian trade little money changes hands. The purchases of beans by Japanese traders from Chinese dealers affords the latter credit upon which they buy cotton goods from the former."[34]

As another convenience, Mitsui allowed Chinese buyers to select cotton textiles from stock in local warehouses that it owned in all of Northeast China's major cities: Dalian, Niuzhuang, Andong, Fengtian, Tieling, Jilin, Changchun, Harbin. As a result, it eliminated the local buyers' uncertainties about long-distance trade—fluctuating costs for interregional transportation, interprovincial tariffs, local exchange rates on currencies—and allowed them the opportunity to examine goods before buying and to hear prices quoted on the spot. As summarized by Odell in a folksy American metaphor, "The Japanese have practically reduced their piece-goods business [in China] to the basis of buying groceries at home at the corner store with a charge account to the good customer."[35]

All of these advantages for customers depended on the efficiency of Mitsui's overall operations, especially its coordination with cotton mills in Japan to assure that its marketing system in China was adequately supplied. To keep these Japanese cotton mills operating on schedule, Mitsui did not buy them. Instead it kept them beholden to it and responsive to its management as their creditor. By 1910 and 1911 no less than twenty-three Japanese cotton mills were in debt to Mitsui for a total of more than 10 million yen. It extended credit to the mills for buying equipment and raw materials that it acquired through its global purchasing system; in particular, it sold them machinery made in England and raw cotton grown not only in China (where Mitsui had established its headquarters for purchasing at Shanghai as early as 1877) but also India and the United States (where it established headquarters at Bombay in 1907 and Houston in 1911).[36]

In exchange for this credit and other financial services, Mitsui was assured of Japanese manufacturers' adherence to agreements for producing according to its schedule and supplying exclusively to meet its needs.[37] As the American consular official George Anderson observed at the time,

> The Japanese . . . exporting is done principally through one firm, which carries on an immense export and import business. [The Japanese manufacturers of cotton textiles] operate through this firm and similar concerns as one organization. If questions arise they are settled at home, in Japan, and the [non-Japanese] foreigner knows nothing of them. Their agents in the field represent all of them, one way or another.[38]

This close Japanese coordination, Anderson noted, was all the more striking because of the lack of it in the American cotton textiles trade and because of the American manufacturers' need for a relationship "between seller and buyer similar to that effected in Manchuria and in some districts around Shanghai by the Japanese cotton interests."[39]

Thus Mitsui's low prices and other financial services were made possible by its efficient coordination of marketing with manufacturing and purchasing. By aggressively promoting its cotton textiles, the Japanese company regained lost ground in its competition with American rivals. As shown in tables 6 and 7, it soon returned the value of its sales of cotton yarn and cloth in China to the levels that it had earlier achieved while the Japanese government had protected it from American competition during the aftermath of the Russo-Japanese War. As a result, between 1908 and 1911 Japan's share of China's trade in foreign-made cotton textiles grew at the expense of the American share. (See table 5.)

AMERICAN RETALIATION

Unable to compete in Northeast China, American manufacturers tried to retaliate by adopting an approach parallel to the one used by their Japanese rivals. Even as Japanese cotton textiles manufacturers had succeeded by marketing through a large Japanese-owned distributing company, Mitsui, so American manufacturers began to market their cotton textiles through British-American Tobacco Company. Although BAT had specialized in cigarettes since its founding and its entrance into China's market in 1902, it announced in 1911 that it would use its cigarette distributors to market American-made cotton cloth in China and called on American textiles manufacturers (who, like BAT's chairman of the board, James Duke, and like BAT's top management in China, were from the American South) to rally against the Japanese competition.[40]

By 1911 BAT, like Mitsui, had already posted foreign (in its case Western) salaried representatives in all of China's major regional markets, including Northeast China.[41] Moreover, it, again like Mitsui, had a marketing staff well positioned to avoid paying commissions to Chinese compradors and interregional wholesalers managing the Shanghai-Dalian trade. As local Chinese wholesalers in the northeastern cities of Changchun and Jilin reported at the time, BAT used its salaried representatives to market cloth in the Northeast with the aim of "cutting out Shanghai with its attendant extra expenses and selling through a local agent, either foreign or Chinese."[42]

At the same time BAT stopped short of adopting Mitsui's practice of granting credit to local Chinese wholesalers of cotton textiles. BAT did grant credit to Chinese cigarette distributors at the time, so it probably refused credit to Chinese cotton cloth distributors on instructions from American cotton textiles manufacturers and exporters such as an American partner in the largest New York-based exporter of cotton piece goods in China who made this critique of the Japanese approach: "The methods of the Japanese are hazardous and would not help if there were not the lower prices to carry their goods into consumption. You know that it is impossible to give credit to the casual interior merchant, and that the Chinese dealers themselves do not do it."[43] An American holding these views had no reason to authorize BAT to grant credit to Chinese distributors of cotton cloth.

As a result BAT proved unable to win over local Chinese wholesalers of cotton textiles. According to an agent of the U.S. Department of Commerce who interviewed Chinese wholesalers in Changchun and Jilin in 1913, BAT representatives' "campaign [to sell American-made cloth] might have been successful if they had worked at it longer, but they started out with the idea of selling for cash only and did not get in with the [Chinese] merchants because they would not cater to the established business customs of the local trade."[44] In 1912, less than a year after BAT began marketing cotton cloth, it conceded defeat by ceasing to carry the item.

BAT's defeat made Mitsui's victory conclusive. In 1910, just before BAT's ill-fated experiment with cotton cloth, Mitsui was already sending at least 35 percent of its total exports of Japanese-made cotton cloth to the Northeast—more than to all the other regions of China combined. In 1911, BAT's one year in the cotton cloth market, Japan exported to Northeast China a total of 8,449,170 yards of cotton cloth, 265 times more than the total (of 31,884 yards) in 1902. In 1912, immediately after BAT's withdrawal, the Japan Cotton Cloth Export Association hailed its victory by announcing its dissolution. With Japanese cloth predominant in the Northeast, the association was no longer needed.[45]

NORTHEAST CHINA AS MITSUI'S MODEL

After triumphing in the Northeast on the eve of World War I, Mitsui developed somewhat similar regional distributing systems in other parts of China. As shown in table 8, between 1909 and 1919 it greatly expanded its staff in the metropolis at the core of each of China's regions, raising the number of staff members in Dalian (for the Northeast) from 16 to 127, in Tianjin (for the North) from 18 to 66, in Shanghai (for the Lower Yangzi) from 48 to 173, in Hankou (for the Middle Yangzi) from 19 to 62, in Taipei (for the Southeast) from 25 to 55, and in Hong Kong (for the South) from 41 to 90. Even as it had shipped cotton textiles from Japan directly to Dalian in Northeast China without passing through Shanghai, it began doing the same to Tianjin in North China, Taipei in Southeast China, and Hong Kong for South China,[46] and through Hankou it reached the Middle and Upper Yangzi. Meanwhile,

TABLE 8. NUMBER OF JAPANESE PERSONNEL
IN MITSUI'S OVERSEAS BRANCHES
AND AGENCIES, 1909 AND 1919

Overseas Branch	1909	1919
Northeast China		
Dalian	16	127
Andong	4	7
Niuchuang (Yingkou)	13	11
Hanyang	5	10
Tieling	6	11
Changchun	8	14
Harbin	11	22
North China		
Tianjin	18	66
Beijing		5
Qingdao	3	52
Jinan		9
Lower Yangzi in China		
Shanghai	48	173
Wuhu	—	2
Zhefu	5	9
Middle Yangzi in China		
Hankou	19	62
Changsha	—	2
Changde	—	1
Chongqing	—	2
South and Southeast China		
Hong Kong	41	90
Haifang (Vietnam)	—	5
Saigon Vietnam)	—	6
Shantou	—	6
Guangzhou	5	16
Fuzhou	3	7
Xiamen	3	8
Taiwan		
Taibei	25	55
Jilong		2
Tainan	21	36
Taizhong		4
Dagou		12
China trainees	9	33
Apprentices in trade	1	—

(*continued*)

TABLE 8   (*continued*)

Overseas Branch	1909	1919
Outside China and Japan		
Seoul	16	61
Pusan	2	22
Jinseng	5	4
Sydney	2	21
Melbourne		4
Manila	5	15
Singapore	10	42
Bangkok	1	7
Medan		1
Java	3	
Surabaya		32
Samarang		7
Batavia		15
Bombay	22	63
Karachi		1
Colombo		3
Calcutta	1	41
Rangoon		11
London	18	41
Lyons	3	13
Marseilles	—	7
Hamburg	7	
New York	28	105
Dallas		19
San Francisco	4	20
Seattle		19
Portland	1	2
Buenos Aires		3

SOURCE: *KMBK*, 339, table 6; 340, table 7.
Note: In Mitsui's organizational hierarchy, branch offices ranked above its agencies. The locations of its branch offices are listed at the margin, and the locations of its agencies are indented.

it did not neglect the Lower Yangzi, retaining its headquarters for China at Shanghai and assigning more of its Japanese representatives there than to any other city in China or, for that matter, the world.

CONCLUSION

As noted at the end of chapter 2, the history of Standard Oil is an exception to the thesis that Western businesses never competed with Chinese networks for control of China's markets, and as the advocates of this thesis have applied it not merely to Western but to foreign businesses in China, the history of Mitsui should be recognized as an even more striking exception. Compared to Standard Oil, Mitsui rejected more decisively and categorically the practice of depending on Chinese to market goods in China. Standard Oil and BAT also employed foreigners in China, but relatively few were genuinely fluent in Chinese or able to market goods without the help of Chinese interpreters and other intermediaries. Mitsui's corps of salaried representatives (who were all Japanese) was not as large as Standard Oil's or BAT's (who included Chinese as well as Westerners), but Mitsui went farther than Standard Oil, BAT, or any other business regardless of nationality in eliminating Chinese from marketing and replacing them with Chinese-speaking foreigners. Its Japanese China specialists supplanted not only Chinese compradors and wholesalers in Shanghai but also Chinese long-distance traders and other merchants distributing goods at core cities in all of China's regions.

Mitsui's president, Masuda, claimed to be eliminating Chinese compradors in 1898 because they were too expensive, but his company's heavy investments in training Japanese replacements suggest that the decision was not based solely on short-term calculations of costs. Equally if not more important was Mitsui's paternalistic desire to find employees likely to regard themselves as members of a company family. By recruiting Japanese "China trainees" on the basis of their "indomitable spirit," Mitsui showed its concern for employees' loyalty to the company, and in allowing each of them to study Chinese full time for three years, it assumed that they would subsequently serve the company for life (which they generally did).[47] Similarly, when Japanese manager Fukui congratulated young salaried representatives for making sales at the local level in China, he praised them for their dedication to the company and its ideals. In all of these ways, Mitsui treated its employees more paternalistically than Standard Oil or BAT did in China.

In China Mitsui also distinguished itself from Standard Oil and BAT by using its management to take fuller advantage of its relations with its home government. Standard Oil and BAT resembled Mitsui insofar as they benefited from unequal Sino-foreign treaties that prevented China from raising tariffs above a low ceiling and granted extraterritoriality and other privileges to foreigners in China's treaty ports, but the Western companies did not receive direct official aid from Western governments of the kind received by Mitsui from the Japanese government.[48] At the time of Japan's victory over America in the battle for China's textiles market, American businessmen bitterly complained that the competition was unfair because their Japanese rivals benefited from the Japanese government's intervention.[49] In retrospect, historians have found no justification for this complaint and have explained the outcome by blaming it on the American businessmen's failures[50] or attributing it to Japan's comparative advantages in endowments.[51] The findings in this chapter indicate that historians have been wrong to dismiss the American businessmen's complaints as groundless, and the more interesting question raised here is when and how—not whether—the company benefited from political intervention by the Japanese government.

As American businessmen suspected, Mitsui's extensive official contacts undeniably worked to its advantage. In fact, Mitsui exercised political influence on the Chinese as well as the Japanese government at the time. For example, some of Mitsui's Japanese China specialists, notably Mori Kaku, supplied loans to Sun Yat-sen on the founding of the Republic of China in late 1911, and after Sun resigned as provisional president in early 1912, they continued to lobby aggressively with other leaders of China's new government.[52] And yet, contrary to American businessmen's complaints, Mitsui relied on Japanese direct official aid in Manchuria only briefly between 1906 and 1907. Thereafter it counted on its integrated corporate hierarchy, not official aid, to overcome its American rivals in Manchuria's market.

Mitsui's decisive victory for Japanese over Americans should not imply that either side's approach was foolproof. On the contrary, each approach had its own rationale and ran its own risks. Mitsui justified its heavy investment in marketing by having its numerous and highly trained staff members handle a wide variety of goods and thus achieved (in the rhetoric of economic theorists) economies of scope;[53] and it ran the risk of not recruiting the right number of manufacturers to keep its marketing system adequately supplied. Mitsui's American rivals, by contrast, had less justification for investing in marketing because they specialized in only one product. When they began to suffer from competition, they had the option of investing in an elaborate marketing system to sell only one product (as Standard Oil did) or to sell numerous products (as Mitsui did). But after seeking and receiving help from BAT's marketing organization without success, they chose not to pursue any such option and instead surrendered their share of China's market to Mitsui.

Whatever decided the contest in Mitsui's favor, the company was hailed in Japan for achieving the first major Japanese victory in inter-

national commerce over Western rivals. Before Mitsui's truimph and
BAT's withdrawal from China's market for imported cotton textiles
in 1912, Japanese manufacturers of cotton textiles had cautiously refrained from building mills in China in the face of Western competition
there. After witnessing Mitsui's success, however, they began to make
their first direct investments in China, and one of them, the Naigai Cotton Company, led the way.

CHAPTER 5

Naigai Cotton Company

In 1911 Naigai Cotton Company (Naigai wata kabushiki kaisha) opened at Shanghai the first cotton mill ever constructed from the ground up by Japanese anywhere outside Japan. Since the 1880s Japanese cotton mills had operated on a large scale in Japan, and since the 1890s they had been guaranteed the legal privilege of manufacturing on Chinese soil—a concession granted under the Sino-Japanese Treaty of Shimonoseki in 1895 after Japan's military victory over China in the war of 1894–95—but for more than a decade their Japanese owners had cautiously refrained from making direct investments in China until Naigai took the lead.[1]

As the premier Japanese manufacturer in China, Naigai became the first to assign Japanese managers the task of exercising direct control over Chinese workers. Only a few years earlier industrial managers within Japan had begun a critical transition from indirect to direct control over workers. In the late nineteenth century Japanese managers had exercised only indirect control in the sense that their central personnel offices had not recruited, hired, trained, and paid all of their workers; instead they had left responsibility for these face-to-face dealings to independent labor recruiters, brokers, and bosses. Then at the turn of the century Japanese industrial managers made two fundamental changes in management-labor relations. On management's side, the companies instituted corporate hierarchies that replaced Japanese labor recruiters, brokers, and bosses or incorporated them into managerial positions. On labor's side, the cotton mills created a labor force of girls and young women, recruiting them from the countryside, training them as apprentices, and housing them in dormitories. It was because of this new system of direct managerial control, according to the Japanese historian Patricia Tsurumi, that Japanese cotton mills in Japan had so few strikes after 1900. "Before compulsory residence in dormitories and long delays between earning and payment of wages became norms" around the turn of the century, she has observed, "united efforts by [Japanese] mill women to assert their interests against 'unfair' employers [in Japan] met with some success." But after Japanese mill owners achieved control by setting up hierarchies of salaried managers, confining workers to dormitories, and paying their wages directly, these "measures . . . made strikes almost impossible to sustain."[2]

These Japanese managerial techniques for controlling workers and preventing strikes were transferred to China by Naigai in two phases. First, between 1911 and 1924, it appointed Japanese China specialists to serve as managers and introduce company welfare programs for Chinese workers. Then, in the mid-1920s, it began training girls and young women in an apprentice program that in China (as in Japan) was designed to prevent strikes but, ironically, gave rise to a wave of strikes and forced the company to revise its Japanese approach to relations with Chinese workers.

ASSERTING MANAGERIAL CONTROL
DURING THE "GOLDEN AGE," 1911–1924

In retrospect Naigai's management characterized the period between 1911 and 1924 as a "golden age" because it was a time of growth and prosperity for the company and other Japanese cotton mills in China. During this time, Naigai built fourteen cotton mills in China—eleven in Shanghai and three in Qingdao—and, following in its wake during this same decade, thirteen other Japanese companies added twenty-one more. As a result the Japanese share of China's total spindles for spinning yarn leapt from 10 percent in 1914 to 33 percent in 1924 while the Western share fell from 24 to 7 percent. By 1924 Naigai employed 25,000 Chinese workers to operate 328,304 spindles, which amounted to 2 percent more than the number of spindles in all of China's Western-owned mills combined. With Nagai setting the pace, other big manufacturers such as Kanegafuchi and Dai Nippon also built large cotton mills in China, but none surpassed Naigai. In the early 1920s Nagai made use of more spindles than any other cotton textiles manufacturer and employed more workers than any other foreign industrial enterprise manufacturing consumer goods in the country.[3]

Operating on this large scale and in a foreign country, Naigai's Japanese management faced a formidable task in seeking direct control over the company's Chinese workers. Nonetheless, in its initial thrust into China it very nearly accomplished this task by transferring trained managers and corporate policies from its cotton mills in Japan and adapting them to China.

TRAINING JAPANESE CHINA SPECIALISTS

Before Naigai opened its first cotton mill in China in 1911, it already had a corps of experienced Japanese China specialists whom it had trained and employed while it had been a trading company in China for more than thirty years. As early as 1877 Naigai's founders had begun employing Japanese China specialists to buy cotton and sell yarn and cloth in China.[4] This early start gave Naigai longer experience in China than any other Japanese trading company except Mitsui (which had been founded in 1876), and in the late nineteenth century it had ranked with Mitsui and Nihon Menka as one of the "Big Three" Japanese trading companies in China. Not until the Sino-Japanese War of 1894–95 had Naigai's trading operations in China begun to falter, and not until the recession following the Russo-Japanese War of 1904–5 had it dismantled its marketing system in China altogether.[5] When the company relieved its Japanese China specialists of their duties as cotton buyers and textiles sellers in China, it did not let their training in the Chinese language and their accumulated experience in China go to waste.

As soon as Naigai brought its Japanese China specialists back to Japan, it began preparing them for future work in its (as yet unbuilt) mills in China by training them in its newly purchased cotton mills. In 1903 Naigai paid 260,000 yen for a factory at Denpo in the Nishihara district of Osaka prefecture, and in 1905 it invested another 550,000 yen to acquire a plant at Nishinomiya. Subsequently, as it dismantled Naigai's marketing system in China, it added machinery in these Japan-based mills, giving them a total of 29,000 spindles and 837 looms and making Naigai the third-largest weaving enterprise in Japan by 1907.[6] By then the company had already begun to set up training programs for China-bound employees at Naigai's mills in Japan.

The first program began in 1906, five years before Naigai inaugurated production in China. To this program Naigai assigned Japanese China specialists who had served as purchasing agents and sales managers in China while it had operated as a trading company there, and it converted them into factory managers in anticipation of its entrance into China as a manufacturing company. Naigai's second training program in Japan was for Chinese foremen who had been recruited to supervise Chinese workers in the company's first mill at Shanghai. In August 1909, two years before the opening of this first mill, the company sent thirty prospective Chinese foremen to Japan for training in its mills there.[7]

By thus training Japanese managers and Chinese foremen in advance, Naigai worked on the premise that its techniques for managing Japanese workers in Osaka could be successfully applied to Chinese workers in Shanghai and Qingdao. On opening mills in China, it put this premise to the test.

CONTENDING WITH CHINESE NUMBER ONES

From the beginning as a manufacturer in China, Naigai took pride in its success at using Japanese managers and managerial techniques to instill more discipline in Chinese factory workers than Western- or Chinese-owned mills were able to do. As early as 1913, barely one year after the company's first mill in China had inaugurated production in Shanghai, one of its Japanese executives paid a visit and made this observation:

> Whereas in spinning companies under Chinese or German management everything is done according to Chinese methods and confusion reigns within the mill, in this company Chinese go to work under the same systematic rules that Japanese do, and since the labor force is mixed, twelve- and thirteen-year-old boys obediently follow the work orders of girls.[8]

This characterization expresses Naigai's intention to distinguish its approach from Western and Chinese approaches. Its claim that Naigai caused Chinese workers to behave "obediently" might well sound exaggerated (not to mention condescending and smug), but in fact Naigai did make remarkable strides toward achieving its goal of ousting Chinese Number Ones and dealing directly with Chinese workers.

In the early 1920s, little more than a decade after Naigai opened its first factory in China, a Japanese reporter named Nishikawa Kiichi noted, "Lately the system [of delegating managerial authority to Chinese Number Ones] has become a shadow of its former self and is al-

most never seen any more in Japanese mills." Writing on the basis of
his own eyewitness observations in Shanghai, he added, "A majority of
the managerial staff are Japanese, and the supervision of workers [is] all
done by Japanese without using Chinese."[9] Chinese and Western observers recorded similar impressions in the 1920s.[10]

In one of the most detailed descriptions of staff members in Shanghai's cotton mills, the Chinese reporter B. Y. Lee noticed that Chinese
Number Ones behaved differently under Chinese management than they
did under Japanese management:

> Under purely Chinese management, [Chinese] head-mechanics and women
> "number ones" practically controlled everything concerning the working
> forces and enjoyed the various sorts of "squeeze." This class of "super up-
> per" workman . . . generally do not do much work nor know much and usu-
> ally do not stay in the mills all the time. Most Chinese managers are afraid of
> them and would not dare to do or say anything directly against their will even
> when wrong-doings done by them are discovered.[11]

"What happens," Lee asked, "when such men are placed inside a Japa-
nese-managed mill?" In Japanese-owned mills, the managers "put their
nationals in charge of various departments and positions of importance," and even at relatively low levels in the hierarchy these Japanese displaced "many Chinese foremen, labor-heads, and machinists
and other classes of labor." As for the remaining Chinese Number Ones,

> instead of doing what they please they have to do whatever they are ordered
> and directed. They are surrounded by [Japanese] foremen in each depart-
> ment and are being closely watched. . . . Good work is rewarded and bad is
> punished. "Squeeze," as customarily practiced in Chinese mills, can not be
> very well done nor large sums of bonus . . . be given.[12]

Exactly how many Chinese Number Ones were retained and "sur-
rounded" in Japanese-owned mills is difficult to say, but after consult-
ing the voluminous records of several Japanese cotton mills, the leading
Japanese historian of the cotton textiles industry, Takamura Naosuke,
has reached this conclusion: "By the mid-1920s, only a small number of
Japanese spinning mills in China retained the system of Number Ones,
and even they used a very limited part of the production process where
the finishing was done."[13]

Japanese supervisors' interventions with Chinese Number Ones did
not necessarily protect Chinese workers from abuses of authority. On
the contrary, Japanese supervisors were at least as harsh as Chinese
Number Ones, if not more so, with male and female Chinese workers.

Lee, the Chinese reporter quoted above, while praising the Japanese mills for reducing "squeeze," achieving a "high degree of efficiency," and practicing "honest and able management," sharply criticized them for their Japanese supervisors' "barbarous" beatings of Chinese male workers. "Striking or beating workmen is very seldom . . . employed in Chinese or British mills," he claimed, first because the Chinese Number Ones recruited the workers and kept them "loyal and obedient" and second because "the social fidelity of the workmen themselves [is] so inter-related and complicated." In Japanese-owned mills, by contrast, Japanese foremen and supervisors, unconstrained by involvement in Chinese social networks, used corporal punishment. In fact, Japanese supervisors were encouraged by the mills' regulations to be detached from and hostile toward Chinese social networks. As a result "whenever a [Chinese] man [was] caught smoking or a [Chinese] child [was] caught idling or violating any mill regulations, instead of punishing him on a fine system employed in the Chinese mills, he [might] be physically struck with a stick or anything which happened to be handy to the Japanese foreman."[14] These charges were corroborated by Japanese observers at the time.[15]

With Chinese women workers, Naigai's Japanese supervisors were also stricter than were their counterparts in Chinese-owned mills. Unlike Chinese-owned mills, Naigai prohibited women workers from bringing children to the factory or breast-feeding babies during working hours. It also differed from Chinese mills in requiring its workers to stand continuously, except during each shift's single thirty-minute meal, and it limited its workers to a fixed number of trips to the lavatory, which they could enter only with a "lavatory pass" (*cesuo pai*). Such close supervision continued every day right up to the workers' quitting time. As they filed out of Naigai's factories, its guards subjected them to thorough body searches on the suspicion that they were stealing yarn, cloth, and other materials.[16]

FROM INFORMAL TO FORMAL WELFARE BENEFITS

While Japanese managers at Naigai and other Japanese cotton mills tried to change Chinese Number Ones' techniques for managing workers, they also introduced personnel offices that circumvented Number Ones and dealt directly with workers. Naigai's personnel office paid wages to workers directly—not through Number Ones—and it gave them direct access to company welfare programs as substitutes for the informal arrangements that Number Ones had made for their room and board. Like mills in Japan, Naigai and other Japanese-owned mills in China set the levels of their wages and benefits less for the purpose of attracting new recruits than for retaining experienced ones.

Overall, Japanese cotton mills paid higher average wages per worker than Western- and Chinese-owned mills did. According to Takamura, if wages in British-owned mills are assigned an index of 100, then overall wage levels in China's cotton mills during the mid-1920s varied as follows:

Wages in British-owned mills	100
Wages in Chinese-owned mills	105
Wages in Japanese-owned mills	127[17]

However, Japanese-owned mills' wages for new recruits were lower than could be found in the mills of Chinese- and British-owned rivals. By the same token, they paid much higher wages to experienced workers at the upper end of the scale.[18]

To discourage experienced workers from leaving the company, Naigai also offered periodic bonuses. As in Japan, it did not make workers wait until the end of the year to see what management had decided their bonuses would be. Instead Naigai's bonuses were given at the end of every month, every half year, and every full year of continuous employment with the company. Altogether its bonuses had the potential to increase an experienced worker's wages by 30 to 40 percent or more per year.[19]

Besides appealing to experienced workers through graduated wage scales and regularly scheduled bonuses, Naigai offered them company welfare benefits, especially housing. As it built its factories in Shanghai, it added within walking distance tenements of row houses (*mune wari nagaya*): 1,400 two-story and 500 one-story dwellings. This housing was rented to workers at 2 to 4 yuan per month, not provided free of charge like the cotton mills' dormitories for workers in Japan.[20]

According to contemporary Japanese investigators, the rented housing in China was superior to the free dormitories at cotton mills in Japan. Each house had electricity, running water, a kitchen for cooking, and a porch for drying clothes. But in Shanghai the houses were extremely crowded. Each one measured thirty by thirty feet (five by five ken) and was designed to hold eight or nine workers (who, if sharing the monthly rent payments equally, would have paid about thirty cents

Figure 8.   Naigai's housing (the gabled buildings) in Shanghai about a mile from the mills, 1920. Reprinted from Pearse, *Cotton Industry of Japan and China,* 166.

each). But, contrary to this design, in practice each unit commonly held several workers' families rather than a few individual workers. Of the 402 families in Naigai's housing surveyed by an American sociologist in 1932, one-fourth had one room per family, more than one-half had slightly less than one room per family, and nearly one-fifth had only one-half room per family. As a Chinese social worker representing the YMCA reported in the mid-1920s, Naigai's housing was so subdivided and heavily populated that it resembled the "overcrowded steerage quarters on a Chinese river boat." [21]

Compared to Japanese mills' dormitories for Japanese workers in Japan, Naigai's housing was architecturally less confining but subject to the same close scrutiny. Whereas Japanese companies in Japan built dormitories contiguous with the mills and prevented workers from leaving the company compound, Naigai built its housing in Shanghai outside the mills and within walking distance for the workers. Naigai, like the mills in Japan, issued paternalistic rules governing proper manners and personal hygiene on and off the job, and it enforced them by assigning as house mothers older Chinese women who, in turn, reported to Japanese superintendents (*kan shi nin*).[22]

Along with housing, Naigai offered some health care. Although it did not add infirmaries for workers until after 1924, in its early years it arranged for its workers in Shanghai to be treated at the local Renji Hospital. It covered the costs of treating a worker's job-related injuries or illnesses, including hospitalization at 45 cents (*xian*) per day (which was nearly equivalent to a worker's wages of 50.5 cents per day), and it paid up to 50 to 70 percent of a worker's wages during hospitalization. Among its other services were company stores (*mai dian*) that sold daily necessities (including coal at a subsidized price in its factories during cold winters at Qingdao in North China) and company schools for workers' children under the age of thirteen.[23]

HIGH PROFITS DURING THE GOLDEN AGE

Training for managers, close supervision for previously independent foremen, graduated wages, and company welfare programs for workers—all had been characteristic of Japanese mills in Japan, and when transferred to China they immediately helped Naigai earn high profits there. Between 1909 and 1920 Naigai's dividends in China were as high or higher than those of Japanese mills at the time in Japan, and between 1921 and 1924 its profits in China reached at an astonishingly high average annual rate of 96.5 percent. (See tables 9 and 10.) Thus in the early 1920s, even while Chinese-owned cotton mills suffered from a crisis as a result of falling yarn prices and rising cotton prices,[24] Naigai's profit rates reached their peak. The company enjoyed these high profits, at least in part, because it suffered hardly at all from strikes or other labor protests before 1925.

DEALING WITH WORKERS' PROTESTS, 1925–1927

As noted in chapter 3, BAT's director, Arnold Rose, was convinced that Japanese companies were more successful than his own at avoiding strikes in China because of their company welfare programs for workers. "The Japanese cotton mills are the only factories in Shanghai that have not suffered from workers' protests so far," Rose wrote from Shanghai in a private letter to BAT's Western manager in Hankou in 1923. The reason, according to Rose, was that "in Shanghai Japanese cotton mills provide housing for almost all of their workers."[25]

Although Rose was burning with envy, his assessment only slightly overstated the case, especially for Naigai. Despite this Japanese company's growth into China's biggest foreign employer of Chinese industrial workers, before 1924 it experienced only one strike, a seven-day walkout by fifty-five hundred workers workers from three of its mills

SOURCE: Takamura, *Kindai*, 81, table 5.

TABLE 9. COMPARISON OF DIVIDEND RATES IN CHINESE
AND JAPANESE SPINNING COMPANIES, 1903–1920 (%)

	Yihe (Ch.)	Lao jing-mao (Ch.)	Hong-yuan (Ch.)	Ruiji (Ch.)	Gongyi (Ch.)	Yangshu pu (J)	Shanghai (J) 1st half/2d half	Naigai (J) 1st half/2d half	Japanese Domestic Spinning Companies 1st half	2d half
1903	8	—	—	—	—	—	8	—	8.1	8.3
1904	—	—	—	—	—	—	10	—	6.5	9.6
1905	16	8	—	5	—	—	20	—	17.7	21.9
1906	20	8	8	10	—	—	—	—	22.4	24.6
1907	5	—	—	—	—	—	—	—	22.9	21.9
1908	10	8	—	7	—	—	15	—	11.9	10.2
1909	22	6	10	—	—	—	8	12	11.7	11.8
1910	8	—	—	—	—	—	8	12	10.9	8.3
1911	14	5	—	10	12	—	16	10	9.9	10.5
1912	22	11	8	12	15	—	20	20	12.1	14.6
1913	30	12	13.3	—	15	—	22	15	15.2	15.3
1914	24	—	6.7	—	12	—	15	10	16.4	13.5
1915	32	—	7.5	—	15	—	12	12	15.0	15.5
1916	18	—	—	—	9	—	12	20	19.8	25.2
1917	40	2.5	16.7	—	20	25	24	35	35.0	42.1
1918	24	7	—	8.3	16	5.3	36	45	55.6	51.9
1919	36	50	—	50	50	20	—	50	51.2	54.2
1920	180	65	—	40	80	100	147	162	58.3	27.8

SOURCE: Takamura, *Kindai*, 81, table 5.
Note: Dividends shown as percentage of paid-in capital.

(Nos. 3, 4, and 5), on June 5–11, 1919, at the height of the May Fourth movement, which was a political protest against the Japanese government's seizure of Chinese territory. Meanwhile, Rose's company, BAT, was the scene of at least eight strikes by 1924.[26]

And then, after experiencing only one strike between 1911 and 1924, Naigai became the site of no less than 44 strikes between February 1925 and November 1927. This extraordinary record—by far the largest number of strikes in a three-year period against any business in Chinese history—was attributable in part to leadership from Chinese Communists, Nationalists, and local gangsters who helped to organize and sustain politically charged strikes during the May Thirtieth movement of 1925 and Chiang Kai-shek's Northern Expedition of 1926–27. But for Naigai's management, the most shocking in this series of 44 strikes was the very first one, which originated not as a political incident but as a protest against the company's effort to carry out the second phase of its Japanese approach to management in China.

THE STRIKE OF FEBRUARY–MARCH 1925

In February 1925 Naigai's first strike during the high tide of labor protests in 1925–27 started when the company tried to fire more than forty male workers in its No. 8 Mill and replace them with women and girls. For Naigai's management this step represented the culmination of its long-term policy of instituting Japanese-style labor-management relations. As shown earlier in this chapter, Naigai had completed phase one of its corporate strategy by using Japanese staff members and company welfare benefits to undermine and oust Chinese Number Ones in China (just as it had undermined and ousted independent Japanese labor brokers and bosses in Japan). Now Naigai proposed to complete phase two in China (as it had in Japan) by replacing male workers with newly trained girls and young women, age fourteen to twenty. Before taking this step, it had recruited Chinese female workers directly from the countryside, housed them in dormitories near the factories, trained them for three to six months, and received their pledges (*baozhengshu*) that they would work at the company for at least three years and would not go on strike. In February 1925 all that remained in Naigai's plans for Japanese-style labor-management relations in China was to put these Chinese female apprentices (*yangchenggong*) to work in place of Chinese male "old workers" (*lao gongren*) or "regular workers" (*zhengshi gongren*).[27]

TABLE 10.   PROFIT RATES OF JAPANESE-OWNED
COTTON MILLS IN CHINA, 1921–1937 (IN %)

	Naigai		Shanghai		Shanhai Seizo		Nikka		Doko	
	1st half	2d half	1st half	2d half	1st half	2d half	1st half	2d half	1st half	2d half
1921	131.6	131.3	70.7	46.8			33.5	32.1		
1922	127.1	127.5	46.8	8.1			24.7	17.9	2.1	7.7
1923	92.1	63.1	8.1	−11.8	11.3	3.8	17.3	14.3	8.4	7.9
1924	50.5	48.7	11.8	1.2	5.7	2.2	13.1	15.6	13.9	11.7
1925	39.7	16.0	1.2	3.0	9.9	5.7	15.6	−3.5	14.3	8.6
1926	24.7	20.7	9.8	9.9	9.2	13.0	3.9	8.0	12.8	14.8
1927	16.6	21.1	16.2	11.1	9.9	16.6	−2.5	−12.2	14.4	13.4
1928	22.4	25.9	14.7	15.1	18.1	21.6	−1.4	8.2	12.0	12.4
1929	29.6	28.1	19.7	26.8	24.3	19.3	13.5	11.5	14.1	13.9
1930	24.9	24.4	31.1	27.1	21.1	25.8	11.5	10.5	12.2	13.0
1931	25.9	41.1	27.2	30.8	33.5	31.4	10.9	6.1	12.2	12.4
1932	19.7	23.4	17.3	21.4	27.6	29.7	−13.2	−15.4	8.9	10.9
1933	22.9	22.6	21.8	28.2	26.6	27.0	−11.2	−5.3	13.3	9.7
1934	22.8	23.3	29.0	40.8	31.6	31.0	3.3	5.8	12.2	14.5
1935	22.8	22.6	48.8	37.0	30.2	29.5	2.5	−21.3	13.9	14.2
1936	27.0	26.4	46.5	50.3	29.6	29.8	10.1	14.3	14.6	16.0
1937	45.7		72.2		38.2		2.9		29.4	

SOURCE: Takamura, *Kindai,* 125, table 8.

On February 2, 1925, Naigai's management dismissed the men for insubordination because they had complained about the beating that a Japanese supervisor had given to a Chinese girl in the mill.[28] To the men being fired, Naigai's actions seemed arbitrary and its subsequent explanation dishonest. According to the recollections of one of Naigai's male workers, the company's Japanese management tried to convince the workers that it was reducing the size of the workforce for financial reasons and was not planning to replace the dismissed men. In his words, "[Japanese managers claimed,] 'Our factory is going bankrupt and cannot keep running. We will give you some money, and you can go look for other ways of making a living.' . . . Just like that they eliminated us one by one, and then recruited women to do our jobs."[29] The Japanese managers' unstated assumption at Naigai, as Honig has pointed out, was that women and especially young girls would be "both easier to manage and less expensive than adult men."[30]

Toka		Yuho		Average		Average among All Mills in Japan		Average among Three Leading Mills in Japan	
1st half	2d half	1st half	2d half	1st half	2d half	1st half	2d half	1st half	2d half
				88.8	57.2	27.9	48.2	45.3	64.3
38.2	4.7			51.3	40.7	41.2	33.4	57.8	50.7
−18.4	2.9			24.3	24.6	29.2	15.1	50.1	31.7
5.2	−3.1			24.0	20.9	24.3	25.3	46.7	44.0
−2.9	−4.5			19.7	6.5	26.7	19.2	44.8	42.3
−8.1	10.7			11.7	14.6	18.7	19.3	40.1	36.8
3.6	−5.8			9.6	7.2	18.0	22.2	34.7	35.3
0.1	0.4			10.7	14.2	21.2	22.8	35.3	36.1
5.9	14.9		16.8	18.4	19.1	23.1	19.2	35.8	24.4
15.0	12.8	18.4	18.4	17.7	17.4	6.1	−0.2	29.3	20.4
13.2	12.8	20.0	17.2	18.0	22.4	16.4	17.5	26.2	26.1
−13.8	−12.8	9.2	9.2	7.9	10.0	18.6	22.2	27.6	29.5
−4.9	−4.8	10.2	14.7	11.6	12.8	24.6	29.3	31.6	33.2
1.0	2.6	18.1	23.4	15.8	17.6	28.4	29.8	37.4	36.1
−5.8	−3.8	25.0	28.4	19.5	10.5	25.3	24.0	36.1	37.2
−16.2	0.4	22.3	20.0	21.5	22.4	22.3	24.8	37.6	37.4
22.6		22.2		32.3		32.0		41.0	

On February 9, a week after Naigai dismissed the men, Naigai's carefully laid plans were disrupted when Chinese male workers, led by Number Ones, went on strike and took as their battle cry "No firing of regular workers without just cause."[31] As Martin W. Frazier has shown in his close study of this strike, of all the suspected strike leaders arrested by the police, no less than twenty-seven out of forty-seven were Chinese Number Ones. In fact, Number Ones played such a prominent role that a police inspector attributed the strike entirely to their leadership. "There was no discontent apparent among the workers," the inspector reported. The "strikes [were] led by a handful of No. 1's."[32]

Besides taking command within the mills, Chinese Number Ones formed liaisons with Communist labor organizers outside the mills. They held meetings with Communists in local restaurants and teahouses, and they agreed to cooperate with party members based at the West Shanghai Recreation Club, which had been founded by Commu-

nists in 1924 with a local branch at Naigai. In the chain of contacts one
key link was the Naigai worker Tao Jingxuan. Before the firings on February 1, he had become a Communist and an activist at the club and
had persuaded leaders of five native-place gangs at his mill to become
sworn brothers pledging loyalty to each other and to himself as the
"elder brother." When Tao heard about Naigai's decision to fire male
workers, he used his contacts in the mills and in the Communist party
to help organize and publicize the strike.[33]

Men took the lead in the strike against the replacement of men with
women, and they seem not to have had the willing support of women
workers. In fact, the head of the Communists' Trade Union Secretariat
at the time, Zhang Guotao, later recalled that male strikers, "under the
slogan 'Oppose Japan,' had adopted the technique of preventing large
numbers of women and child workers from going to their jobs." [34]

Voluntarily or not, as many as thirty-five thousand men and women
went on strike at Naigai and twenty-one other Japanese-owned cotton
mills, idling six hundred thousand spindles between February 18 and
March 9. Never before in China had so many workers from one industry participated in a strike, and their collective action had a jarring effect on Japanese managers at Naigai and other mills. In negotiations
labor was represented by unions, and management was represented
by Japanese negotiators working through Chinese mediators from the
Shanghai General Chamber of Commerce. In the course of bargaining,
the unions agreed to shorten their list of demands, but to the end they
were adamant that there be no firing of workers without just cause, and
ultimately the Japanese cotton mills acceded to this demand.[35]

This strike marked the first major challenge to Naigai's plans for
instituting Japanese-style management-labor relations in China. Since
1911 Naigai had steadily built up its corporate hierarchies and elaborated its paternalistic company welfare programs with the aim of ridding
itself of Chinese Number Ones, and it had come close to achieving this
goal. But during the strike of February–March 1925, Chinese Number
Ones took the lead and strengthened their social networks by making
contacts with Communists and other labor organizers outside the mills.
In the span of a few short weeks, Naigai's two options—Japanese corporate hierarchies, on the one hand, or Chinese social networks, on the
other—had both begun to change, and before Naigai made a decision
about whether to shift responsibility from Japanese supervisors to Chinese Number Ones, its mills became the scene of an incident that started
the most famous strike in Chinese history.

THE MAY THIRTIETH STRIKE OF 1925

On May 15, 1925, at Naigai's No. 5 Mill in Shanghai—a big factory made of reinforced concrete and regarded by the company as the "model mill"—a Japanese guard shot and killed a Chinese mill worker, Gu Zhenghong, and thereby triggered a vehement and sustained series of Chinese protests. The same day and the next day, male workers rioted at Naigai's mills and (as in the February strike) women workers unwillingly followed. According to a contemporary account, "Because the women workers were afraid of the male workers' rioting, they fled from the south to the exit and then ran outside the mill."[36] Two weeks later, on May 30, 1925, three thousand Chinese students marched down Nanjing Road into the center of Shanghai's commercial district to protest the shooting at Naigai, and when fifty of these demonstrators were shot and ten were killed by a British-led police squad, others demonstrated against this outrage by citing the Naigai incident in a series of anti-imperialist strikes and boycotts known as the May Thirtieth movement.[37]

Naigai's management responded by negotiating with the family of the victim of the May 15 shooting and with Naigai's Number Ones rather than with labor unions. On May 7 Naigai and other members of the Association of Japanese Cotton Textile Manufacturers in Shanghai had banned unions from their factories, and wherever the unions had continued to be active, Naigai's management had carried out a policy of lockouts; in fact, it was one of these lockouts that the worker Gu Zhenghong had been protesting when he was killed. On May 31, 1925 (the day after the killings on Nanjing Road), when the Shanghai General Labor Union was founded under Communist leadership, Naigai and other Japanese mills immediately adopted a negotiating strategy designed to avoid it. In the words of the General Labor Union's bitter protest, the Japanese cotton mill owners "linked up with foremen and seduced [workers] with trivial benefits, such as frequently asking them to banquets, increasing wages for the foremen, and opening schools and hospitals. All of this was to divide workers and create conflicts in order to hurt the union."[38] Naigai's negotiators began by contacting Gu Xueqiao, a relative of the worker killed on May 15 at Naigai's mill and a gang boss himself. Naigai's negotiators convinced Gu Xueqiao to accept 10,000 yuan as compensation for Gu Zhenghong's death and to call for an end to the strike, but the General Labor Union rejected the offer, insisted on compensation of 50,000 yuan, and refused to stop the strike until the full amount was paid.[39]

Figure 9.   Chinese strikers in Shanghai joining the May Thirtieth movement
of 1925 under banners indicating that they are from Naigai's cotton mills.
Reprinted from Wusa yundong bianxie zubian, *Wusa yundong,* preceding 1.

After the strike continued all summer, Naigai's negotiators finally met
for talks with one hundred Number Ones on August 22. They discussed
the Number Ones' complaint that Naigai paid its Number Ones far less
than Chinese-owned cotton mills paid theirs, keeping wages for Number Ones at Naigai only slightly above those for its ordinary workers.[40]
In response Naigai offered to widen the difference between Number
Ones' and ordinary workers' wages by giving a 20 percent raise to workers and a 100 percent raise to Number Ones. In addition, Naigai agreed
to waive rent that had gone unpaid for rooms in Naigai's company housing during the strike and once again acceded to the demand that regular
workers would not be fired without just cause. When Number Ones expressed their approval of this proposal, the General Labor Union reluctantly endorsed Naigai's original offer of 10,000 yuan in compensation
for the killing of the worker, and the May Thirtieth strike against Naigai
and other Japanese mills ended on August 25, 1925. Lasting one hundred days, this strike had hit Naigai harder than any other company. All
eleven of its mills in Shanghai had been closed, and 18,400 of its workers had been on strike.[41]

During the following year Naigai tried to regain authority for its

Japanese managers and supervisors, but it repeatedly encountered opposition from strikers. In early June 1926, for example, twelve hundred
workers at Naigai's No. 13 Mill struck for four days to protest the presence of Japanese supervisors on the night shift, and later in the same
month workers struck because of the misbehavior of four supervisors,
who were accused of being "bullies." In the settlement following the
latter strike, Naigai tried to reassert its authority by insisting "that the
mills shall have the right to recruit mill hands without interference
on the part of the workers,"[42] but strike after strike called this "right"
into question, and in March 1927 the Shanghai Cotton Textiles Union
(Shanghai shachang gonghui) formulated the strikers' persistent demand as a general principle: "From now on, mills should retain all
regular workers, stop recruiting apprentices, and hire only new workers
recommended by the Union."[43] With its apprentice program repeatedly
under fire, Naigai's management was forced to consider alternatives to
Japanese direct managerial control over workers.

In early 1927 Naigai's management was presented with a new alternative for its relations with labor as a result of Chiang Kai-shek's successful military expedition that originated in the southern city of Guangzhou and culminated in the capture of Shanghai. Between 1925 and
early 1927 Naigai had dealt with Chinese social networks that included
Communists, but soon after Chiang arrived in Shanghai, the Communists came under attack.

This attack, "the tragedy of the Chinese Revolution" as Harold
Isaacs has called it, was led by members of the Green Gang.[44] The "god-
father" of the Green Gang, Huang Jinrong, had as many as twenty thousand followers and took advantage of connections with major political
figures, including Chiang Kai-shek who had pledged his discipleship to
Huang at Shanghai in the early 1920s. In March 1927, on Chiang's tri-
umphant return to Shanghai as commander of the Northern Expedition,
Huang was there to greet him, and a few weeks later, in April 1927,
another of Huang's followers, Du Yuesheng, financed and directed the
combination of gangsters and military forces that carried out the attack,
smashing unions, killing hundreds of workers and labor organizers, and
driving Communists out of Shanghai. While serving Chiang's political
purpose by ridding him of Communists and other leftist political rivals,
this attack also opened the way for Du's emergence as Shanghai's leading labor organizer.[45] During the next decade, 1928–37, Du and other
members of the Green Gang played prominent roles as mediators between labor and management, and in one of their major rackets they be-

gan to profit from supplying Naigai and other cotton mills with workers under a system of contract labor.

EMPLOYING CONTRACT LABOR, 1928–1937

From the standpoint of Naigai's management, the Green Gang's mediation with labor had the immediate advantage of bringing three years of almost continuous strikes to an abrupt end. After its forty-four strikes between 1925 and 1927, the company experienced during the following decade only three more: an eighteen-day strike by 2,036 workers in July 1928; a nine-day strike by 1,079 workers in January and February 1929; and a general strike against all Japanese-owned cotton mills in Shanghai during 1936.[46] In dealing with the Green Gang, Naigai once again faced the issue of whether to continue its quest for direct managerial control through Japanese corporate hierarchies or surrender this control to Chinese social networks. Between 1911 and 1925 it had aggressively attacked Chinese Number Ones and their relatively small and informal networks, using its Japanese corporate hierarchies to discipline and displace Chinese Number Ones. Then, between 1925 and 1927, it had contended with Chinese Number Ones who had aligned their networks with Communists and other labor organizers, and, under pressure from strikes, it had temporarily retreated, agreeing not to replace male Chinese Number Ones and their networks with Chinese women and girls under direct Japanese managerial control. Now, in the late 1920s and 1930s, confronted by the Green Gang, Naigai decisively changed its strategy. For the first time it delegated long-term responsibility for recruitment of workers to Chinese networks.

RELINQUISHING CONTROL OVER RECRUITMENT

Between 1928 and 1937, after the labor protests of the mid-1920s had ended and Chiang Kai-shek's Nationalist government had become established, Naigai accepted more and more workers from Chinese labor contractors who were relatively autonomous from the company. These contractors were not formally on Naigai's staff or payroll. Instead they were connected with the company informally through the social networks of Naigai's Chinese Number Ones. Under this system of contract labor (*baoshengong*), Chinese contractors (*baogongtou* or *baolaoban*) recruited girls from rural families in the countryside for Chinese Number Ones in the mills. They looked for girls between the ages of twelve and sixteen, and they convinced the girls' families to sign three-year contracts. Under the contracts, each family received a small sum (20–30 yuan), each girl became obligated to work at a mill in Shanghai for the labor contractor, and each contractor was supposed to take care of the girl's food, clothing, shelter, and medical care. A small-scale labor contractor handled thirty to fifty girls, and a large-scale contractor had as many as one hundred fifty.[47]

In the late 1920s and early 1930s Naigai shifted a large measure of responsibility for labor recruitment into the hands of the labor contractors. In the early 1920s it had sent its own salaried agents directly into villages near Shanghai to recruit girls and to give them physical examinations and simple tests for literacy and manual dexterity before admitting them as apprentices. But by the early 1930s it became known as one of Shanghai's leading employers of contract laborers in an industry where two out of every three workers were contract laborers. Under the contract system, Naigai's transactions with workers became much more indirect. Its wage payments passed through the hands of Chinese Number Ones and labor contractors before reaching workers, and its houses were leased to Number Ones and labor contractors who set room rates and collected rents from workers.[48]

Naigai and other cotton mills (whether owned by Chinese, Westerners, or Japanese) all accommodated labor contractors, according to Honig, because they were "in the stranglehold" of the Green Gang.[49] And yet, as Naigai became more dependent on the Green Gang's network, it by no means withdrew its Japanese managers. In fact, between 1928 and 1937 it strengthened its staff of Japanese managers and supervisors.

REINFORCING JAPANESE MANAGERIAL CONTROL

In 1929 Arno Pearse, a British cotton textiles expert who had traveled to Shanghai to investigate the industry there, made this report: "Several Chinese mill owners had praised to me the superiority of the Japanese system of training the Chinese workpeople by having a comparatively large number of young female overseers and by instituting greater discipline."[50] This "greater discipline"—the envy of Chinese mill managers —was achieved by employing numerous Japanese in highly structured corporate hierarchies.

In the early 1930s Naigai and other Japanese mills employed far more foreign staff members than did their Western- and Chinese-owned counterparts. In 1930 Naigai had no less than 402 Japanese staff members

in its mills, and several other Japanese cotton mills also employed large
numbers: Kanegafuchi had 264; Dai Nippon, 160; Osaka Godo, 75;
Toyo, 70; and Fuji, 26. At Naigai's factories Japanese managers served
at one of four levels in rank order. At the top three levels were the chief
production manager (*daban*), his assistants (*erban*), and the supervisors
of the shops (*sanban*), all of whom had offices in the factory but not on
the shop floor; and at the fourth level were the supervisor's assistants,
known to Chinese workers by the derogatory name "little Asians" (*xiao
dongyang*), who worked full time on the shop floor and stayed in close
proximity to Chinese workers, even to the point of routinely taking
responsibility for using oil cans to lubricate the machinery. For these
Japanese managers, Chinese served formally or informally as mediators
with Chinese workers in one of three capacities: as Number Ones (under the title "overseers," *jianchayuan*), trainers (*zhidaoyuan*), or labor
contractors, who were also known as recruiters (*tangguan*).[51]

Naigai's use of numerous Japanese managers gave it a hybrid approach to labor-management relations. On the one hand, it recruited
workers through Chinese networks outside the mills; on the other, it
supervised workers through Japanese corporate hierarchies inside the
mills. Although this approach deviated from Naigai's original, purely
Japanese vision for itself in China, it did not raise the cost of Chinese labor in China above the cost of Japanese labor in Japan. According to a
Japanese survey in 1929, for example, the labor costs for producing one
bale of twenty-count cotton yarn was 9.20 yen in China compared to
20 yen in Japan.[52] These relatively low costs undoubtedly boosted Naigai's profit rates in China between 1925 and 1937.

THE SILVER AGE

In the late 1920s and the 1930s Naigai did not maintain profit rates
quite as high as in the early 1920s, but it distributed its goods more
widely in China than ever before. As always since its conversion from a
trading company into a manufacturing firm in 1908, it distributed its
finished goods and bought its raw materials through Japanese trading
companies, notably C. Itoh (Ito chu shoji kabushiki kaisha), which by
1936 grew into the largest Japanese distributor of cotton textiles and
the largest Japanese purchaser of raw cotton in China.[53] During the late
1920s and 1930s Naigai's best-known brand of yarn, Moon on the Water (Shui yue), was distributed by Japanese trading companies far beyond its mills in Shanghai and Qingdao and reached all nine of China's

regions: the Northeast, North, and Northwest (as well as Inner Mongolia); the Lower, Middle, and Upper Yangzi; and the Southeast, South, and Southwest (including both of the southwestern provinces of Yunnan and Guizhou).[54] Because of this widely known brand, Chinese commonly referred to its manufacturer as Moon on the Water Yarn Mills (Shui yue shachang) rather than Naigai (which is pronounced "Neiwai" in Chinese).

Naigai's wide distribution allowed it to make speedy recoveries from numerous anti-Japanese boycotts (which were generally less effective outside Shanghai than within it) and to maintain relatively high profits. Like other Japanese-owned cotton mills in China, it never restored its profit rates to the extraordinary levels of the pre-1925 "golden age," and again like other Japanese-owned mills in China, it suffered from falling profit rates during each boycott. Nonetheless, between 1925 and 1937 Naigai maintained an average annual profit rate of 25.6 percent, which compared favorably with the average annual profit rate of 21.3 percent earned by all cotton mills in Japan during these years, if not with the average annual profit of 34.1 percent earned by the three biggest mills in Japan at the time (see table 10). On the basis of these figures, if the period between 1925 and 1937 was not a golden age for the company, it may be characterized without exaggeration as a silver age.

CONCLUSION

Paradoxically, Naigai's history in China provides examples in support of both sides of the debate (as summarized in chapter 1) over the question of whether Japanese businesses exercised managerial control over Chinese workers. In China during Naigai's first thirteen years, 1911–24, it demonstrated an impressive capacity for transferring Japanese corporate hierarchies from Japan and putting them to use in China. In carrying out this process, Naigai resembled Mitsui. Even as Mitsui trained Chinese-speaking Japanese to manage purchasing and distributing in China's markets, so Naigai trained Chinese-speaking Japanese to supervise the manufacturing of goods in China-based factories. Just as Mitsui paternalistically aimed to imbue its staff members with loyalty to the company, Naigai did the same, combining appealing benefits (housing, medical care, regular bonuses, graduated wage scales) with tight discipline and close scrutiny on and off the job. By these means both of the Japanese businesses made headway against Chinese intermediaries, but Naigai did not consolidate its gains as fully or permanently as Mitsui did. Whereas Mitsui replaced Chinese compradors and merchants with Japanese China specialists, Naigai disciplined Chinese Number Ones and did not replace them. Nonetheless, like Mitsui, Naigai achieved a high degree of managerial control as measured by its success at preventing strikes—before 1925.

If Naigai's record between 1911 and 1924 shows its success at gaining managerial control over networks of Chinese workers, its record between 1925 and 1937 shows its failure to sustain this control. Between 1925 and 1927 Naigai's campaign to eliminate Chinese Number Ones was interrupted by the high tide of the Chinese labor movement that made Naigai the prime target. Thereafter Naigai retreated from its earlier campaign to institute a Japanese corporate organization of Japanese managers and Chinese women workers who were supposed to be recruited, housed, trained, and supervised like their counterparts in Japan. Instead it settled for a hybrid organization in which Chinese workers were supervised by Japanese managers but were recruited by Chinese labor contractors and the Green Gang through Chinese social networks.

The ultimate failures of Naigai and BAT (both foreign-owned firms) to sustain managerial control over their factory workers raises the question of whether Chinese-owned industrial enterprises had any greater success along these lines. If Western and Japanese corporate hierarchies did not permanently prevail over networks of Chinese factory workers, did a business using Chinese social networks for managerial purposes fare any better? Since BAT and Naigai were both big manufacturers of consumer goods, it is worth comparing them with China's biggest Chinese-owned manufacturer of cotton textiles, Shenxin Cotton Mills.

CHAPTER 6

Shenxin Cotton Mills

In the early twentieth century Shenxin Cotton Mills (Shenxin shachang) became the biggest Chinese-owned business in China's leading industrial sector, cotton textiles. Founded in 1915, by 1932 Shenxin employed 31,717 workers (the most of any firm in China) who spun yarn on 561,592 spindles (the most of any firm in China) and wove cloth on 5,357 looms (the most of any firm in China except one, the Japanese-owned Kanegafuchi Cotton Mills).[1] Continuing to operate as a privately owned company until the founding of the People's Republic, Shenxin made its owners, a family named Rong, the richest businesspeople in China. According to an official nationwide audit done in 1956, the Rongs were worth 60 million yuan—far more than any other capitalist family in the country.[2]

Shenxin's founder, Rong Zongjing, achieved success by adapting a Chinese social network of people from his family and native place. He turned to his family members and native-place associates as investors and managers in Shenxin and as lobbyists with the government. And yet it would be wrong to assume that his heavy reliance on his network resulted in an egalitarian consensus or freed him from conflicts with investors, managers, workers, and officials. On the contrary, Rong established Shenxin and retained managerial control of it by forming a corporate hierarchy with himself at the top, and he developed Shenxin into a large and profitable enterprise by overcoming opponents who included family members and native-place associates within his network.

OVERCOMING OPPOSITION FROM
FAMILY AND NATIVE PLACE

In 1915, when Rong Zongjing founded Shenxin Cotton Mills in Shanghai, its prospects for expansion were not bright because its financial base was severely restricted. Rong Zongjing and his brother, Rong Desheng, obtained a majority (53 percent) of the company's stock by investing 159,000 yuan out of its total of 300,000 yuan in initial capital, and Rong deliberately foreclosed the option of selling a majority of Shenxin's shares to other stockholders.[3] Instead he founded Shenxin Cotton Mills as an unlimited liability company—a closed partnership in which Rong Zongjing as general manager and Rong Desheng retained full responsibility for all decisions—and these two brothers continued to hold a majority of Shenxin's stock for the next twenty-three years until Rong Zongjing's death in 1938. Rong Zongjing made the decision not to raise capital through the sale of a majority of Shenxin's stock because he was determined to carry out his plans for expansion and because in managing previous enterprises he had encountered opposition to his plans for expansion from stockholders—even stockholders bound to him by family and native-place ties.

FAMILY TIES

Before founding Shenxin in Shanghai in 1915, Rong Zongjing had spent more than twenty-five years in the city, and throughout this quarter century his family had consistently instructed him to raise capital that was to be remitted to his native Wuxi, a city 120 kilometers (75 miles) west of Shanghai. His decision in 1915 to fly in the face of his family's instructions by opening Shenxin Cotton Mills in Shanghai rather than Wuxi deviated from the norms not only of his own family but of Chinese merchant families in general.

Rong Zongjing's sojourn to Shanghai and remittances to Wuxi before founding Shenxin followed a classic pattern in late imperial Chinese history. According to this pattern, as identified by G. William Skinner, a Chinese merchant family commonly achieved upward mobility by sending a young son along a "merchant-financier track" up an urban hierarchy from the family's native place to a larger and more central city where the boy did an apprenticeship in commerce or finance and then "plundered [the larger city] for the benefit of his own" native place.[4] Whether the sojourner came from a village, a marketing community, or a town, he abided by financial decisions originating in "leadership councils" in his native place where he expected ultimately to return and retire.[5]

Until 1915 Rong Zongjing unwaveringly conformed to this well-established pattern. The firstborn son in a merchant family, he emerged at a young age as the family favorite, especially compared to his younger brother, Rong Desheng, who seemed dim-witted as a child and did not speak before the age of four, earning for himself the family nickname "Blockhead No. 2 Son" (er mutou). As the son chosen to lead his family up the economic ladder, Rong Zongjing was sent at the age of fifteen from Wuxi to Shanghai, the largest city in the Lower Yangzi region and, for that matter, in all of China, where he took up an apprenticeship at the Yu Yuan Native Bank for three years and then accepted a job at the Sen Tai Rong Native Bank for another four years.[6] Thus trained, Rong Zongjing proceeded to "plunder" his host city between 1896 and 1912 in the sense that he presided over financial institutions that channeled capital out of Shanghai and into Wuxi.

In early 1896 Rong Zongjing opened the first of these Shanghai financial institutions, the Guangsheng Native Bank. He bought this bank in partnership with his father, Rong Xitai, and his brother, Rong Desheng, who had overcome his tongue-tied childhood and completed a banking apprenticeship comparable to Rong Zongjing's. Less than four months later, in June 1896, the brothers' father died, but Rong Zongjing, then twenty-three, did not dispose of the Guangsheng Native Bank in Shanghai and return to Wuxi to manage his family's business, a silk cocoon trading company (can hang). Instead he continued to raise capital through the Guangsheng Native Bank in Shanghai and sent his brother back to Wuxi to open and manage a branch bank that received remittances from Shanghai. Moreover, he solidified ties between his Shanghai bank and Wuxi's silk industry by betrothing his infant daughter to the son of Xue Nanming, the leading silk manufacturer in Wuxi and probably in all of China.[7] In all of these maneuvers—sojourning "up" from Wuxi to Shanghai, opening a Shanghai-Wuxi native bank, and forming a Wuxi marriage alliance—Rong Zongjing positioned himself to remit funds from his host city to his native place.

In July 1905, after channeling funds from Shanghai to Wuxi through the Guangsheng Native Bank for nearly ten years, Rong Zongjing increased this flow of capital by adding a second conduit, the Yu Da Xiang Commercial House (Yu da xiang shang hao) of Shanghai. Rong Zongjing and his brother became members of this financial house at the invi-

Figure 10.   Rong Zongjing, founder and head of Shenxin
Cotton Mills. Reprinted from *Men of Shanghai and North
China*, 699.

tation of Rong Ruixing, a member of their lineage from Wuxi who held
a position as a Shanghai comprador for Jardine, Matheson and Company. Within the next few years the Yu Da Xiang Commercial House
served as an effective vehicle for transferring capital from Shanghai to
Wuxi. In fact, it made redundant the Guangsheng Native Bank, which
Rong Zongjing closed in 1909.[8]

By 1915 Rong Zongjing's efforts at raising capital in Shanghai had
visible effects on Wuxi. His remittances were used to finance several
Wuxi enterprises under the Rong family's ownership: a silk trading company that had been the family's original business; Baoxing Flour Mill,
established in 1900; Maoxin Flour Mill, which succeeded Baoxin in
1903; and Zhenxin Cotton Mill, founded in 1906.[9] Moreover, the Rong

family's success with these ventures set an example that was followed by other Wuxi families, notably the Yangs, Xues, Tangs, and Zhous who, along with the Rongs, became known as Wuxi's "Five Families of Big Industrialists." Like the Rongs before 1915, the other four families invested exclusively in Wuxi, and even after 1915 they continued to do so until forced out of Wuxi by the Japanese military occupation of 1937. With the Five Families supplying 70 percent of the capital for industrial investments (principally in flour, textiles, and silk mills), Wuxi was swiftly transformed into "Little Shanghai" (as it was called), China's fifth most industrialized city, which ranked only behind the much larger metropolises of Shanghai, Hankou, Tianjin, and Guangzhou.[10]

For twenty-five years Rong Zongjing seemed content to play this role as a Shanghai financier "plundering" his adopted city for the benefit of his native place. Not until 1914 did he propose that funds raised in Shanghai should be invested anywhere besides Wuxi.

RONG ZONGJING'S CLASH
WITH HIS NATIVE-PLACE ASSOCIATES

In 1914 Rong Zongjing called on the board of directors of his family's biggest business, Zhenxin Cotton Mill, to make a decisive departure from their past practices by building factories outside Wuxi. As chairman of the board, he exhorted Zhenxin's board members to open four new cotton mills—two in Shanghai and one each in Ningbo and Zhengzhou. As a first step, he had already selected a site for the factory at Zhengzhou and had made all arrangements for purchasing the property pending approval from Zhenxin's board of directors. It was time, he told the members of the board, for expansion beyond the boundaries of their native place.

To Rong Zongjing's dismay, he failed to win approval for the purchase of land for one additional factory, much less for his overall scheme. No matter how much he insisted that these new factories would be worthwhile long-term investments, he was defeated by his opponents, led by Rong Ruixing, who preferred to take short-term profits in Wuxi and complained about the lack of dividends during the preceding year. As the conflict deepened Rong Desheng was accused by the board of directors of mismanaging Zhenxin's factory in Wuxi and demoted from factory manager to assistant manager in early 1915.

Angered by the board's treatment of both his brother and himself, Rong Zongjing abruptly resigned as chairman of Zhenxin's board, ceased to play any role in its leadership, and withdrew almost entirely from it. To dissociate themselves as fully as possible from Rong Ruixing, the brothers Rong Zongjing and Rong Desheng exchanged the majority of their Zhenxin stock for Rong Ruixing's stock in their Maoxin Flour Mill, leaving them with 30,000 yuan worth of stock in Zhenxin and him with none in Maoxin.[11]

By breaking away from these native-place associates, Rong Zongjing freed himself to invest outside Wuxi, but he also cut himself off from his enterprises' major financial backers. Before 1915 virtually all of his Wuxi businesses had been financed by Wuxi natives—some residing in Wuxi and others (like Rong Ruixing) in Shanghai or South China—[12] and, if he intended to expand his business without taking their investments and giving them authority, he had to raise capital elsewhere.

FINANCING FROM JAPANESE-OWNED BANKS

To finance his and his brother's controlling interest in Shenxin, Rong Zongjing turned for the first time to foreign-owned banks that had no ties to financial institutions owned by his family or anyone else from Wuxi. In 1917 and 1918 he borrowed from Japanese-owned banks loans valued at 300,000 yen, 400,000 yen, and 250,000 yen. In the first of these loan agreements (which survives and is probably similar to his subsequent ones) he promised to pay interest at an annual rate of 8 percent and agreed to put up as security all properties belonging to Shenxin Cotton Mill and to his Fuxin Flour Mills Nos. 1 and 3. According to this contract, if he failed to make payments on time, then the bank had the right to "dispose of the mortgages at will."[13]

By taking advantage of this financing, Rong Zongjing quickly enlarged Shenxin's capital base without surrendering control to other shareholders. Initially capitalized in 1915 at 0.3 million yuan, by 1922 Shenxin was worth more than fifty times as much—nearly 16 million yuan. During the same period, Rong Zongjing and Rong Desheng not only maintained but increased their majority share from 53 percent in 1915 to 63.3 percent in 1922 (see table 11). To give them a say in all sales of Shenxin's stock, they stipulated in Shenxin's bylaws that any of its shareholders wishing to sell stock to investors outside the company could do so only with the unanimous consent of all shareholders.[14]

In theory Rong Zongjing shared authority with his brother, but in practice he invariably prevailed. In 1919, for example, when the two brothers argued over a suitable location for Shenxin's second factory,

TABLE 11. CAPITAL, SPINDLES, AND LOOMS AT SHENXIN
AND OTHER FIRMS IN CHINA, 1916–1932

Year	Shenxin's Total Capital (yuan)	Shenxin's Spindles	All Chinese-owned Spindles	Japanese-owned Spindles	Shenxin's Looms	All Chinese-owned Looms	Japanese-owned Looms
1915	300,000						
1916	649,350	12,960					
1917		12,960					
1918		12,960	647,570	240,904	350	3,502	1,636
1919		55,872	658,748	332,922	600	2,650	1,486
1920	5,890,770	74,280			700		
1921		78,280			1,111		
1922	15,911,620	134,907	1,506,630	621,830	1,111	6,767	
1923	17,303,310	140,008			1,615		
1924	17,273,000	140,008					
1925	23,269,510	184,620	1,866,232	1,268,176	1,615	11,121	17,205
1926		189,804					
1927		189,804					1,888
1928		197,896					
1929	37,318,260	280,532	2,146,150	1,462,160	2,708	15,205	13,554
1930		327,352	2,345,070	1,587,780	2,836	15,718	15,983
1931		460,000	2,453,300	1,715,790	4,757	17,629	19,081
1932	64,231,800	521,552	2,625,410			5,357	

SOURCE: *RJ*, 104, 109, 110, 111, 114, 143, 144, 154, 264, 265, 266, 267, 268, 269, 278, 280, 281, 285, 613, 615.

Rong Zongjing got his way. He insisted that it, like the company's first factory, should be in Shanghai, and he announced a plan to buy and refurbish a twenty-year-old plant, the Hengchangyuan Cotton Mill. He brushed aside his younger brother's protests that the Hengchang-yuan mill's machines were obsolete and that Shenxin Cotton Mill No. 2 should be located in Wuxi rather than Shanghai, and he demanded and received his younger brother's financial backing. After yielding to Rong Zongjing and putting up 40 percent of the capital needed to buy and up-grade the old Hengchangyuan mill, Rong Desheng meekly noted in his journal: "I did not disobey elder brother's orders." [15]

At the Shenxin Cotton Mills, Rong Zongjing took greater risks and earned higher profits than he had done previously. His big loans in 1922 were borrowed at a relatively high interest rate of 11.5 percent (at a time when the average interest rate in industrialized countries was about 3 percent),[16] but he quickly paid them off by benefiting from China's booming cotton textiles market, which brought spectacularly high profit rates—no less than 96 percent per annum between 1918 and 1920 at Shenxin Cotton Mill No. 1 (see tables 12 and 13). Strengthened by these results, Rong Zongjing moved the headquarters for all of his family's enterprises to Shanghai.

DIRECTING EXPANSION FROM HEADQUARTERS IN SHANGHAI

In 1921 Rong Zongjing completed the transfer of authority from Wuxi by opening in Shanghai his General Corporation (Zong gongsi), which served as headquarters for all of the Rong family's industrial enterprises —Maoxin and Fuxin flour mills as well as Shenxin Cotton Mills. Rong's choice of a site in Shanghai for his new headquarters symbolized his de-termination to supervise personally the expansion and the operation of his business. His brother and other colleagues from Wuxi urged him to choose a location that they selected in Shanghai on the basis of geo-mancy (*feng shui*), but Rong rejected it in favor of a more central place on Jiangxi Road near Shanghai's Bund, saying, according to an entry at the time in his brother's journal, "At the first site the feng shui might be good, but the telephone service is no good." [17] Once he had his head-quarters in place, Rong Zongjing showed that he was serious about us-ing Shanghai's telephone service. As his business grew, he required all of his factory managers to telephone him for instructions during noontime every working day.[18]

TABLE 12.   SHENXIN COTTON MILLS'
PRODUCTION, SALES, AND PROFITS, 1916–1936

Year	Yarn in Pieces (*jian*)	Cloth in Bolts (*pi*)	Gross Sales (yuan)	Profits (yuan)
1915				20,000
1916	3,584			
1917	9,723	29,002		400,000
1918	9,811	128,719		800,000
1920		180,000		1,000,000
1921	36,300			
1922	80,356	359,530		
1923	75,343	701,871		
1924	82,081			
1925	97,264	976,441		
1926	116,667	1,021,730		
1927	86,741	1,068,393		
1928	143,550	1,462,784		1,824,540
1929	165,127	1,704,068		2,984,910
1930	182,925	1,742,310		
1931	221,213	2,432,207		
1932	306,248	2,798,486	69,334,220	
1933	294,805	2,376,940		
1934	304,567	2,346,448		
1935	285,928	2,432,050		
1936	319,653	2,884,272		

SOURCES: *RJ*, 104, 109, 152, 218, 264, 266, 281, 615; Takamura, *Kindai*, 106.

TABLE 13.   SHENXIN MILL NO. 1'S CAPITAL AND
PROFITS, 1918–1921

Year	Capital (yuan)	Net Profit (yuan)	Profit Rate (%)
1918	300,000	222,506	71.2
1919	800,000	1,048,056	131.0
1920	1,500,000	1,275,878	85.1
1921	2,400,000	728,051	30.3

SOURCE: *RJ*, 84.

With telephone in hand, Rong Zongjing took advantage of Shanghai as a center for communications, finance, and shipping and steadily expanded Shenxin's manufacturing, marketing, and purchasing operations during the 1920s and early 1930s. He capitalized on Shanghai as a financial center by borrowing from Japanese banks to cover the cost of

Shenxin's expansion. In 1922, the first year after he founded the General Corporation, he took out a loan for 3.5 million yen at an annual interest rate of 11.5 percent from the Japanese-owned Toa Trading Company in Shanghai.[19] He also financed Shenxin's expansion by transferring capital from Maoxin and Fuxin flour mills, which he administered through the General Corporation even though he did not hold a majority of stock in them. By investing these funds in the 1920s, Rong raised the number of Shenxin's cotton mills from two to eight: six in Shanghai, one in Wuxi, and one in Hankou.[20] Despite a depression that sharply curtailed overall production in China's textiles industry between 1922 and 1924, he steered a steady course toward expansion, adding new spindles to Shenxin's factories between 1922 and 1932 every year except the worst year of the postwar depression, 1924 (see table 11).

By taking advantage of Shanghai as a shipping center, Rong also expanded his marketing network and earned high profits in places not reached by his rivals. As Shenxin's plant managers noted in a 1935 review of its long-standing marketing policies:

> From the beginning this company's selling method for reaching ports outside Shanghai [wai pu] has been to set up branch distributors [fen zhuang] right in the localities so that we would be more familiar with local demand and purchasing power, better able to penetrate deeply into the hinterland [neidi], and better positioned [compared to the competition]. It has shipped all of its products directly and has kept the shipping costs extremely low. Since the selling prices in the hinterland have been higher than in Shanghai, this method has been very effective.[21]

These "extremely low" shipping costs were attributable to a special contract (hetong) that Shenxin negotiated with China Merchants' Steam Navigation Company (Lunchuan zhaoshang ju). Under it Shenxin paid lower rates and received higher tonnage limits than any other customer.[22]

Rong Zongjing took advantage of Shanghai as a center for communications to lengthen Shenxin's reach in purchasing. Even as he used the telephone to instruct his factory managers and used steamships to transport finished products, so too did he use the telegraph to discuss purchases of raw cotton with Shenxin's agents who were stationed outside Shanghai in agricultural areas of the Lower Yangzi region. Although telegraphed from distant Shanghai, his decisions had serious consequences in the cotton-growing areas because local sellers regularly withheld their cotton from other companies' buyers until hearing his offer.[23]

RONG ZONGJING VERSUS HIS WUXI NETWORK

The above examples all point to the conclusion that Shenxin became China's biggest business because its founder, Rong Zongjing, overcame his family members' and native-place associates' objections to expansion outside Wuxi by transferring authority into his own hands and capitalizing on Shanghai's economic centrality. As general manager of Shenxin and the General Corporation—both unlimited liability companies—Rong Zongjing achieved paramount authority over financial decision making and overrode objections from other managers and stockholders at Shenxin. When he heard complaints from his brother, Rong Desheng, and his Wuxi partner, Wang Yuqing, that he made indiscriminate investments—even in native banks not owned by people from their native place of Wuxi—he brushed aside their criticisms. "It'll be a long time before they understand my philosophy," he observed. "If I buy 10,000 shares [in a native bank], I can take out loans worth ten or twenty times that amount." [24] In fact, this estimate was conservative. In 1931 and 1932 Rong Zongjing invested 0.25 million yuan in five native banks and one modern bank, and in 1932 he borrowed from these six financial institutions a total of 43.74 million yuan—175 times the value of his investment. [25]

Fully in charge, he set the agenda for making all the major decisions and convened meetings entirely at his own discretion. As one of his bankers later recalled:

> All matters great and small were decided by Rong Zongjing himself. . . . He was always busy, walking in and out. People seldom saw him sitting behind his desk reading official papers or quietly considering something, and he never called staff meetings of top managers to discuss business matters in his office. . . . Any important meeting was held in his home rather than at the office. [26]

In settling "all matters great and small" for China's biggest business, Rong Zongjing's decisions were, in a word, binding.

Rong Zongjing's strategy for gathering authority into his own hands and shifting his family's investments from Wuxi to Shanghai ran the risk of alienating his brother and other Wuxi associates and tearing apart his network based on ties to family and native place. But even while he aggressively excluded his brother and native-place associates from the formulation of Shenxin's policies, he fully included them in the implementation of these policies by appointing them as members of Shenxin's administrative staff and relying on them to control its factory workers.

TRAINING MANAGERS AND CONTROLLING WORKERS

In dealing with workers, Shenxin's management compiled a remarkable record in avoiding strikes. In Shanghai during Shenxin's first decade, 1915–25, its workers went on strike only once and then for only one day, March 5, 1922. Between 1925 and 1927 the high tide of China's labor movement, Shenxin's mills in Shanghai had only six strikes—far less than its Japanese rivals Naigai (which had 44), Japan-China Spinning and Weaving Company (Nikka) (which had 13), and Toa Seima Kaisha (Toka) (which had 12), and no more than its leading Chinese rival, Yong'an (which, like Shenxin, had 6).[27] Data on strikes outside Shanghai are scarce, but by all available indications, Shenxin's mills in Wuxi and Hankou went on strike even less often than its mills in Shanghai did.

Why were strikes by workers in Shenxin's mills so rare and so brief? Part of the answer may be that Chinese Communists made a relatively weak effort to organize Shenxin's workers. The most serious attempt on record lasted only a few months. After sending fifty-two workers from Shenxin's Mill No. 1 in Shanghai for two months of secret training in Guangzhou, the Chinese Communist party began to form a union in the mill early in 1927, but on April 12, 1927, during the crackdown on Communists and other labor activists in Shanghai, the union's leader was killed and its organization smashed.[28] Another possible explanation for Shenxin's small number of strikes might be the nationality of Shenxin's ownership. As a Chinese-owned company, it might have been spared nationalistic strikes and boycotts that targeted its foreign rivals.

In light of Elizabeth Perry's important new book, neither of these explanations is adequate.[29] As she has convincingly shown, the Chinese Communist party was not the sole or even the most prominent cause of strikes in the history of Shanghai, and, according to her reading of Chinese workers' memoirs, they were not strongly motivated by antiforeign nationalism: "Resentment against profits more than against foreign ownership" caused Chinese factory workers to go on strike.[30] A likelier explanation for the infrequency of strikes at Shenxin's big and prosperous Chinese-owned mills lies in the Rongs' approach to relations with Shenxin's workers.

RECRUITING A STAFF FROM FAMILY,
LINEAGE, AND NATIVE PLACE

In the 1920s and 1930s, even after moving the headquarters of their business to Shanghai, the Rongs continued to fill most of their companies' staff positions with people from their family and native place of Wuxi. At the highest administrative levels, they appointed members of their family as managers in each of their factories, and below them they assigned additional family members as assistant managers (*xieli*). In 1928, for example, they employed 117 members of the Rong family, representing 12.2 percent of their business's administrative jobs.[31]

Among these "family" members were more than the two brothers' own sons. Shenxin's managers and assistant managers also included their sons-in-law, the products of marriage alliances with powerful families mostly from their native place. In fact, all ten of their sons-in-law held high managerial positions in either the Rong family's enterprises or large Chinese-owned banks, shipping firms, or other companies. Of the Rongs' marriage alliances with families from Wuxi, perhaps the most significant for administrative purposes were the weddings of Rong Zongjing's son and daughter to the offspring of Wang Yuqing, a Wuxi native who in 1912 had been one of the founding members of the Fuxin Flour Mills and by 1928 had become manager of four of Fuxin's mills in Shanghai. Of the Rongs' marriage alliances with families from outside Wuxi, perhaps the most useful for financial purposes was the wedding of Rong Desheng's daughter to the son of Song Hanzhang, an influential official at the Bank of China's branch in Shanghai throughout the republican period.[32]

While the Rongs generally reserved positions in top management for family members, they filled most of the much more numerous staff positions with other people from their native place. In the same year cited above, 1928, of the 957 staff members that they employed, no less than 617—64.5 percent—hailed from Wuxi.[33]

FOUNDING SCHOOLS FOR TRAINING
MANAGERS IN A NATIVE PLACE

The Rong brothers not only recruited managers from Wuxi but also trained them there. Before founding Shenxin, they had practiced a kind of educational philanthropy typical of preindustrial China. In 1906 they had opened in their native place a school for their lineage, the Rong Clan School (Rong shi jia shu), and between 1906 and 1917 they had founded eight Wuxi primary schools (four named Gong Yi for boys and four named Jing Hua for girls) plus the Gong Yi Library.[34] Then in the late 1910s and 1920s, as Shenxin added new factories, they began introducing vocational and technical institutes.

The Rongs became aware of the need for training when their appointments of family members and native-place associates failed to acquire specialized expertise appropriate for their business. For example, marrying Rong Desheng's eldest daughter to a Wuxi-born, well-educated engineer, Li Guowei, a graduate of Tangshan University, did not immediately produce a manager with ideal credentials. As Li later remarked:

> Because I was his [Rong Desheng's] son-in-law, he and Mr. Rong Zongjing persuaded me to give up my work as an engineer building railroads and join their business. I was first appointed to be assistant manager and chief engineer of Fuxin Flour Mill No. 5 and was later promoted to be manager of both Fuxin Flour Mill No. 5 and Shenxin Cotton Mill No. 4. But what I had studied was civil engineering, and I was really a novice at the textile and flour industries, so I made many mistakes in my work.[35]

To acquire appropriate expertise, the Rongs opened two centers at Wuxi, one in 1917 for vocational training and another in 1928 for managerial training. The first, known as the Gong Yi Middle School for Industry and Commerce (Gongyi gong shang zhong xue), taught prospective staff members to make economic transactions. It included simulated workshops, stores, and banks where students put into practice lessons learned in the classroom. In 1919, to solidify the linkage between Gong Yi Middle School's curriculum and their own factories, they added at Wuxi the Gong Yi Machine Shop, a simulated factory where students tested their skills under controlled but realistic conditions.[36]

In 1928 the Rongs introduced at Wuxi their managerial training center, the Staff Training Institute (Zhigong yangcheng suo), directed by Shen Banyuan, a respected specialist who had studied and worked in the textile business in Japan and Britain for ten years. Under Shen's regimen, in the mornings students in the Wuxi training program attended classes taught by Chinese instructors who had been educated in Britain or Japan, and in the afternoons they had opportunities for practical application in a simulated factory. During the school's first four years, 1928–32, it offered a yearlong course and produced eighty-one graduates, most of whom worked in Shenxin Cotton Mills.[37]

During these same years, Rong Zongjing and Rong Desheng acquired additional technical expertise for their business by educating members of their family at schools abroad. In 1928 they sent Rong Desheng's son, Rong Yiren, to Lowell, Massachusetts, where he earned a bachelor's degree at the Lowell Textile School, which was renowned at the time as the leading institution of its kind.[38] Subsequently the Rong brothers sent to the Lowell Textile School one of Rong Desheng's sons-in-law, and eventually they funded educations abroad for other sons and sons-in-law. Despite the outbreak of the Sino-Japanese War in 1937, the Rongs continued to maintain their training center at Wuxi, and when the war ended in 1945 they enlarged it. Between 1937 and 1945 the Rongs who remained in Japanese-occupied Wuxi operated the Staff Training Institute there, and the ones who withdrew to unoccupied Chongqing in Sichuan province and Baoqi in Shaanxi province started training courses there. These institutes placed most of their graduates within the company. After the war the Rongs once again concentrated their investments in training at Wuxi, especially as founders of Jiangnan University, opened in 1947, whose comprehensive curriculum in the arts, sciences, agriculture, and engineering included the first course ever offered in China on the flour industry.[39]

DEALING WITH NUMBER ONES

While training managers at Wuxi, the Rongs began to deal with Wuxi's Chinese foremen and forewomen, the Number Ones. Before the mid-1920s the Rongs had not extended their authority in the factory over Number Ones, who had retained the power to hire and fire their subordinates. As a former technician at Shenxin Mill No. 3 in Wuxi later recalled:

> The Rong family relied heavily on Number Ones to manage [*guanli*] the workers, so these Number Ones had great power and influence. All important and highly paid jobs in workshops were filled with these Number Ones' family members, relatives [*qinqi*], fellow native-place people and other cronies [*banghui*], and former apprentices.[40]

Although the Rongs were similarly dependent on Number Ones at their factories in Shanghai and had much bigger operations there, they chose their native place as the site for two attempts to block Number Ones: a failed attempt in 1924–25 and a successful one in 1933.

In 1924 the Rongs introduced the "student system" (*xuesheng zhi*) under which young Chinese "engineers" (*gongcheng shi*) and "new administrators" (*xin zhiyuan*), as they were called, were sent into the factory to circumvent Number Ones and give workers direct supervision. Although not fully trained professional engineers, these young men had earned degrees from vocational institutes such as the Hangzhou No. 1 School of Industry (Hangzhou jiazhong gongye xuexiao—the precursor of Zhejiang University) and had acquired experience at big Japanese-owned cotton mills such as Toyota, which, as Rong Zongjing pointed out at the time, had higher worker productivity than his own Shenxin Mills. These young engineers set out to reform the Rongs' Wuxi factory, Shenxin Mill No. 3, by adding a laboratory and maintenance department and, above all, by establishing managerial hierarchies and issuing their own instructions directly to workers.[41]

Shortly after the Rongs introduced the student system, they encountered vehement opposition that had been organized by Number Ones. Before the Rongs introduced this system, Number Ones in Wuxi had formed their own group, the Committee for the Alliance of the Six Mills' Workers (Liu chang gongren lianhe weiyuanhui), and on April 15, 1925, the committee's leaders, including Shenxin's leading Number One, Wang Abao, had met in Wuxi's Zhide Temple and resolved to mobilize workers and drive the new student system, out of Shenxin's mill. On the appointed day, April 21, 1925, workers defied the authority of the newly hired young engineers and beat them up. To stop the fighting, Rong Desheng called the police and closed the mill. He did not reopen it until after he had acquiesced to demands from Wang Abao, representing the workers, to abolish the new student system, withdraw the new engineers and administrators, and restore the old system under Number Ones.[42]

In 1933, eight years after the failure of this short-lived experiment, the Rongs resorted to a much more comprehensive and costly approach for restructuring labor-management relations: the Community for Self-Governing Workers (Laogong zizhi qu). Consciously following the example set earlier by Japanese cotton mills in Shanghai, they built the community in a large company compound that functioned like a company town unto itself within the town of Wuxi. The community rented to Shenxin's employees four sets of residential quarters—one for staff members' families, one for workers' families, one for single male workers, one for single female workers—and provided dining halls, public bathhouses, clinics, primary schools for workers' children, day schools and night schools for workers, libraries, theaters, and cinemas.

Through the community Shenxin's management began to monitor workers' activities both on and off the job. The residential quarters for single women, which housed 1,628 of the 4,050 women and men employed in Shenxin Mill No. 3, was organized to serve the purpose of surveillance much like the "watch group" (*bao jia*) system of mutual surveillance long used in urban and rural China. These quarters consisted of eight buildings (*cun*—lit., villages), each with its own building head; and each of these buildings had between fourteen and twenty-six rooms, each with its own room head. These heads reported disputes to the Court for Workers' Self-governance (Gongren zizhi fating) on which sat five judges elected by Shenxin's workers. To eliminate doubts about who held ultimate judicial authority, the company gave unsatisfied litigants the opportunity to appeal this court's decisions to Shenxin's general office (*zong guanli chu*), making Rong Zongjing's headquarters in Shanghai the court of last resort.

Of all the buildings in the Community of Self-Governing Workers, perhaps its two temples most fully embodied the values that Shenxin's management sought to inculcate in its residents. One, named the Hall of Wisdom (Zhun xian tang), stood next to the Court for Self-Governance. Even as the court had five presiding judges, so the temple featured five presiding canonized historical heroes, all of them patriots (including three famous figures from Chinese history, Guan Yu, Yue Fei, and Qi Jiguang). Another temple, known as the Temple of Merit and Virtue (Gong de si), had a different pantheon of deities. At its altars religious practitioners were offered opportunities to pay respects to model workers who had died after serving the company faithfully for ten or more years.[43]

By introducing the community, Shenxin's management established corporate authority, undercut the authority of Number Ones, and rid its Wuxi factory of them. Once management, not Number Ones, supplied workers with housing and access to a full-scale community, it tempted some Number Ones (including Wang Abao) into early retirement and reassigned others, causing them to resign. Shenxin's management then replaced Number Ones with staff members in a corporate hierarchy, and these staff members, in turn, immediately laid off a number of workers. Between 1933 and 1934, while continuing to run ten thousand spindles at the Wuxi cotton mill, they reduced the number of spindle operators from 450 to 297 and later to 270, and they cut in half the number of loom operators, who each began tending four machines rather than two.[44]

Within their native place, the Rong brothers thus succeeded in re-structuring relations with labor, ousting Number Ones, and cutting la-bor costs. In carrying out this project at Wuxi, they took advantage of their mills' proximity to their management training center, which was also located in their native place. But they did not confine their experi-ment to Wuxi. Once it began to succeed there, they tried it elsewhere.

FROM WUXI TO HANKOU

In 1934, only one year after opening the Community for Self-Governing Workers in Wuxi, the Rongs introduced a similar compound for work-ers at their factories in Hankou. Previously, during the late 1920s and early 1930s, under the direction of Rong Desheng's son-in-law Li Guowei, Shenxin had tried in vain to discipline Number Ones in its Hankou mill. Li began to make these reforms effective only in 1934, af-ter the Rongs sent graduates from their Gong Yi training center in Wuxi to Hankou where these graduates formed a cohesive band of man-agers known within the company as the Industry and Commerce Group (Gong shang pai).[45] Because Li and the other managers were from Wuxi, they did not have the advantage of having the same native place as their workers, who hailed from Hankou or places near it. Nonethe-less, the Industry and Commerce Group adopted Shenxin's Wuxi model and put it into effect with surprising speed.

In late 1934 and early 1935 within a mere ten months, Shenxin's staff members introduced at Hankou the corporate structure from Wuxi and completed the recruitment of workers. They built housing for 1,200 of the factory's 1,770 workers and added dining rooms (where meals were subsidized), employee banks (where interest paid on workers' savings was higher than at local banks), and company stores (known as "con-sumer cooperatives" [xiaofei hezuo she] where flour and cloth from the Rongs' factories were sold more cheaply than in local markets), hospi-tals, pension funds, and other company welfare programs.[46] At the same time they alerted ward heads (qu zhang), the subordinates of county magistrates, around Hankou as to where and when admission tests for prospective workers would be held, and later they sent recruiters di-rectly into the countryside.

According to Shenxin's hiring policy, it accepted as candidates women aged fifteen to eighteen who were unmarried, functionally liter-ate, and healthy and had unbound feet. Before taking the admission test, each examinee handed over a letter guaranteeing her integrity plus

5 yuan in earnest money, and to pass the test she had to show her manual dexterity, aptitude for the work, and ability to read, write, and count. Those passing the test became apprentices and began a three-month course during which they attended three hours of classes and practiced for eight hours in workshops every day. On successful completion of the course, they worked as trainees for three years before becoming wage-earning "regular workers." Throughout the training period, they were given free room and board and a small allowance but no wages.

By mid-1935 the management of Shenxin Mill No. 4 in Hankou recruited no less than one thousand young women and trained them to the point where they completed their apprenticeships. These workers never finished the final three-year phase of the training program because it was interrupted by the Japanese military invasion of China, which reached Hankou in 1938. Nonetheless, by then Shenxin's staff began exercising direct managerial control over recruitment and training of workers there as effectively as in Wuxi. According to an investigation conducted after 1949 by the Wuhan Bureau of Industry and Commerce and the Wuhan Textiles Bureau, Shenxin's "welfare institutions" (fuli sheshi) in Hankou were fully developed and highly successful before 1937.[47]

This record shows that a corporate scheme originally introduced in the Rongs' native place of Wuxi was successfully transferred to a larger city, Hankou, and it implies that their scheme had the potential to restructure their and other mill owners' relations with factory workers in any of China's cities. And yet, paradoxically, they had less complete success with efforts to transfer the Wuxi model to Shanghai, the site of more than three-fourths of Shenxin's investments.

APPLYING THE WUXI MODEL IN SHANGHAI

The Rongs had more at stake in Shanghai than in Wuxi or Hankou. By 1932 they invested 77 percent of their capital in Shanghai (compared to 11 percent in Wuxi, 9 percent in Hankou, and 3 percent in Jinan),[48] and they employed 78.3 percent of their workers in Shanghai (compared to 13.5 percent in Wuxi, 9.2 percent in Hankou, and 0.3 percent in Jinan). And yet, despite the financial incentives to cut labor costs in Shanghai, they were not able to exercise control as fully over all workers there as they did in Wuxi and Hankou.

In 1931, even before establishing the Community for Self-Governing Workers in Wuxi, the Rongs instructed two of Rong Desheng's sons,

Rong Weiren and Rong Erren, to oversee the establishment of a similar community for workers in Shanghai. These two young men were supposed to begin with Shenxin Mill No. 6, which had only recently been moved from Changzhou to Shanghai, and then they were to restructure all seven of Shenxin's Shanghai cotton mills along the same lines. As instructed, they opened a "welfare department" (*huigongke*) and built dormitories and social clubs for workers and schools for workers' children—facilities that, in the words of a study of labor conditions in the 1930s, "have been established with good intentions and are not as fully developed and as good as they were supposed to be."[49]

Regardless of these "good intentions," Shenxin's welfare department in Shanghai left some Number Ones firmly in place, especially at its largest mills, No. 1 and No. 9. As late as 1937 Shenxin Mill No. 9, which employed a total of 4,680 workers, retained 1,200 contract laborers (25 percent of the mill's workers) under the control of twenty Number Ones. Unlike workers under Shenxin's managerial control, these contract laborers received their wages, housing, and uniforms through Number Ones, not directly from the company.[50]

Rong Zongjing's failure to carry out his plans for workers as fully in Shanghai as in Wuxi and Hankou is not explained in available documentation, but circumstantial evidence suggests that it resulted from his defeats at the hands of Du Yuesheng, the leading figure in Shanghai's underworld and the head of the Green Gang. Before the 1930s Rong Zongjing had skillfully blocked Du's attempts to assume influential positions in Shanghai's cotton textiles and flour industries. Then in 1931, at the very time when Rong began trying to introduce communities for workers in Shanghai, he lost a legal suit, which allowed Du to join the board of the Shanghai Cotton Textiles Exchange, and suffered an election defeat in which his candidate was replaced by Du as director of the Shanghai Flour Trade Association (Shanghai mianfen ye gonghui).[51]

By 1931 Rong had reason to defer to Du, who had become widely influential in Shanghai. Between 1927 and 1931 Du first hunted down Communists and other labor leaders on behalf of Chiang Kai-shek's Nationalist government and then became the city's most prominent labor negotiator. During this period, by Perry's reckoning, Du "was invited to intervene in virtually every major strike that broke out in the city [and his] intervention in strikes helped the gangster chieftain shed his unsavory reputation and become a celebrity in Shanghai."[52]

Unlike the Rongs, Du did not oust Number Ones and replace them with salaried foremen and forewomen. Instead he incorporated Number Ones into his own social network, which reached down through criminals and labor contractors to skilled and unskilled workers. To keep Number Ones and workers under surveillance, Du stationed members of his Green Gang as guards at each mill's gate.[53]

And yet, while Rong Zongjing yielded some ground to Du, he did not surrender all of his control over Shenxin's workers in Shanghai. As noted earlier, by 1937 Shenxin relied on contract laborers to hold only a minority of the jobs in its Shanghai mills, employing in most positions salaried workers who were supervised by the company's own salaried foremen and forewomen. In fact, Rong Zongjing did not relinquish all control even over Shenxin's contract laborers. Extending his reach once again through his social network of native-place associates, he recruited from the ranks of Du's Green Gang a Shanghai sojourner from Wuxi, Rong Binggen, to serve as Shenxin's adviser on the Green Gang's handling of contract laborers.[54]

PREVENTING STRIKES

The account of labor-management relations above suggests that Rong Zongjing prevented strikes by confining workers in company towns, paying wages directly to them, and exercising managerial control over them through a corporate hierarchy of staff members who were recruited from his social network. In the 1920s this staff, even when reinforced by the addition of trained technicians with previous experience in Japanese-owned mills, failed to oust Number Ones or to deal directly with workers, but in the 1930s Shenxin's staff largely succeeded at this task by building company towns within the cities of Wuxi, Hankou, and Shanghai and by supplying workers with housing and other basic services more fully and systematically than Number Ones had done. In Shanghai Rong Zongjing yielded authority over some contract laborers to Du Yuesheng and the Green Gang, but even in this case Rong exercised indirect influence through a Wuxi associate who was a member of the Green Gang in Shanghai. In all of these dealings with workers—whether directly within Shenxin's mills or indirectly through the Green Gang—Rong consistently relied on staff members who were bound to him by personal ties, and he trained and deployed these staff members in a corporate hierarchy to exercise managerial control and prevent strikes.

DEFLECTING OFFICIAL INTERVENTION

While Shenxin was not frequently a target for strikes in the late 1920s and early 1930s, its founder, Rong Zongjing, was a target of three campaigns waged by officials in Chiang Kai-shek's Nationalist government. First, in May 1927, only a few months after Chiang's army arrived in Shanghai from South China and established its capital at Nanjing, Chiang himself ordered Rong's arrest. Second, in 1933 Chiang's minister of finance, T. V. Soong (Song Ziwen), accused Rong of sabotaging the implementation of a cotton loan that Soong had negotiated with the United States, and after the bungling of the loan led to Soong's resignation, Soong vowed to retaliate by bringing Rong down. Third, less than a year later, in July 1934, officials in the government-controlled Bank of China did bring Rong down by forcing him to resign from his post as general manager of Shenxin.

How did Rong Zongjing cope with these three attempts at political intervention at Shenxin? In each case he faced a threat from a different faction in the Nationalist government, and in each case he used his social network to limit, redirect, or deflect official policies.

RESISTING ARREST

On May 15, 1927, one day after the Nationalist government arrested the son of another wealthy merchant, Xue Baorong, Chiang Kai-shek ordered that Rong Zongjing be arrested. Chiang's immediate aim was to secure funds. A few weeks earlier his government had told Rong, as head of the Association of Chinese Cotton Mill Owners (Hua shang shachang lianhehui) that the association should buy 500,000 yuan worth of government bonds (er wu kujuan), and Chiang had ordered Rong's arrest after hearing Rong's reply that the association could afford to hand over no more than 125,000 yuan—only one-fourth as much as Chiang requested. On the day after Chiang issued orders for Rong's arrest, Chiang received assurance from the association that it would buy government bonds in the full amount, 500,000 yuan, but he did not immediately rescind the order for Rong's arrest. According to this order, Rong was charged with being "close" to Sun Chuanfang, the warlord whose forces had held Shanghai and the five provinces nearest to it before being defeated by Chiang's army in 1926 and 1927; and Rong was further accused of "producing various types of propaganda inimical to [Chiang's] revolutionary forces." Under these vague charges, Rong seemed vulnerable to additional financial demands, because the order for his arrest specified that his property would be placed "under legal protection until his case is settled." [55]

In late May and early June 1927, as Chiang's government attempted to carry out the order for Rong's arrest, the Rongs actively resisted it. In Wuxi, when the local authorities came to confiscate Rong Zongjing's property, Rong Desheng insisted that his brother's property was all in Shanghai, and he surrendered no possessions other than some pottery that was carefully labeled and placed in a warehouse. At Shenxin's mill in Wuxi Rong Desheng allowed the local magistrate to post guards. Otherwise he continued to operate the plant as usual. At the same time, in the newspapers on May 22, 1927, Rong Desheng and other members of the Wuxi County Merchants Association (Wuxi xian shangmin xie-hui) denounced the order to arrest Rong Zongjing as "slanderous and inspired by hatred," and they demanded "that the Commander-in-Chief [Chiang Kai-shek] redress this slander and end the impoundment [of Rong's property]." A week later a similar statement was published in the newspapers by the Association of Wuxi Sojourners in Shanghai.[56]

Meanwhile, in Shanghai Rong Zongjing took advantage of his social network to gain access to Chiang Kai-shek. In particular, he communicated through Wu Zhihui, Rong's associate from Wuxi, who had served in high positions with the Nationalist party (Guomindang) since its First National Congress in 1924 and had become one of the "four elder statesmen," as they were called, a quartet of Chiang's most trusted advisers. On May 22 Wu initially pressed Rong's case with Chiang in Shanghai at a memorial service for one of Chiang's fallen colleagues, and subsequently Wu's support for Rong was reinforced in Chiang's consultations with two of the other four elder statesmen, Cai Yuanpei and Zhang Renjie.

On June 4, 1927, less than three weeks after Chiang had issued the order for Rong's arrest, the Rongs' lobbying efforts brought results. Chiang Kai-shek reiterated his belief that Rong Zongjing "had used his money to do evil, traces of which can be found everywhere," but he also cancelled the order for Rong's arrest, saying that he had been reassured because Rong had received endorsements from both "gentry and merchants" (*shen shang*). In addition, Chiang granted Rong other concessions: a promise to allow the Association of Chinese Cotton Mill Owners to redeem its government bonds in full at 500,000 yuan plus 8.4 percent interest (which the Nationalist government punctually repaid to the association during the following two and one-half years) and a preferential tax break (which went into effect for Shenxin in June 1927—earlier than for any other company).[57]

In assessing this initial encounter between Rong Zongjing and Chiang Kai-shek, it is undeniable that Rong was a target of Chiang's strong-arm tactics and that he was coerced into buying more government bonds than he wanted. At the same time it would be misleading to characterize Rong as a passive victim. By activating his network in Wuxi and Shanghai, Rong evaded Chiang's order for his arrest (which was never carried out), continued to work in his office every day, and persuaded Chiang to rescind the arrest order without any additional financial demands on himself, Shenxin, or the Association of Chinese Cotton Mill Owners. Whether or not Rong won as much as he lost in this first struggle with Chiang, he unquestionably showed that he and his network were capable of penetrating Chiang's inner circle of advisers and influencing Chiang's policies.

INFLUENCING OFFICIAL DECISIONS

After evading Chiang's arrest order, Rong Zongjing maintained two different relationships with the government, one public and one private. Publicly he continued to serve as head of the Association of Chinese Cotton Mill Owners, and he accepted numerous official appointments: in 1928, as adviser to the Ministry of Industry and Commerce; in 1929, as a member of the board of directors of the government-controlled Bank of China; in 1931, as a member of the National Economic Council (Quanguo jingji weiyuanhui); and in 1932, as an overseer (*jianshi*) on the board of directors of the government-controlled China Merchants' Steam Navigation Company. In official business-government relations between 1928 and 1933, Rong appeared to align himself with Soong, Chiang's minister of finance, and to support Soong's economic policies because they were anti-Japanese.[58]

Meanwhile, Rong behaved differently behind the scenes than he did in public. In his unofficial maneuvers he showed little interest in Soong's anti-Japanese policies and used his personal contacts with Soong to promote policies favorable specifically or even exclusively to Shenxin. In fact, Rong's zealous campaigning to promote his own business proved to be very costly for Soong in at least one critical case, a large cotton and wheat loan from the United States.

Between 1931 and 1933 Rong indefatigably campaigned for this loan. In autumn 1931 he complained to the Nationalist government that Japan's invasion of Manchuria and a disastrous flood in the Lower Yangzi Valley had cut off supplies of wheat and cotton from the two regions on which Shanghai industrialists such as himself had most heavily depended. In June 1932 he arranged for a purchase of 400,000 bales of American cotton and won Song's approval for its financial guarantee by the Nationalist government, but the U.S. Congress blocked the sale. Undeterred, Rong in October 1932 appealed to the Reconstruction Finance Corporation (RFC) in the American government for credit to purchase 100 million bales of cotton and 100 million bushels of wheat over a three-year period, and he offered as security his own personal note and a mortgage on his mills. This time he found the RFC eager to dispose of surplus agricultural goods that were a drag on rural America's recovery during the Great Depression, but its prices were too high to tempt Rong beyond preliminary negotiations. Unable to put through these deals, Rong implored the Nationalist government's highest officials to join his campaign, and at a meeting with Soong in spring 1933 he finally received assurance that Soong would seek a cotton and wheat loan during a forthcoming trip to the United States.[59]

On reaching Washington in April 1933, Soong immediately requested a loan of cotton and wheat, and he relied on Rong Zongjing for advice through the subsequent negotiations. Soong's proposal prompted the RFC to offer him a loan of cotton valued at U.S. $40 million and wheat valued at U.S. $10 million—far more than the U.S. $5 million worth of each that Soong had originally intended to borrow. Initially dubious, Soong turned to Rong for assurance that such a large amount of cotton would not go to waste. In response Soong received telegrams from the Ministry of Finance in China quoting Rong as saying that China's current stocks of cotton were "sufficient for one month only" and that Rong alone "could use 50,000 bales per month for 12 months" —that is, a total of 600,000 bales within the coming year. Early consummation of the cotton loan was needed, Rong told Soong, because only with its help could Chinese-owned textile companies survive and overcome the "cut-throat competition of government-subsidized Japanese mills."[60] Reassured, Soong signed a loan agreement in May 1933 with the understanding that China would buy 600,000 bales of cotton using a loan valued at U.S. $40 million.

Within a few weeks the consequences of Rong's influence in this matter became evident to all concerned and painfully evident to Soong. The first sign that Rong's advice should not have been accepted uncritically came in June 1933, barely one month after the loan agreement was concluded, when Soong received a telegram from the Ministry of Finance warning that Shanghai usually consumed no more than 300,000 bales of imported American cotton per year. Incredulous, Soong replied that he had understood that Rong alone had asked for 600,000 bales; therefore, Soong insisted, the Ministry of Finance's figure of 300,000 must be a mistake. Taking a bureaucratic dodge, Soong's staff answered, "It is true that Y. K. Yung [Rong Zongjing] said he could use 600,000 bales, but we did not endorse his statement and merely transmitted it." [61] Thus was Soong given the first inkling that he had made a decision in foreign relations based too trustingly on Rong's advice.

With no apologies for misleading Soong, Rong continued his campaign for low cotton prices. In September 1933 he exhorted the Nationalist government to give him and other Chinese industrialists preferential deals on the borrowed American cotton, explaining that they were buying less imported cotton than usual that season because China happened to have a bumper cotton crop 20 percent above normal. At this time the demand for cotton was driven still lower by two other developments. In 1933 China's urban economy entered a depression that caused some cotton mills to close, and in early 1934 the Japanese government (which objected to American support of any kind for Chiang's government) issued orders forbidding Japanese-owned mills from buying American-grown cotton in China. As a result all purchasers in China combined during 1933 and 1934 ended up buying a total of only sixty thousand bales of imported American cotton—a mere 10 percent of the amount that Rong had originally projected he alone would buy.[62]

Rong's savings from these low cotton prices cost Soong dearly. Soong's handling of the loan antagonized three governments: the Japanese government, because it suspected that Soong was securing resources from the United States to finance anti-Japanese military movements in China; the American government, because it blamed Soong for reneging on the agreement to borrow cotton valued at $40 million, which he eventually had to scale back to $10 million; and Soong's rivals in the Chinese government, who claimed that these foreign governments' complaints showed Soong's incompetence. On October 25, 1933, under attack for this and other reasons, Soong resigned as minister of finance.[63]

For his role in the cotton loan episode, Rong earned the enmity of Soong and several other high officials in the Nationalist government. Soong vowed to remove Rong from his position as head of the Association of Chinese Cotton Mill Owners, and at the end of 1933 Rong was, in fact, voted out of this office.[64] With the help of a Wuxi associate in the association, Rong succeeded in delaying his successor's appointment until mid-1934, but by then Rong faced a much severer threat—political intervention that deprived him of authority over his own company.

REGAINING AUTHORITY

In spring and summer 1934 Rong Zongjing was ordered to resign as general manager of Shenxin. He found himself under attack from a formidable array of groups: bankers and officials often identified with the Political Study Clique of political figures, business associates from his own social network, and supporters of Wang Jingwei, one of Chiang Kai-shek's leading rivals in the Nationalist government.

The principal charges against Rong were made by two members of the Political Study Clique, Zhang Jia'ao, head of the government-controlled Bank of China, and Chen Guangfu, founder and owner of the Shanghai Commercial and Savings Bank. Rong had failed to make payments on past debts owed to their banks as well as to the British-owned Hongkong and Shanghai Banking Corporation and between forty and fifty Chinese-owned native banks, and, to cover these debts, he had applied to the Bank of China for an additional loan of 5 million yuan. In June 1934 Zhang Jia'ao released to him 2.8 million yuan of this 5 million yuan loan, but on July 4, 1934, Zhang denied him the remaining 2.2 million yuan because Rong had spent the first part without heeding Zhang's demands for reforms in Shenxin's cost accounting and other business practices. Unable to persuade Zhang and Chen through their networks in the Political Study Clique or by any other means, Rong found himself in an untenable financial position, and on July 4, 1934, he resigned as Shenxin's general manager.[65]

A week earlier, in late June 1934, Rong had made an eleventh hour appeal to his Wuxi associate and business partner Wang Yuqing. Rong had proposed to shift funds within the General Corporation from Fuxin and Maoxin flour mills to Shenxin Cotton Mills so that he could cover his overdue bank loans that were secured against Shenxin. But Wang, who had gained control over Maoxin and Fuxin flour mills, had blocked this maneuver and refused to help on the grounds that Rong and Rong's eldest son, Rong Hongyuan, had imprudently plunged Shenxin into debt.[66]

On resigning as head of Shenxin, Rong Zongjing immediately began to campaign both officially and unofficially to reverse the Bank of China's decision on his loan. Officially, he appealed for help from the

Ministry of Industry, but he had little influence with its head, Chen Gongbo, or with Wang Jingwei, Chen's patron who was head of a major faction in the Nationalist party and was president of the government's Executive Yuan. Showing no sympathy for Rong, Chen conducted an investigation that concluded that Rong's Shenxin Cotton Mills had no budgetary planning, no calculation of costs, and no balancing of accounts, and Chen expressed his willingness to help Rong's company only if he could prevent Rong's "restoration" (*fupi*—the term used to describe an emperor's restoration). To block Rong's resumption of authority as head of Shenxin, Chen appointed a committee to "reform" (*zhengli*) the company.

While seeking support through official channels, Rong Zongjing once again lobbied unofficially through his Wuxi associate Wu Zhihui, who presented the case for Rong both publicly in the press and privately to Chiang Kai-shek. In Chinese newspapers Wu published open letters to Minister of Industry Chen Gongbo and argued that by denying Rong's loan the Bank of China had discouraged Chinese "risk takers" whose enterprising spirit benefited the economy and encouraged Chinese "hoarders" whose cynicism and pessimism did it harm.[67]

Privately Wu spoke directly and repeatedly to Chiang Kai-shek and urged him to align himself with Rong and against Rong's accusers, both Chen Gongbo and Chen's patron, Wang Jingwei. In fact, Wu lobbied so many times at Rong's urging that he began to lose patience with Rong. "I can't do any more for you," Wu wrote to Rong's intermediary, Xue Mingjian, who was also from Wuxi, on July 24, 1934. "If you ask me to tell Chiang Kai-shek 'Help Rong for the sake of giving me face,' people will laugh at me. People will think I'm crazy [*fengzi*]. You are asking me to say more to Chiang Kai-shek, but what more is there to say!"[68]

Yet Wu had apparently said enough. A few weeks later, in mid-August 1934, Rong Zongjing's campaign achieved the desired result. Rong regained his position as general manager of Shenxin Cotton Mills and received a loan of 4 million yuan from the Bank of China and the Shanghai Commercial and Savings Bank. His loan was released to him as the result of intervention by Soong's successor as the minister of finance, H. H. Kong. Again he was told (this time by Kong) that he had received the loan on the condition that he would reform his company's managerial structure and accounting methods. And again he kept the reformers at bay, this time by allowing the "overseers" (*jiandu*) of the loan from the banks only to audit his finances and monitor his cotton purchasing—not to assume any authority over production and sales.[69]

The completeness of Rong Zongjing's victory was implicit in the exasperation of the overseers, who reported to the banks at the end of the year, on December 18, 1934. "Since we control purchasing and not sales," they complained, "when Shenxin suffers losses, we suffer losses, but when Shenxin enjoys profits, we do not enjoy profits."[70] In other dealings with the Nationalist government, as Richard Bush has shown, Rong Zongjing benefited from similar outcomes, and he never again resigned as Shenxin's general manager.[71]

In retrospect the significance of the episode of 1934 lies less in Rong Zongjing's resignation than in the speed of his recovery. In this case he survived attacks from some of the most powerful factions in the Nationalist government and lost the backing of his own business partner, but he still managed to regain his position as the head of Shenxin. His success shows that his business, based largely on a social network of family members and native-place associates, was effective at dealing with high officials in government as well as merchants in markets and workers in factories.[72]

CONCLUSION

As noted in chapter 1, historians have debated the issue of whether Chinese businesses have adopted Western-style impersonal corporate structures or relied on Chinese social networks, and the case of Shenxin Cotton Mills is directly relevant to this debate (and has been cited in it).[73] By refusing to distinguish sharply between ownership and management, Rong Zongjing decisively rejected a Western-style impersonal corporate structure. He established Shenxin as an unlimited liability company for the avowed purpose of avoiding interference by stockholders from outside his family and then drew heavily on his social network to staff Shenxin, appointing his family members as its top managers and his native-place associates to 60 percent of its administrative positions. As China's biggest Chinese-owned firm, Shenxin is perhaps the supreme example in Chinese history of a business using Chinese social networks to build itself into a large, profitable, and competitive enterprise.

While reaching this conclusion, it is important to emphasize that Rong Zongjing did not passively conform to the dictates of his social network or leave it as he found it. On the contrary, he battled with it every step of the way. When he founded Shenxin he did so over objections from his native-place associates who opposed his plans for expansion of a business outside Wuxi, and he departed from his previous practice of relying on their financial support by taking out loans from Shanghai banks owned by Japanese and Chinese who were not from Wuxi.

Ultimately Rong carried out a comprehensive reform of his social network that allowed it to achieve some functional equivalencies to Western and Japanese corporate hierarchies. Although Rong did not experiment with joint-stock financing and related financial arrangements that were found in Western and Japanese corporations, he did mold his Chinese networks into a highly structured and integrated managerial hierarchy. Like many other large Chinese networks, Rong's network was hierarchical before he began to reform it,[74] and it became even more so under his leadership. While Rong retained this hierarchy, he also transformed it. In delegating authority, he passed over his senior associates and chose young members of his network for admission to Shenxin's own schools and for study abroad. On their graduation he assigned them to manage all aspects of his business—purchasing, manufacturing, and marketing—and gave them authority to carry out reforms such as the introduction of company welfare programs to undermine Number Ones and achieve direct managerial control over workers. In so doing he adapted his hierarchical social network into a corporate hierarchy for the purpose of integrating his business. Perhaps Rong's approach bore a closer resemblance to personal capitalism than to managerial capitalism because he kept a tenacious grip on authority over top-level decision making rather than delegate it to his staff, but he nonetheless created an extensive hierarchy of managers who encountered networks of Chinese factory workers and sought to achieve optimum managerial control over them in much the same way that Western-owned BAT and Japanese-owned Naigai did (see chaps. 3 and 5).

Rong Zongjing's success at adapting his social network for managerial purposes raises the question of whether Chinese businesses had any need for Western or Japanese corporate models. If Chinese social networks could be used to achieve equivalency with Western and Japanese corporate hierarchies, then why should a Chinese business bother to follow these foreign examples? The rationale for taking such a step may be found in the Western-style organizations and practices put to use by another of China's biggest Chinese-owned businesses, China Match Company.

CHAPTER 7

China Match Company

China Match Company (Da Zhonghua huochai gongsi) was established in 1930 and immediately became China's biggest manufacturer of matches, employing between two thousand and three thousand workers and holding the largest market share of any match company in the country. China Match's spectacular entrance into China's market in 1930 was especially dramatic because at the time its leading rival, the Western-owned Swedish Match Company, controlled no less than 62 percent of all the matches manufactured in the world.[1] China Match's founder, Liu Hongsheng, amassed a fortune from selling matches and several other industrial products, and when audited by the government of the People's Republic in 1956, he and his family ranked behind Rong Zongjing's descendants and ahead of virtually all other Chinese among the richest capitalist families in the country.[2]

In founding and building up China Match, Liu Hongsheng formed some Western-style corporate hierarchies and bureaucratic organizations that Rong Zongjing had avoided.[3] In 1930 Liu established and registered China Match as a joint-stock limited liability company, and he and his family never held a majority of its stock or exercised decisive financial control over it (as Rong Zongjing and his brother did over Shenxin). Subsequently, in the mid-1930s, Liu formed and presided over first a cartel of match manufacturers and then a national monopoly of the match industry in which almost all of the members were from outside his family and native place. And yet Liu Hongsheng by no means ignored his Chinese social network in his approach to business. In fact, like Chinese before him, throughout his career he cultivated a wide variety of contacts based on family, native place, school ties, and other institutional affiliations.

THE FOUNDER AND HIS CONNECTIONS

Liu Hongsheng formed China Match as a merger of Shanghai's three largest Chinese-owned match companies. When the three businesses pooled their capital, he and his brother jointly received 29.57 percent of China Match's stock, an amount roughly proportionate to their share of the three businesses' total investments.[4] Although Liu's Hongsheng Match Mills was only the second largest of the three, he instigated the merger, became China Match Company's first general manager, and subsequently presided over China's interregional match cartel and national match monopoly. Liu became the head of China Match in 1930 (and later of the cartel and monopoly) partially because of his extraordinary connections. By 1930, at the age of forty-two, before founding China Match and without having done business abroad, he had already made contacts of lasting importance in China through Western as well as Chinese institutions: an American-sponsored school, a British-owned big business, and a Chinese native-place association.

SCHOOL TIES

Without studying overseas, Liu Hongsheng learned English and formed school ties with other English-speaking Chinese in Shanghai at St. John's Middle School and St. John's University—two educational institutions founded by the American Episcopal Mission. In the 1890s St. John's had become one of the first Christian colleges in China to offer non-Christian students a liberal arts education that was taught in English, and, according to Yeh Wen-hsin, in the 1920s and 1930s it eventually gave "young Chinese from affluent financial, commercial, industrial, and professional backgrounds an unabashedly Western-oriented education."[5] Compared to his fellow students, Liu did not come from an especially affluent background, and in 1905, after attending St. John's Middle School for four years and St. John's University for less than two, he was forced to leave college because he lost his scholarship. According to the Liu family's lore, Liu was forced out of school by the American president of St. John's, F. L. Hawks Pott, who angrily withdrew Liu's

Figure 11. Liu Hongsheng, founder and head of China
Match Company. Reprinted from *Men of Shanghai and
North China*, 339.

scholarship when Liu declined Hawks Pott's offer to finance Liu's education for the Christian ministry at a theological seminary in the United
States.[6]

Liu's premature departure from St. John's University and his lack of
a degree did not prevent him from becoming its most influential organizer of alumni. In 1922 he founded St. John's University's alumni club,
known as Fanhuang Du Julobu, where he regularly met with St. John's
classmates. In the late 1920s he became chairman of St. John's University's board of directors, and in 1930 he received an honorary LL.D. degree from St. John's for his service and contributions to the university.[7]

In the 1920s and 1930s, as Liu invested in industrial enterprises and
built up his businesses, he turned his St. John's school ties to his commercial and political advantage. During these years, for example, he
appointed several of his St. John's classmates to key posts as managers,

bankers, and accountants in his enterprises.[8] In addition, Liu maintained close contact with two of his politically influential classmates, the brothers T. V. Soong and S. L. Soong (Song Ziliang). Later, between 1928 and 1933, when T. V. Soong served as minister of finance under Chiang Kai-shek, Liu's contacts with the Soong brothers helped him gain access to Chiang.

Liu also derived long-term benefits from his training in English at St. John's. According to one of his close associates, he regularly used his reading knowledge of English to study science and technology, although he showed no interest in books on economics or literature.[9] Perhaps still more important to his financial success, he used his command of spoken English on the job for decades with British businessmen at the Kailuan Mining Administration in China.

MANAGERIAL TIES

Throughout the 1910s, 1920s, and 1930s, Liu Hongsheng worked for British employers at the Kailuan Mining Administration. In 1909 he originally landed a job with this firm (which had been under Chinese ownership from its founding in 1877 until it was taken over by the British in 1900 and then became a Sino-British joint venture in 1912), and as an employee there he accumulated the capital that he used to open industrial enterprises, including his first match factory, Hongsheng Match Mill (established in 1920), a cement plant (started in 1923), and a woolen mill and a briquette factory (both opened in 1926).

Liu favorably impressed his British colleagues and swiftly rose up the coal mining company's corporate hierarchy, because he was able to capture for it the coal market in the Lower Yangzi region around his birthplace and hometown, Shanghai. Initially Liu accepted a low-level position as a traveling salesman (*paojie*). He was posted in Tianjin rather than Shanghai because the company had set up its head office there and had built up a large organization for marketing coal around Tianjin in North China where its mines were located. At Shanghai, by contrast, Kailuan had at the time only a tiny office that distributed little coal to foreign customers and virtually none to Chinese in the Lower Yangzi region. Nonetheless, during his first year with the firm, 1909, Liu convinced his British supervisor to transfer him back to Shanghai and give him sole responsibility for the accounts of all the company's small number of Chinese customers in the Lower Yangzi region.[10]

On returning to Shanghai, Liu recruited his brother, Liu Jisheng, to join him, and they began drumming up business with Chinese customers in Shanghai and along the Beijing-Shanghai Railroad. As their sales rose the Liu brothers added coal warehouses (*mei zhan*) and coal sales offices (*mei hao*) along the railroad and assigned Chinese commission agents to staff these distributing points, notably in the cities of Shanghai, Suzhou, Wuxi, Yixing, Changzhou, Zhenjiang, Nantong, Jiangyin, and Pukou. Spurred on by the Liu brothers, the company then began selling a greater share of its coal in the Lower Yangzi region. Whereas in 1906 it had distributed only 27.7 percent of its goods through Shanghai and other coastal ports, between 1909 and 1911 it raised the share going to these same cities to 40 percent.[11]

In 1914, with the outbreak of World War I in Europe, Liu seized on new opportunities for enlarging his responsibilities within the company. As wartime shipping in Europe forced Western industrial enterprises to cut back in China, Liu's Chinese clients around Shanghai expanded their factories and increased their orders for Kailuan's coal, and as Kailuan's own British staff members were drafted into military service, the company allowed Liu to take over its accounts with foreign customers in Shanghai even while he retained his accounts with his Chinese customers there.

During World War I and its aftermath, Liu's profits from handling Kailuan's coal provided by far his largest source of income. In 1917 and 1918 he earned 1.3 million yuan in this way. As of 1926, even after he had opened several industrial enterprises, his profits from coal sales at 1.5 million yuan dwarfed the profits from the most profitable of his other enterprises, his cement plant (665,500 yuan) and his match mill (142,500 yuan). Through Kailuan, Liu became rich in contacts as well as money. He moved easily among foreigners in China, and in the 1920s he employed several German and Japanese engineers, accountants, and other technical specialists whom he replaced with Western-trained Chinese in the 1930s.[12]

Thus, before 1930, even without any training or experience at trading outside China, Liu learned about Western business practices from a Western company, made contacts with foreign businesspeople, and earned an income that provided his initial capital for investment. These experiences of learning English from Americans at St. John's and working with Englishmen at Kailuan undeniably contributed to his success in business. And yet, while benefiting from his education at a Western-sponsored school and from employment in a Western-owned business, Liu by no means divorced himself from Chinese institutions.

NATIVE-PLACE TIES

Between 1920 and 1937 Liu Hongsheng was head of the Association of Ningbo Sojourners of Shanghai,[13] and throughout his life he remained heavily dependent on family members and other native-place associates from Ningbo, a prefecture containing his family's home county of Dinghai, which was about 150 kilometers southeast of Shanghai. In fact, his success with the Kailuan Mining Administration, which on the surface might seem to have been entirely a matter of his relations with Westerners, was directly attributable to his relations with native-place associates from Ningbo.

CHINESE MERCHANTS

Liu was placed in his job at Kailuan in 1909 by the head of the Association of Ningbo Sojourners in Shanghai, Zhou Yangshan. For the preceding fourteen years, since the death of his father in 1896, Liu had regarded Zhou as a kind of surrogate father, and in 1906, three years before being given the job at Kailuan, Liu had greatly strengthened his family's Ningbo ties by marrying Ye Suzhen, a member of one of Shanghai's wealthiest Ningbo families and the granddaughter of Ye Chengzhong, the merchant who had risen from rags to riches in the nineteenth century by migrating from Ningbo to Shanghai and creating an interregional network for distributing Standard Oil's kerosene, among other products (see chap. 2). In 1909, once Liu was placed by Zhou at Kailuan, he began sending Zhou monthly payments—gratuities that he never ceased to deliver for the rest of Zhou's life—and he became Zhou's partner first in coal trading and later in match manufacturing.[14]

After landing his position at Kailuan through the Ningbo sojourners' renowned job placement system,[15] Liu took full advantage of his Ningbo ties to succeed on the job. While his British employers thought that Liu personally captured the Lower Yangzi's market and directly administered coal distribution in the region, he secretly left responsibility for distribution in the hands of an experienced Ningbo merchant, Du Jiakun, whose well-established trading company, Yitaixing, marketed coal by relying on its own docks, ships, and distributing network. In the late 1910s and early 1920s, under this sub rosa agreement, Liu handed over Kailuan's coal to Du and in return received 30 percent of Yitaixing's profits, all quite apart from the salary paid to him by Kailuan.

In 1924, when Kailuan's British managers discovered that Liu was not personally supervising distribution and was collecting a separate income, they insisted that Liu terminate this arrangement, and they established a Shanghai branch in which Kailuan and Liu each invested 50 percent of the capital and each retained 50 percent of the profits. Even then, unbeknown to Kailuan, Liu continued to cooperate with Du, who put up half of Liu's share of the capital in Kailuan's Shanghai branch and received half of Liu's share of the profits throughout the 1920s.[16]

STAFF MEMBERS AND WORKERS

Liu also tried, with less success, to use native-place ties to exercise managerial control over his staff members and workers. In 1920 he prepared the way for recruiting and training Ningbo employees by donating funds to establish two schools in Ningbo prefecture at his home county of Dinghai: the Dinghai County Middle School (Dinghai zhong xue) for boys and the Dinghai Middle School for Girls (Dinghai nuzi zhong xue).[17] Then, in the late 1920s, he began to channel the schools' graduates from Ningbo into his Shanghai businesses, especially the Zhanghua Woolen Mills and the Zhanghua Wharf Company.

At the Zhanghua Woolen Mills, founded in Shanghai in 1929, Liu employed graduates of his Ningbo school as supervisors of Ningbo workers. To the young male graduates, he offered positions as trainees (lianxisheng), and, on their successful completion of the training course, he gave some of them additional training in Japan and appointments in Zhanghua as salaried supervisors and staff members (zhiyuan). To the young female graduates, he offered positions as Number Ones supervising other Ningbo women—altogether more than a thousand of them— who were brought from Ningbo to Shanghai to serve first for three years as apprentices with no wages and then as full-fledged workers in the Zhanghua Woolen Mill.[18]

Once Liu's managers and workers had all arrived from Ningbo and had begun working at his mill in Shanghai, he tried to exercise direct control over them by taking advantage of his native-place ties. In 1930 he attempted to circumvent Number Ones at the Zhanghua Woolen Mill by introducing the Labor Investigation Section (kao gong ke) in which overseers (guanli yuan) were supposed to deal directly with workers and send reports to their superiors who were known as "labor investigators" (kao gong yuan). But soon he withdrew the overseers because they were unable to gain access to workers, leaving his labor investigators dependent on Number Ones and leaving Number Ones with undiminished authority to retain or dismiss workers. In 1932, according to an investigation done at the time by journalists in the Zhanghua

Woolen Mill, "workmen [were] engaged . . . on the recommendation of the foremen," and "women work[ed] under forewomen." [19]

At the Zhonghua Wharf Company (Zhonghua matou gufen youxian gongsi) Liu also employed graduates of the schools that he sponsored in Ningbo, and, as at the Zhanghua Woolen Mill, he had virtually no success at using them to achieve managerial control over workers. Whereas all of the Zhonghua Wharf's staff members were young male graduates of the Dinghai Middle School in Ningbo, the company's managers hailed from elsewhere and left the recruitment and management of dockworkers entirely in the hands of Shanghai's leading gangsters according to the memoirs of Liu's son.[20]

"From the very beginning of the Zhonghua Wharf Company," Liu's son recalled, "the docks were all under the control of the gangs, and my father knew the heads of the gangs such as Du Yuesheng, Huang Jinrong, and Zhang Xiaolin." [21] Liu Hongsheng used a term of great familiarity, "brother" (cheng xiong dao di) to address these three men—the best-known gangsters in Shanghai—and in 1936 he urged his twenty-five-year-old son to acknowledge the authority of the top man, Du Yuesheng, by "paying respects to him as an elder" (bai lao touzi). These instructions struck Liu's son as sadly ironic. As he later recalled,

> By then [1936], my father was the manager of more than ten enterprises and a multimillionaire [qian bai wan fuweng]. He was the head of the Association of Ningbo Sojourners in Shanghai, a Chinese member of the Shanghai Municipal Council, which governed the International Settlement, and the general manager of the China Steam Navigation Company. And he was the no. 1 or no. 2 celebrity [wen ren] among Shanghai's capitalists. Yet, with all this, he still had to let Du Yuesheng behave as lord and master [cheng wang cheng ba] on his docks.[22]

Writing this passage in the early 1980s at the age of seventy, Liu's son might have exaggerated Liu's deference to Du, but all available accounts point to the conclusion that Liu exercised no direct managerial control over workers on the docks at the Zhonghua Wharf Company.[23]

Although Liu's record in labor-management relations before 1930 at his match mills is less well documented than his record at the Zhanghua Woolen Mill and the Zhonghua Wharf Company, the evidence suggests that he did not exercise direct managerial control over workers at his Hongsheng Match Mill either. In it, as in his woolen mill and wharf, he employed graduates of the schools that he sponsored in Ningbo, but because it was located in Suzhou, 100 kilometers from his headquarters in

Shanghai, he seems to have remained even more distant from its workers than from the ones in some of his other factories.[24]

USING CONNECTIONS TO FORM CHINA MATCH COMPANY

In founding China Match Company, Liu Hongsheng took advantage of his experience in dealing with Western businessmen and his connections with capitalists and workers among his native-place associates from Ningbo. His aim was to convince the Chinese owners of two other match companies, Yingchang Mills and Zhonghua Mills, to merge with his own Hongsheng Match Mills and to make himself general manager, even though the three companies had learned to distrust each other during fierce battles for the match market in the 1920s and even though his firm was not the biggest of the three.

Between 1928 and 1930 Liu urged his two potential partners to carry out the merger and make him general manager, maintaining that this strategy would help them defeat their Western rival, Swedish Match Company. He had shown as recently as 1926, when Swedish Match had tried to buy out his Hongsheng Match Mills, that he could stand up to this Western company, deal with its owners in English, and refuse offers that did not meet his terms. In 1929 and 1930 Liu's call for a united front against Swedish Match became more and more persuasive as the Chinese companies suffered the consequences of price wars with Swedish Match in Shanghai, especially during the first half of 1930 when Yingchang lost 93,000 yuan and Zhonghua lost 17,000 yuan.[25]

In nominating himself general manager of China Match Company, Liu was able to invoke his native-place tie with Shao Erkang, the owner of Yingchang Match Mills, which was the biggest company in the planned merger. Liu and Shao both hailed from Ningbo, and, as members of sojourning families, they had both established the headquarters for their businesses in Shanghai. For them, this native-place tie was more than sentimental. As they were well aware, Liu's native-place network included close contacts with the Ningbo Bank (Siming yinhang) through which he could arrange financing for the merger.[26]

While their Ningbo tie dispelled some distrust, Liu still found that Shao bargained hard from beginning to end. Even at the last minute, in summer 1930, after two years of negotiations, Shao insisted on one last concession: a 20 percent increase in the evaluation of all three companies' assets—fixed assets, liquid capital, and even the value of their brand names' reputations and goodwill. As the assets of Liu's match company were considerably smaller than Yingchang's, he fully realized that making this concession would be costly for him, but he acceded to it anyway.[27]

In July 1930 all three companies formally agreed to merge under the name China Match Company (Da Zhonghua huochai gongsi), and they appointed Liu Hongsheng its general manager. Although not holding a majority of China Match's stock, Liu quickly extended his administrative authority over the company. Within its first year he established a central office (*zong shiwusuo*) directly under his authority and divided it into seven departments: general affairs, management, manufacturing, accounting, labor supervision, technical services, and purchasing. He bought the two largest match companies in the Middle Yangzi region and several smaller ones, and he assigned to each of China Match's mills an accountant, an engineer, and a labor supervisor who all reported directly to him in the company's general office at Shanghai.[28]

Following the same pattern as at the Zhanghua Woolen Mill, Liu immediately tried to tighten his management's control over China Match Company's two thousand workers by hiring fellow Ningbo natives, creating the Labor Investigation Section, and strengthening it with the help of a Ningbo contact, Pan Gongzhan, the head of the Nationalist government's Social Affairs Bureau in Shanghai. But through these maneuvers, he controlled workers no more closely or directly at China Match Company than at the Zhanghua Woolen Mill.[29]

Beginning in 1930, on the completion of the merger and the founding of China Match Company, Liu began to devote himself primarily to this one business. In the 1920s he had used his impressive array of contacts to mobilize capital and open a variety of enterprises making cement, woolens, and briquettes as well as matches. But in the 1930s he concentrated on China Match Company, and he built it up by retaining his social network, founding bureaucratic organizations, and developing corporate hierarchies.

DEFEATING RIVALS AND FORMING A CARTEL

In the early 1930s China Match Company became China's leading distributor of matches by instituting the most far-reaching and effective marketing organization in the industry. As commander in chief of this organization, Liu Hongsheng used it to prepare the way for a cartel by attacking rivals and then signing truces with each of them in succession: Swedish Match Company between 1930 and 1933; smaller Chinese-owned match mills in 1934 and 1935; and big Japanese-owned mills in 1935.

DEFEATING A LARGER WESTERN RIVAL

On its founding in 1930, China Match Company put in place a marketing system that equaled Swedish Match's in some respects and surpassed it in others. Like Swedish Match (and other big foreign distributing companies, as shown in earlier chapters), China Match appointed salaried employees to its sales staff and made them responsible for recruiting and monitoring local Chinese commission agents. Unlike Swedish Match, Liu's China Match Company appointed only Chinese to serve in its marketing organization, assigned some of them to several cities and towns in the Lower Yangzi region not reached by Swedish Match, and authorized them to let commission agents sell on consignment.

China Match's commitment to marketing in cities outside Shanghai in the Lower Yangzi region was evident at every level of its marketing hierarchy. At the top, unlike Swedish Match, it divided its sales department (*yingye ke*) in two. One part was responsible for "distant points" (*yuan qu*) in the same metropolises of the Middle Yangzi and the Southeast where Swedish Match had its offices; the other part, for which Swedish Match had no corresponding organization, was responsible for "nearby points" (*jin qu*) within the Lower Yangzi region outside Shanghai. As shown in table 14, China Match thus extended its marketing reach not only to its "divisional offices" (*fen shiwusuo*) at the level reached by Swedish Match Company but also to subdivisional offices or "marketing outlets" in twenty-four counties at smaller and more peripheral cities and towns than the ones reached by Swedish Match. At this local level China Match's Chinese salaried representatives dealt with Chinese commission agents who, in turn, distributed through small Chinese wholesale merchants (*xiao pifa shang*) and retail stores (*lingshou dian*).

This finely articulated marketing system gave China Match's headquarters in Shanghai the means for gathering commercial information, regulating prices, and driving Swedish Match's goods out of local markets. When China Match was formed in 1930, its management immediately had all of its local representatives conduct surveys to determine which of its more than sixty brands were most popular around each

TABLE 14. LOCATIONS OF MATCH COMPANIES'
SALARIED REPRESENTATIVES IN CHINA, 1930S

	Swedish Match Company	China Match Company
Headquarters for China	Shanghai	Shanghai
Divisional offices at the regional level	NE (2 cities) LY (1 city MY (1 city) So (1 city)	LY (5 cities) MY (4 cities) SE (3 cities)
Subdivisional offices at the county level		LY (24 counties)

SOURCES: *LHS*, vol. 1, 153; vol. 2, 149; vol. 3, 65; *ZMHG*, 71–72.
Abbreviations: NE: Northeast; LY: Lower Yangzi; MY: Middle Yangzi; So: South; SE: Southeast.

divisional office. On the basis of this information its management designated each division's "important trademark" (*zhuyao shangbiao*),
which generally reflected a feature of the locality. (In Suzhou, for example, Bao Ta, named after a local pagoda, was the important trademark). To deepen consumers' loyalties to an important trademark wherever possible, the company proceeded to eliminate forty of its brands
and to lower the price of its important trademark in each locality, making the amounts of the decrease proportionate to the strength of the local competition in each place.

Once the local market was cornered, China Match raised prices and
took high profits. In 1930, for example, it drove out Swedish Match and
other competitors between Shanghai and Nanjing by selling one brand
at the low price of 34.17 yuan per case; in 1931, after cornering the market, it raised the price to 48.94 yuan per case. The net gain from this one
area was an increase in revenue of 1.8 million yuan. By 1932 several
divisional offices had their important trademarks fully established, and
they were instructed by Shanghai to resort again to these same tactics—
"first lower prices, then raise prices"—if any rival tried to return and
break into the local market.[30]

Liu kept this multilayered and interregional marketing organization
responsive to his leadership by adopting a philosophy summarized in
the slogan "Generous benefits, strict control" (*Daiyu congyou, guanli
congyan*). "Generous benefits" in the form of salaries and bonuses were

paid according to rank in the sales organization's corporate hierarchy. In China Match's central headquarters at Shanghai, heads and deputy heads of the sales department received 300 yuan per month; standard bonuses (*zhiyuan huahong*), given to all staff members according to their seniority, attendance, and supervisors' evaluations; and special bonuses (*zhiyuan techou*), given at Liu Hongsheng's discretion. At the middle level heads of divisional offices made 100 to 120 yuan per month plus standard bonuses. At the lowest level subordinates to divisional heads earned 50 to 100 yuan per month plus standard bonuses.

"Strict control" was exercised through a "guarantee system" (*baozheng zhidu*) that required employees to have guarantors post bond on their behalf. Executives at the high and middle levels were exempted from this process, but bond for each employee below the rank of divisional head had to be posted in amounts that varied according to the volume of goods and cash that the employee handled: a bond of 20,000 yuan for a head cashier; 10,000 yuan for a bill collector (*kuanji*); 5,000 yuan for a clerk (*zhanfang*), a stockkeeper (*shouzhi yuan*), or a canvasser (*waipu fenxiao paojie*); and 500 to 2,000 yuan for a staff member holding a lesser position.[31]

Introduced between 1930 and 1932, this administrative organization gave China Match Company a distinct advantage over Swedish Match in attracting Chinese local commission agents, because, unlike Swedish Match, its salaried representatives released goods on consignment without requiring cash deposits. As Sigvard Eurén of Swedish Match observed, "[China Match's] sales system is different from ours. They stock up their dealers with one to two month's supply held by the dealers in consignment."[32]

With its Chinese salaried representatives "stocking up" Chinese dealers on consignment, Liu's company surpassed Swedish Match and became the biggest distributor in the market between 1930 and 1932. At the height of the anti-Japanese boycott between July 1931 and June 1932, China Match supplied 46.2 percent (100,753 cases) of the matches sold in the Lower Yangzi and 72.7 percent (20,045 cases) of those sold in the Middle Yangzi. In competition with Swedish Match and its other rivals, its marketing system followed the "first lower prices, then raise prices" strategy to reap high profits. Between its opening in July 1930 and the end of 1931 it quadrupled its average prices (from 14.47 yuan per case to 43.33 yuan per case).[33] As table 15 shows, in 1931 its total profits also quadrupled (from 125,535 to 545,823 yuan), and its profit rate rose to 23.06 percent—higher than ever before or ever

TABLE 15. CHINA MATCH COMPANY'S PRICES, COSTS, PROFITS, RATES OF PROFIT, PRODUCTION, AND CAPITAL, 1930–1944

Year	Price per Average Case (yuan)	Production Costs per Average Case (yuan)	Profits (yuan)	Profit Rate (%)	Production (cases)	Capital (yuan)
1930 (July–Dec.)	34.17	28.27	125,535	6.57	64,500	1,910,080
1931	48.94	31.17	545,823	23.06	140,410	2,367,300
1932	48.97	31.89	415,186	15.98	120,549	2,598,480
1933	41.88	30.51	62,197	2.07	129,254	3,000,000
1934	34.06	26.93	−423,793	−11.61	147,596	3,650,000
1935	30.92	24.05	−506,579	−13.88	150,093	3,650,000
1936	40.55	26.01	838,062	22.96	146,950	3,650,000
1937	41.94	26.68	333,056	9.12	96,711	3,650,000
1938	—	—	1,770,092		33,230	
1939	—	—	1,021,925		67,128	
1940	—	—	2,354,515		54,956	
1941	387.00	236.00	2,862,660		40,766	
1942	733.00	503.00	6,731,927		16,779	
1943	2,752.00	1,635.00	16,542,783		10,812	
1944	41,979.00	22,440.00	111,712,667		13,831	

SOURCES: LHS, vol. 2, 170–71, 248; vol. 3, 96–97; ZMHG, 75, 82.
Note: Currency for 1937–41 is in *fabi*; for 1942–44, in the Wang Jingwei government's *chu zhuan*.

again in its history. In 1932 its profits slipped downward (to 415,186 yuan at a profit rate of 15.98 percent), but by then Liu had thrown Swedish Match fully on the defensive. "Yes, we had a sort of competition with Krueger [the founder of Swedish Match]." Liu wrote with more than a touch of pride to his sons in 1932, "But that belongs to the past now. . . . [O]ur matches are more preferred." His victory was so complete that he tried in 1932 to buy out Swedish Match's operations in China, and even though he did not convince Swedish Match to sell, thereafter he dealt with its Western management on his own terms.[34]

ALLYING WITH A WESTERN RIVAL

In the wake of China Match Company's victories, Swedish Match's management readily conceded defeat, acknowledged Liu's control over the market, and appealed to him to end the fierce competition between the two companies. This surrender was declared in Stockholm by Fred Ljungberg, chairman of Swedish Match's board of directors and head of its worldwide operations, and was carried out by Sigvard Eurén, its Shanghai manager.

"As he [Liu] is evidently entirely unscrupulous in the methods he uses to fight his opponents," Ljungberg wrote privately from Stockholm to Eurén in Shanghai in 1934, "he is, of course, a hard nut to crack." Unwilling to vie with China Match for control of China's match industry, Ljungberg instructed Eurén that he should "frankly tell him [Liu] that our aim is not to obtain any kind of control or predominant position in the market but merely to secure a reasonable yield on our investment in the Shanghai factory." To avoid further losses, "we wish to be guided by the principle 'live and let live' in China," Ljungberg told Eurén. In fact, he left Eurén with no alternative to this policy, concluding that "cooperation with Chinese manufacturers still appears to be the only remedy to the present situation."[35]

In the new alliance, Liu and Eurén of Swedish Match worked together closely, exchanging price lists, discussing market conditions, and taking joint actions. As Eurén secretly reported from Shanghai to his superiors in Sweden, "We are still in close contact with the China Match Co.," which wanted to lower prices because "the smaller factories not affiliated with the China Match Co. were cutting into the China Match Co.'s market. . . . The price reduction [by Swedish Match] was therefore made in full agreement with the China Match Co."[36]

And yet, despite this close cooperation between Liu's China Match

Company and Swedish Match Company, the two giants suffered large losses in China between 1933 and 1935. As shown in table 15, after China Match Company entered the market and successfully built up profits at Swedish Match's expense between 1930 and 1932, it then lost much of the market, selling barely above cost in 1933 and plunging deeply into debt in 1934 and 1935. In fact, China Match Company lost nearly as much during 1934 and 1935 (930,372 yuan) as it had made during its two best years, 1931 and 1932 (961,009 yuan). These losses were largely attributable to price wars with smaller Chinese match companies that began to enter the Shanghai market in these years.

MOUNTING A MARKETING OFFENSIVE

Ironically, although Liu successfully subdued and formed cooperative agreements with his major competitor, he had difficulty doing the same with his minor ones. To end his losses, he first tried to obliterate his opposition. As part of this combative approach, in March 1933 he underpriced the smaller Chinese firms in the Lower Yangzi region, seven of which had been attracted to the booming market within the preceding year. When this tactic failed, he launched a new marketing offensive.

In 1934 he mobilized China Match's salaried staff (*yingye renyuan*) in divisional offices by introducing the Sales Bonus System (Xiaohuo jiangli zhidu). This system provided new incentives for raising sales by permitting local divisional offices to retain a percentage of annual sales revenue for over-quota sales on an incremental scale: 1 percent on sales 1–10 percent above quota, 1.2 percent on sales 11–20 percent above quota, 1.4 percent on sales 21–30 percent above quota, 1.6 percent on sales 31–40 percent above quota, and 1.8 percent on sales 41–50 percent or more above quota. Conversely, this system withheld portions of regular annual bonuses from divisional offices that failed either to sell their full quota or to collect all their unpaid debts (*dai zhen*).[37]

To win over local commission agents during price wars, Liu's China Match Company formed the Marketing Association (Jingxiao tongye lianhe hui) in 1934. The company induced Chinese sales agents to join this organization by offering them not only the usual commissions (*yong jin*) but also monthly bonuses (*chou lao fei*) at 0.3 yuan per case and annual bonuses (*jiang li jin*) set at the discretion of salaried supervisors in divisional offices. In return China Match insisted that the agents pledge their allegiance exclusively to it, sell only its brands, and operate at prices and in territories according to its specifications. To check on loyalty, the Marketing Association also gave bonuses to members for making secret reports on other members' violations of rules.[38]

Although aggressive, this marketing offensive failed to stop the kind of commercial guerrilla warfare that small Chinese firms were waging. Repeatedly Liu signed price agreements with his fellow Chinese industrialists only to see the signers ignore the agreements and cut prices. Even in his own native place of Ningbo he was not able to prevail over the locally owned rival, Zhengda Match Mill, which persistently engaged in price wars against him and stubbornly refused to accept his offers to buy it out.[39] As China Match's losses mounted, Swedish Match's management began to take Liu Hongsheng's complaints seriously. "On this occasion," Eurén noted in May 1933, "the China Match Co. were perfectly frank with us. They informed us of the difficulties in making the smaller factories adhere to the price agreement and their own failure to put into effect the new prices agreed upon." Within the one year of 1933, according to Eurén's reckoning, China Match's prices fell by 25 percent (even more than indicated in table 15).[40]

Liu failed to persuade small companies to lower production and raise prices because they expected that a cartel would soon be formed. On this premise every match manufacturer had reason to keep production high between 1933 and 1935 whatever his losses on low prices in the short run, so that later, once the cartel was formed, he would receive high quotas that would earn him high profits in the long run. As Eurén of Swedish Match wrote to his superiors in Stockholm in 1933, "In view of the possibility that quotas are planned, we have delayed as long as possible . . . reducing our output as it is probable that the ultimate quota figure will be based upon previous production figures." The same rationale seems to have guided China Match's planning. Despite its losses, it increased its production between 1933 and 1935 and manufactured more in each of these unprofitable years than it had in each of the preceding profitable years (see table 15). The small companies were accused by Eurén of overproducing because of shortsightedness and incompetence; in his contemptuous assessment, they were nothing more than "small mosquito factories who [did] not keep check on their costs." But they too probably produced at or near capacity in the hope that a cartel would eventually award them high production quotas.[41]

If match manufacturers anticipated that a cartel would be formed, they also anticipated who would form it. "Nobody now suspects us of attempting to control the industry," Eurén wrote from Shanghai to Sweden in March 1934, because Swedish Match's dominance "would obvi-

ously be impossible at present." The only possible candidate for orga-
nizing the cartel was Liu Hongsheng, who in early 1934, Eurén feared,
might have already begun "getting control for himself." [42] In the event,
Eurén's fears proved to be well founded.

FORMING A SHANGHAI-BASED INTERREGIONAL CARTEL

As match manufacturers had anticipated, Liu Hongsheng began to form
a match cartel in the mid-1930s. After broken price agreements and vi-
cious price wars, no one in the industry trusted anyone else to perform
a cartel's most fundamental tasks—setting quotas on production, speci-
fying prices, establishing sales territories—because each industrialist
feared his competitors would exceed their quotas, cut their prices, and
sell across territorial boundaries at his expense. In this atmosphere of
distrust, recruiting rivals into a cartel was easier than convincing them
to abide by its policies.

In forming this cartel, as in negotiating earlier cooperative agreements, Liu recruited members by granting concessions to them and retaining for himself unqualified authority as general manager. In 1934
and 1935 Liu negotiated with nine smaller Chinese-owned match companies that joined together under the name Great China Match Company (Da Zhongguo huochai gongsi) for the purpose of bargaining with
him. He offered them the chance to raise profits by setting quotas on
production and sales, and, at their insistence, he conceded to them the
right to manufacture 40 percent above quota if a factory's production
fell as low as twenty cases per day. From the smaller Chinese firms, in
return, he required acceptance of his decision to base quotas on the Nationalist government's tax records, July 1931–June 1934 (rather than
the number of machines per factory, which would have given smaller
firms higher quotas).

On April 9, 1935, Liu and the Chinese owners of the other nine
match companies signed an agreement establishing a cartel known as
the Joint Sales Office of the National Association of Match Manufacturers (Guochan huochai zhizao tongye lianhe banshichu). Under the
agreement, all members made three pledges: to buy official tax stamps
(needed to make legal sales) through the cartel, not directly from the
government; to arrange for official import permits (needed to buy sulfur
and other indispensable raw material) through the cartel, not directly
from the government; and to open members' factories to the cartel's inspectors. All of the members also acknowledged Liu's leadership. He be-

came chairman of the Joint Sales Office's board, and staff members from his China Match Company occupied six of the eleven seats on the Office's board, three of the five positions on the Office's standing committee, and all of the Office's top administrative posts including general manager, assistant general manager, and heads of general affairs (*zong wu*), accounting (*kuaiji*), and business affairs (*ye wu*).[43]

While winning over smaller Chinese firms, Liu Hongsheng also convinced Swedish Match to work with the Joint Sales Office. On February 24, 1934, more than a year before the cartel was formed, he showed a proposal for it to Swedish Match and found Eurén wary but interested. "Our experience in the past when we have made price agreements," Eurén reminded Liu, "has not been such as would encourage us to relinquish control of our sales. On the other hand, you know that we have strictly kept the price agreements until broken by others."[44]

As negotiations proceeded, Liu allayed Eurén's fears by conceding more administrative authority to Swedish Match than he had surrendered to the Chinese members of the Joint Sales Office. To give Swedish Match a role in decision making, he authorized the creation of a "control committee" consisting of three members, two from the Chinese members of the Office and one from Swedish Match. This committee had the power to consider all major issues that came before the Office—quotas, prices, sales territories—and it resolved issues only when all of its members voted unanimously. With the addition of this committee, Liu induced Swedish Match to sign an agreement to cooperate with the Joint Sales Office on July 27, 1935, three months after the cartel had been established.[45] Thereafter, although never formally becoming a member of the Joint Sales Office, Swedish Match consistently abided by the Office's policies.

At the same time that Liu persuaded his Western rival to sign a separate agreement, he convinced his Japanese rivals to sign one too. In dealing with China's Japanese-owned match mills, he faced somewhat different issues; unlike Swedish Match, China Match, and the other Chinese-owned companies in the cartel, the Japanese-owned companies had located their mills in North China, mainly in the cities of Qingdao and Tianjin. Less concerned with capturing North China's market than with protecting other regional markets, Liu was willing to grant the Japanese companies high quotas as long as they confined their sales to Shandong province (where Qingdao was located) and Hebei province (where Tianjin was located). With this aim in mind, in February 1935 he sent to Tokyo a member of China Match's board of directors, Chen Bofan, a Japanese-speaking Chinese whose father was a naturalized Japanese citizen. Chen accompanied Japanese mill owners on a visit to match mills in Qingdao and Tianjin, and then in July 1935 he brought them to Shanghai to negotiate with Liu Hongsheng. On July 26, 1935, Liu and the Japanese match manufacturers signed a market-sharing agreement, and two months later they enlarged the cartel to encompass existing members plus new Japanese members and gave it a new name: Chinese National Joint Production and Sales Union for Matches (Zhonghua quanguo huochai chanxiao lianyingshe). Liu presided over this larger cartel as chairman, and six Chinese and two Japanese served as members of the board of directors. On their side, the Japanese became members and promised to cease their sales of matches outside Shandong and Hebei provinces. In return Liu granted the Japanese high quotas totaling 101,714 cases per year—second only to China Match's quota of 124,800 cases per year.[46]

Outside Shandong and Hebei provinces, Liu kept quotas for his China Match Company well above those of his other rivals. While granting high quotas to Japanese mills (which competed with Chinese companies in North China not belonging to the new cartel), he saw to it that China Match was guaranteed more than half of the match sales in the Lower and Middle Yangzi and the Southeast. More precisely, the quotas set in July 1935 for eight provinces (Jiangsu, Zhejiang, Fujian, Anhui, Jiangxi, Henan, Hubei, Hunan) allocated 54.87 percent of the market to China Match, 29.31 percent to the other nine Chinese firms, and 15.82 percent to Swedish Match.[47]

At the same time Liu informed the cartel's members of new policies on production, prices, and profits. In July 1935 he instructed them to cut production by 20 percent and during October, November, and December of 1935 told them to raise prices monthly, with increases ranging from 3 to 3.6 yuan per case on large cases and 2.4 to 3 yuan per case on small cases each time.[48] Liu exhorted the members of the cartel to carry out his new policies, but, as before, he had difficulty enforcing its policies on a long-term basis.

THE PROBLEM OF LONG-TERM ENFORCEMENT

At the end of 1935, six months after reaching agreements with Swedish Match and the Chinese and Japanese match companies and instituting the cartel's first major policies, Liu still encountered resistance from smaller Chinese match mills in the cartel. According to a Westerner representing Swedish Match at the cartel's meetings, China Match argued with smaller companies at length about the cartel's policies. "The small factories," he wrote to his superiors at Swedish Match Company in January 1936, "have blocked the most important questions, e.g., the limitation of production and sales to correspond with consumption. Only after months of argument was it possible to get an equalization of sales between the factories in connection with the price increase." The "special weakness" of the system, he noted, was that "each factory has the right to withdraw on short notice" from the cartel.[49]

Liu praised the small Chinese match manufacturers for at least showing enough initiative to join the cartel despite the absence of any external discipline exercised by the Nationalist government.[50] But, as his praise implied, he preferred to have the government legally guarantee that all match companies in China would comply with the cartel's policies, and he tried to achieve this aim by campaigning for an officially sponsored national match monopoly.

WINNING GOVERNMENT SUPPORT FOR A NATIONAL MATCH MONOPOLY, 1936–1937

From the time China Match Company was founded in 1930, Liu Hongsheng lobbied continuously for the Nationalist government to intervene in the match industry and reduce the competition among manufacturers. His ultimate success suggests that Chinese entrepreneurs did not always oppose and suffer from the imposition of monopolies by the Nationalist government (as historians have generally supposed).[51] Despite Liu's numerous proposals for government intervention in the early 1930s, until 1936 his efforts were almost entirely in vain. In 1931 he was gratified by the Nationalist government's decision to raise the tariff on imported matches from 7 to 40 percent, but this policy by no means ended foreign competition in the industry: Swedish Match Company jumped the tariff barrier by acquiring match factories in Shanghai and producing 30 to 40 percent of the matches manufactured there between 1932 and 1936.[52]

In 1933 Liu submitted to the government his "Outline of Regulations for a Control Committee Governing the National Match Industry," which was endorsed by fifteen match factories, including five owned by China Match Company. Although Liu failed to win the government's approval of this proposal, he used it to put on record for officials' future reference a comprehensive description of a match monopoly's potential powers, including the authority to set quotas on production and sales, to close down any mills exceeding quotas, to monitor distribution of chemicals and raw materials to mills, and to prohibit construction of new factories.[53]

In 1935, when Liu formed the match cartel, he finally convinced the Nationalist government to play a role in the industry, albeit a very modest one. At Liu's urging the government's Ministry of Finance instructed the Internal Tax Administration to issue tax stamps to members of the match cartel showing each mill's production quota. In taking this first tentative step toward intervention, the government still was largely passive; it provided no official sanctions for enforcing quotas, closing down violators, regulating the flow of raw materials, or stopping the construction of new factories. Not until 1936 and 1937 did Liu convince the government to form a monopoly with the authority to impose these sanctions.

THE FORMATION OF THE MONOPOLY

On February 21, 1936, the Nationalist government officially sanctioned Liu's cartel, the Chinese National Joint Production and Sales Union for Matches, as a national monopoly and gave it a five-year charter for the period 1936–41. At a joint meeting of the Ministries of Industry, Finance, and Foreign Affairs, the government promised to enforce all of the policies that Liu had advocated, including quotas on production and sales, regulation of chemicals and raw materials, inspection of mills, and closure of companies for violations of the union's policies. The government prohibited anyone from building a new match mill without permission from the union beginning February 15, 1936 (two weeks after the official establishment of the union), and it barred any lapsed match mills from reopening unless they received the union's approval.[54]

The government eliminated all ambiguity about control over marketing by making the union the sole authorized seller of matches. Individual firms were forbidden to sell their own goods and were forced, as a manager at Swedish Match observed at the time, "to give up their present selling organization and sever their, in many cases, long-time relations with the dealers." Besides requiring all Chinese-owned match companies to become members of the union, the government also ordered all foreign-owned match companies to negotiate settlements with the union or submit to arbitration under the supervision of the Ministry of Foreign Affairs.[55]

Liu succeeded in persuading the government to adopt his proposal by arguing that the union would prevent match manufacturers from evading taxes, and, characteristically, he made his case by approaching decision makers through unofficial channels as well as official ones. Liu ingratiated himself with Chiang Kai-shek by invoking native-place ties, as both men hailed from Ningbo. In the early 1930s he frequently joined in discussions restricted to Chiang's most intimate confidants, and in 1932 he received from Chiang an appointment as the general manager of the government-owned China Merchants' Steam Navigation Company over which he presided for two years. Liu had the benefit of an introduction to T. V. Soong, minister of finance between 1928 and 1933, from Soong's brother, T. L. Soong, who had been Liu's classmate at St. John's University. Liu received from T. V. Soong appointments to two of the government's most prestigious advisory bodies, the National Financial Council in June 1932 and the National Economic Council in October 1933.[56]

In 1935 Liu apparently tried to buy the support of another high official, H. H. Kong, Soong's successor as minister of finance. Judging by the results, it is possible that Liu's bribe had the intended effect. In February 1935 Liu signed a three-year lease and began paying rent on one of Kong's houses, which Liu never used, and less than a year later Liu finally won approval for the national match monopoly in an official order that was signed by Kong. Although there is no direct evidence that Liu's payments for rent on Kong's house caused Kong to endorse Liu's proposal, there is evidence of Liu's gratitude to Kong for officially establishing a national match monopoly. Even while other Chinese capitalists compared Kong unfavorably with T. V. Soong, Liu staunchly defended Kong and his economic policies.[57]

Perhaps most important to Liu's negotiations with the government were his relations with another official, Wu Dingchang, who had a long career in banking before joining the government. It is more than a coincidence that Liu's campaign for official intervention finally began to achieve results immediately after Wu assumed his position as minister of industry in December 1935. However assiduously Liu had cultivated Chiang Kai-shek, T. V. Soong, and H. H. Kong, he had found in the government no receptive audience for his proposed monopoly before he began working with Wu, and when the monopoly went into effect, he made a point of thanking Wu for support. On March 13, 1936, following his usual practice of mixing personal concerns with business matters, Liu wrote a private letter to congratulate Wu on the marriage of his daughter, and he added: "I and my fellow industrialists in the match industry are very grateful for your help in winning approval for our proposal to form a union for five years and to limit the construction of new match mills. Your generous support will decisively help us to overcome our current difficulties."[58]

In 1937, during the only legal confrontation between the union and one of its members, Liu enjoyed Wu's unqualified backing. In this case the union under Liu's leadership charged a small match company, Minsheng Match Mills of Suzhou, with falsifying documents that allowed it to take more than its quota of tax stamps; the union further charged that when caught committing this illegal act, Minsheng Match Mills then withdrew from the union, refused to allow the union's inspectors to enter its factories, and began manufacturing and selling matches as a nonunion member. In its defense, Minsheng Match Mills accused the union of unfairly exercising monopoly powers in the match industry and of granting privileges to large firms at the expense of small ones. To end these inequitable policies, Minsheng Match Mills said, the union should be disbanded.

When this case was referred to the Ministry of Industry, Wu Dingchang served as the final arbiter and settled the matter unequivocally in favor of the union. He reaffirmed the validity of the union's charter and ordered Minsheng Match Mills to remain in the union, stay within its quotas, admit inspectors into its factories, and comply with the other provisions of the its charter or close down operations altogether. Announcing his decision on July 8, 1937 (just as Japanese military forces were invading China), Wu pointed out that no other member of the union besides Minsheng Match Mills had violated the union's rules since its founding eighteen months earlier.[59] In light of the earlier price wars and broken agreements in the match industry, Wu's claim might seem difficult to believe, but he was not exaggerating the union's effectiveness in Shanghai and the Lower Yangzi region.

THE UNION'S EFFECTIVENESS IN THE LOWER YANGZI REGION

With its headquarters in Shanghai, the union proved to be very effective at enforcing its policies in the Lower Yangzi region. In its first year between April 1936 and April 1937, it raised average match prices in the region by a total of no less than 50 percent.[60] As a result some members of the union profited handsomely.

The chief beneficiary of the cartel was Liu Hongsheng's China Match Company. As shown in table 15, after having accumulated the biggest debts in its history between 1934 and 1935, China Match then made the highest profits in its history between 1936 and 1937. This dramatic reversal of its fortunes was a direct result of the effectiveness of the cartel.

After the founding of the union, Swedish Match's profits also rose and achieved much higher levels than its Western managers thought was possible. When Eurén and others in Swedish Match's Shanghai office had first seen the proposal for the union in January 1936, they expressed the suspicion that "the whole scheme is intended to give the Chinese a possibility of eliminating Amfea [Swedish Match] as a competitor and of creating a virtual monopoly for Mr. O. S. Lieu's [Liu Hongsheng's] group in Central China." But within the union's first year, these Westerners began to change their minds. In February 1937, writing from Shanghai to his superiors in Sweden, the usually dour Eurén optimistically predicted, "[The union] will furnish a working basis and a fairly satisfactory one considering that we are working in China." Six months later his office jubilantly confirmed that his forecast had been borne out: "Since the 1st of February 1937, competition has been largely eliminated by allotting tax stamps on an agreed quota basis." [61]

The remaining Chinese match companies in the Lower and Middle Yangzi belonging to the union seem to have benefited from membership in it according to each one's size. Middle-sized firms such as Zhongguo Match Mills of Shanghai, Zhengda Match Mills of Ningbo, and Chusheng Match Mills of Hankou were profitable in 1936 and 1937. Some small member firms such as Zhongnan Match Mills in Shanghai and Minsheng Match Mills in Suzhou suffered losses in 1936 and 1937, but the union continued to expand and regulate additional small match mills. By February 1937 the union exercised authority over twenty-one mills in the Lower Yangzi region compared to the ten with which it had begun one year earlier. [62]

THE UNION'S LIMITATIONS OUTSIDE THE LOWER YANGZI REGION

Liu Hongsheng and the union were only somewhat successful in the Middle Yangzi region, less so in North China, and not at all in other regions of China. In the Middle Yangzi Liu overcame the union's initial failure by forming a separate organization whose jurisdiction was confined to this one region. On the founding of the union in February 1936, it had originally recruited this region's match companies and had applied its general rules to them. But within a few months Liu was forced to negotiate a separate agreement because the Middle Yangzi region's biggest locally owned match company, Chusheng Mills, began exceeding its quota by using tax stamps drawn against its allotments for the future. To prevent a resumption of competition, Liu offered to raise Chusheng Mills' quota from 660 to 990 cases per month if it would join China Match and Swedish Match in forming a regional cartel whose sales territory was confined to the Middle Yangzi region (which was specified within the agreement as the territory within the boundaries of Hunan and Hubei provinces). In June 1936 all three companies signed the agreement, which gave China Match and Swedish Match each a quota of 1,200 cases per month. Thereafter in 1936 and 1937 they virtually monopolized the Middle Yangzi's match market.

In North China the union tried to build on its earlier agreement with Japanese-owned firms, but it ran into opposition from Chinese match manufacturers and local warlords. In spring 1936, after setting up an office for Shandong province in the city of Qingdao, the union ordered four local Chinese-owned match mills to close and another twenty to lower production. In closing down the mills, the union's officials cited the Nationalist government's regulations prohibiting the opening of new factories or the reopening of old ones after March 28, 1936, and they sett quotas on production based on the mills' records as taxpayers to the Nationalist government between July 1931 and June 1934.

Many Chinese match manufacturers reacted sharply to these and the union's other policies. Two large Japanese-owned firms and ten Chinese-owned firms joined the union, but twenty Chinese-owned firms formed a rival cartel, and later five of the ten that had originally joined the union withdrew to establish yet another cartel. The two locally founded cartels complained that the union had discriminated against Chinese by granting excessively high quotas to big Japanese firms, and they demanded that the union base its quotas on the number of machines in each mill, not the tax records of the Nationalist government.

When the union and the Nationalist government tried to impose their authority, they failed to overcome local opposition. In February 1936, shortly after the union's founding, its office at Qingdao cut off the supply of official tax stamps to the twenty mills that had refused to join, but these mills disregarded the Nationalist government's regulations and continued to sell their matches without stamps. Determined to discipline the violators, the union sent investigators from Shanghai to Qingdao to document the violations of its policies and the evasion of the Nationalist government's taxes. But as the investigators were about to return to

Shanghai, the local warlord, Han Fuju, sent troops onto their train and confiscated the evidence that they had collected. Thereafter the union exercised authority over no more than a fraction of the match manufacturers in Qingdao. Perhaps its most significant accomplishment was its success in persuading big Japanese-owned match companies in Qingdao to refrain from exporting matches from North China to the Lower and Middle Yangzi regions.

Elsewhere in China the union had little or no effect on match manufacturers. In Tianjin it set up an office similar to the one in Qingdao, but it recruited fewer firms there, and its members paid only lip service to their quotas. In South China the union encountered outright hostility from sixteen match mills that had their own cartel and sent a letter to the union characterizing Liu Hongsheng as "a careerist" (*yexinjia*) and "a criminal in our country's industrial world" (*woguo shiyejiezhi yidazuiren*). In Northwest China, the union conducted formal negotiations with the warlord Yan Xishan who had established a match monopoly in Shanxi province in 1931 and found him unwilling to set up a local office. In other regions of China (notably the Northwest, the Upper Yangzi, and the Southwest), the union did not even attempt to conduct negotiations with local match mills.[63]

Nationwide the union's effectiveness as a monopoly seems to have correlated closely with the Nationalist government's effectiveness as the union's enforcer, according to a survey conducted by Swedish Match Company in spring 1937. Swedish Match found that control over production through the use of official tax stamps was "fairly satisfactory" in the Lower and Middle Yangzi and the Southeast; less so in other regions where provincial governments did not "sincerely support" the Nationalist government's tax regulations; and least of all in "border areas between controlled and loosely controlled territories [where] competition from uncontrolled manufacturers ha[d] been keenly felt." As a general rule, according to this assessment, the union's policies became more "unsatisfactory . . . the longer the distance from Nanking [Nanjing, the Nationalist government's capital]."[64]

PRIVATE INITIATIVE AND GOVERNMENT ENFORCEMENT

In evaluating this collusion between business and government, it is worth emphasizing that the initiative lay with private businessmen, not Nationalist officials. To be sure, before the establishment of the official match monopoly, Liu Hongsheng had not been a private entrepreneur in the sense that he had avoided all contact with the government. On the contrary, long before the founding of China Match Company in 1930 he had befriended influential officials, and in the early 1930s he had accepted official posts on advisory committees and as director of the government-owned shipping line. Nonetheless, in 1930 or even earlier Liu took the initiative as a private entrepreneur to seek official intervention in the match industry and lobbied for years before he finally convinced the government to follow his lead. At the same time, by engineering China Match's merger in 1930 and founding the interregional match cartel in 1935, Liu demonstrated that industrialists could cooperate without the government's leadership. Indeed, when the government finally established a national match monopoly in February 1936 it was bowing to Liu's requests and placing its imprimatur on policies that he had already formulated and tested before the government became involved.

After the national match monopoly began to operate, the Nationalist government sanctioned several other monopolies (on vegetable oil, tea, fish, and consumer goods handled by department stores), which historians have interpreted as vehicles that were used by the Nationalist government to impose policies unilaterally on private entrepreneurs.[65] It is possible that in these other industries officials aggressively proposed monopolies and private entrepreneurs reluctantly accepted the idea, but in the match industry (and perhaps other industries),[66] it was the other way around.

CONCLUSION

As recounted here, China Match Company's management might well seem to have made an irreversible transition from the use of a personal Chinese social network to the use of an impersonal Western-style corporate and bureaucratic hierarchy. Before founding China Match, Liu Hongsheng had built up a powerful social network by forming a marriage alliance with a legendary merchant family that had migrated to Shanghai from his native place, by serving as head of the Association of Ningbo Sojourners in Shanghai continuously from 1920 on, and by cultivating a friendship with his fellow Ningbo men ranging from industrialists and bankers to Chiang Kai-shek. On the eve of China Match's founding, Liu had also used his social network to bring together the co-investors who gave birth to the company. By drawing on native-place ties, he had convinced a fellow Ningbo man who owned a match company bigger than his own to join with him in the merger and yet allow him to be the head of China Match.

Then in 1930, once China Match was founded, Liu seemed to set aside his social network in favor of Western-style impersonal corporate structures and organizational forms that depended on investors and staff members from outside his family and native place. First in 1930 he legally registered China Match as a joint-stock limited liability company in which he and his family were minority shareholders; then in the early 1930s he instituted administrative and distributing systems at China Match that had corporate hierarchies quite similar to the ones in Western businesses; and ultimately in the mid-1930s he recruited into a cartel and later into a national monopoly several Chinese, Western, and Japanese industrialists with whom he had no family or native-place ties. He and they joined together not in informal networks based on family and native place but in formal organizations held together by the fear of suicidal competition and the threat of reprisals from the Nationalist government.

And yet near the end of this period Liu carried out a reorganization of his top management that shows that his transition from a Chinese social network to Western-style corporate hierarchies had not been entirely irreversible. After entrusting authority to professional managers from outside his family since the early 1930s, Liu shifted authority over his business into the hands of his sons in the late 1930s and 1940s. As thirteen of his children reached adulthood and returned from their studies abroad (four sons and one daughter from schools in the United States, four sons and one daughter from schools in England, two sons and one daughter from schools in Japan),[67] Liu appointed his eldest sons to positions as top managers and gave them authority second only to his own. His sons, graduates of Cambridge University Law School and other Western academic institutions as well as Japanese universities, retained and endorsed Western-style accounting and business practices in all of Liu's businesses, but they unequivocally insisted on excluding nonkin from decision making at the highest levels of the business and in 1936 took authority away from Liu's professional managers and gathered it into their own hands.[68]

This reversion from professional to family management shows that Liu's business did not make a definitive or final transition from management by a social network to management by a corporate hierarchy, and it undercuts or at least complicates the conclusion that China Match was a Chinese business in which Western-style management triumphed over a Chinese social network. In this case, as in the cases discussed in the preceding chapters, it is misleading to conclude that any business always operated in China exclusively through either a corporate hierarchy or a social network. In the course of history, all of the businesses under consideration here depended periodically or even simultaneously on both corporate hierarchies and social networks. These conclusions point to the need for a reformulation of the issues with which this book began.

CHAPTER 8

Conclusion

Corporations and Networks

In 1937 the Japanese military invasion of China drastically altered the country's business environment and caused all of the corporations described here to restructure their operations. The year 1937 thus provides an appropriate chronological ending for this book, but it is worth noting that all of the corporations found ways of doing business in China even after the war broke out. During the war Standard Oil and BAT partially closed down and generally confined themselves to parts of China not occupied by the Japanese military. Mitsui and Naigai expanded, especially in the areas under Japanese military occupation. And Shenxin and China Match divided their operations, leaving their old Shanghai headquarters in charge of areas under the Japanese occupation and making their new divisions, based in Chongqing, responsible for areas outside the Japanese occupation.[1] After the war ended in 1945, Mitsui and Naigai withdrew from China along with Japan's defeated troops, and Standard Oil, BAT, Shenxin, and China Match all resumed operations with headquarters at Shanghai until Mao Zedong and the Communists defeated Chiang Kai-shek and the Nationalists and assumed power in 1949.

Since the 1940s all except Naigai have continued to be major multinational corporations or at least have bequeathed legacies to major multinational corporations. Standard Oil's heirs (by various names) have dominated the world's oil industry, and BAT (still by the same name) has been the world's leading manufacturer of cigarettes. Although

Naigai has not reentered international markets since 1945, Mitsui has done so and has become the prototypical Japanese general trading company (*sogo shosha*), serving as a model for numerous Japanese general trading companies that have profoundly shaped the world's economy. Meanwhile, after supervising Shenxin and China Match in their transitions to socialism during the 1950s and becoming targets of Maoist campaigns against capitalists in China during the 1960s and 1970s, the Rong and Liu families have reemerged as influential promoters of Chinese businesses in the 1980s and 1990s. In contemporary China a member of the Rong family, Rong Zongjing's nephew Rong Yiren, has come to personify the country's capitalist legacy. He is the founder of China International Trust Investment Company (CITIC), China's biggest foreign trading company, and he has recently become vice president of China, leaving his position as head of CITIC to his son.[2]

Although this book has not described the post-1937 history of these corporations in detail, its interpretation of their pre-1937 history has implications for the long-term development of business institutions. As noted in chapter 1, previous studies have described Western, Japanese, and Chinese ways of doing business and have identified the Western way and the Japanese way with corporate hierarchies and the Chinese way with social networks. By operating within these categories, scholars have left the impression that every successful firm has been guided by its business culture to make a clear-cut and lasting choice between one of two mutually exclusive ways of doing business: either through corporate hierarchies or through social networks. But the findings in this book suggest that Western, Japanese, and Chinese businesses have not maintained a firm boundary between hierarchies and networks. Over time none of the firms described here always relied solely on hierarchies or solely on networks. Each used both hierarchies and networks.

CORPORATE HIERARCHIES

All six of the corporations described in this book made use of corporate hierarchies for managerial purposes in China. They differed not on the issue of whether to use hierarchies but rather on the question of what kind to adopt or create, and each one formed a corporate hierarchy derived from its management's experience in the West, Japan, or China.

The two Western companies, Standard Oil and BAT, both introduced Western bureaucratic hierarchies by sending Western salaried representatives to China and by training English-speaking Chinese salaried representatives in China during the first decade of the twentieth century. To be sure, the two companies were strikingly different in the sequences that they followed. Standard Oil delegated authority to Chinese social networks for twenty years (1883–1903) and then instituted its corporate hierarchies for direct marketing in China. BAT, by contrast, on its arrival in China almost immediately introduced its corporate hierarchies for direct marketing and then after nearly twenty years (1902–19) shifted primary responsibility into the hands of commission agents in Chinese social networks. Nonetheless, both companies imported, instituted, and adapted their managerial hierarchies in China over long periods.

The two Japanese companies, Mitsui and Naigai, used Japanese hierarchies to exercise control over their operations in China. Compared to Standard Oil and BAT, they staffed their hierarchies with more Chinese-speaking foreign nationals from their home country, and they used these Japanese China specialists to extend their reach in managing Chinese markets and supervising Chinese workers. Like Standard Oil and BAT, Mitsui and Naigai differed from each other in the lengths of time that they operated their managerial hierarchies at maximum strength in China, and both maintained these hierarchies over long periods.

Even the Chinese businesses, Shenxin and China Match, had corporate hierarchies. As noted in chapter 1, Chinese businesses have generally been identified with social networks as opposed to corporate hierarchies, and Shenxin and China Match both made use of social networks, but they made use of corporate hierarchies too. It is true that one of them, Shenxin, had a hierarchy that was quite personal insofar as its founder, Rong Zongjing, retained considerable authority for decision making and employed a staff that largely consisted of members of his family and associates from his native place. But Shenxin still had a strict corporate hierarchy, with Rong presiding at the top and trained managers exercising control in separate departments and at all levels down to and including purchasing agents in cotton fields, distributors in yarn and cloth markets, and workers in factories on the shop floor. Whereas Shenxin's hierarchy was somewhat personal, China Match's was impersonal. China Match's founder, Liu Hongsheng, established a joint-stock limited liability company, and he built up this corporate structure by forming a series of hierarchical organizations—an administrative system for direct marketing, a cartel, and a national monopoly—with himself as head and with investors and staff members almost entirely from outside his family and native place.

In all six cases, then, businesses used corporate hierarchies to exercise control in China. In some cases they introduced these hierarchies to replace or supervise social networks, and in others they followed the opposite pattern by transferring responsibilities from their hierarchies to Chinese networks.

SOCIAL NETWORKS

While making use of hierarchies in China, all six of the corporations described here also delegated authority to Chinese social networks. In the course of their history the management of every one of these corporations encountered and accommodated Chinese networks. These networks were not merely passive, always acted on and never acting. On the contrary, in some instances Chinese networks took the initiative more than corporate hierarchies did.

At both Western corporations networks of Chinese merchants gained control over marketing, but they were unable to retain it at Standard Oil as consistently as they did at BAT. During Standard Oil's first two decades in China (1882–1903) networks of Chinese merchants and compradors took distribution of kerosene into their own hands and paid little heed to the company's organization and business practices. These relatively autonomous Chinese networks showed their tenacity by retaining authority over Standard Oil's goods longer than local networks were able to do in any of the world's other major markets; not until the period from 1903 to 1914 was the company's system for direct distribution installed in China. Once this system was in place, however, the members of Chinese networks were replaced or assigned to positions in which they were held accountable under Standard Oil's regulations and punished for violations of the company's policies.

At BAT, by contrast, once networks of Chinese began to serve as commission agents, they never relinquished control over distribution of the company's goods. During BAT's first two decades in China, 1902–19, they marketed BAT's goods more profitably than the company's corporate hierarchy for direct distribution was able to do. In 1919, when the Chinese networks' superiority became fully apparent to the company, they were given primary responsibility for BAT's distribution, and they retained it during the 1920s, 1930s, and 1940s. Throughout these decades networks of Chinese generally operated beyond the reach of BAT's corporate hierarchy, escaping close supervision by the company's salaried representatives in cigarette factories and tobacco fields as well as cigarette markets.

At the two Japanese corporations, as at the Western ones, networks of Chinese took control and held it longer at one company than at the other. During Mitsui's first twenty-one years in China, 1877–98, compradors and other Chinese merchants took charge of its marketing in much the same way as they did at Standard Oil and other big Western corporations, but in 1898 the compradors were pensioned off, and many of the Chinese merchants were replaced by Japanese China specialists in Mitsui's corporate hierarchy.

By comparison, networks of Chinese workers in Naigai's factories proved to be more durable than did networks of Chinese merchants in Mitsui's marketing system. During the 1910s and early 1920s, Chinese Number Ones were thrown on the defensive by Naigai's aggressive reforms that strengthened the company's hierarchy of labor supervisors, subjected Chinese Number Ones to stern discipline, and undermined the Number Ones' authority by providing housing and other benefits directly to workers. But in the mid-1920s networks of Chinese Number Ones seized the initiative against Naigai by joining with Chinese Communists, Nationalists, and gangsters as leaders of a series of strikes. Taking Naigai as their prime target, these Chinese Number Ones helped to paralyze it in numerous work stoppages between 1925 and 1927, and they achieved a lasting victory that left them (not Naigai's management) in control of recruiting and training Chinese workers throughout the late 1920s, 1930s, and 1940s.

The two Chinese businesses were not spared challenges from Chinese networks simply by virtue of their Chinese ownership. At Shenxin members of Rong Zongjing's own social network opposed his plans for founding a company outside their native place of Wuxi. Although they did not prevent him from opening Shenxin in Shanghai and establishing its headquarters there, they did succeed in placing family members and native-place associates in the majority of Shenxin's administrative positions at all levels of its hierarchy. Other Chinese networks challenged Shenxin's management in the company's cotton mills. Led by Chinese Number Ones, these networks endured throughout the late 1910s and 1920s until they encountered teams of trained managers who descended on them through Shenxin's corporate hierarchy in the early 1930s. Thereafter the Number Ones in Wuxi and Hankou lost their jobs at Shenxin, and the ones in Shanghai were restricted to the extent that they were left with control over a fraction of the company's workforce (approximately 1,200 of Shenxin's 34,000 workers).

At China Match Chinese social networks also took initiatives with factory workers and top management. Whereas networks of Chinese gangsters and labor racketeers struggled with Rong Zongjing over control of Shenxin's workers, they seem to have had less difficulty winning deference from the head of China Match, Liu Hongsheng, who apparently did not resist their recruitment of workers for his businesses. At the highest level of China Match's management, another social network consisting of Liu's sons also received his endorsement. After Liu had devised formal corporate hierarchies and entrusted authority to professional managers since founding China Match in 1930, he transferred responsibility for ultimate decision making from these professional managers to his sons in 1936.

To sum up, Chinese social networks exercised control over both staff members and factory workers with varying degrees of consistency and for varying periods at all six of the corporations described in this book. In light of past studies, this conclusion in itself should not be regarded as surprising. As noted in chapter 1, several historians have emphasized the importance of Chinese social networks for managing staff members and workers in China, and if viewed in a comparative perspective, the tenacity of Chinese Number Ones in China bears a close resemblance to the tenacity of Western and Japanese foremen and gangsters who resisted businesses' efforts to achieve direct control over workers in the West and Japan during the late nineteenth and early twentieth century.[3]

What is surprising about this conclusion is its relationship to the preceding one. In Chinese history, as I have shown here, it is not enough to focus exclusively on either corporate hierarchies or social networks. Over time every corporation was guided in various phases or even simultaneously by initiatives originating in both its own hierarchical organization and Chinese social networks. Corporations did not all make linear transitions, fully liberating themselves from social networks and becoming exclusively dependent on managerial hierarchies, nor did they do the reverse. Instead, in one way or another, corporations and networks all engaged in long-term dynamic interaction.

DYNAMIC INTERACTION

The interaction between corporations and networks was dynamic because neither wholly controlled the other. As corporations grew they tried to extend their hierarchical control as deeply into Chinese society as seemed profitable in the long run, and as networks grew they tried to widen their control as broadly in Chinese society as seemed profitable in the long run, but even the biggest corporations and networks had their limitations in relation to each other.

As shown here all of the corporations allowed for their dependence on networks. Of the two Western-owned firms, Standard Oil replaced social networks with corporate hierarchies while BAT did the opposite, but both took Chinese social networks seriously throughout their history. Even at the height of its managerial control, Standard Oil presided over a nationwide distributing system that did not take the acquiescence of social networks for granted. It contrived means to keep its Chinese staff members away from their networks by assigning them to posts distant from their native places, and it never ceased to threaten these staff members (as well as its local Chinese distributors, jobbers, and commission agents) with punishment for violating company policies. Meanwhile BAT delegated authority to Chinese social networks and remained heavily dependent on them in purchasing tobacco and manufacturing and marketing cigarettes in China throughout the 1920s, 1930s, and 1940s.

The Japanese-owned corporations also had limitations in relation to networks. Mitsui solved the problem of managerial control by replacing Chinese staff members with Chinese-speaking Japanese, but training these staff members was expensive—so expensive that Mitsui was not able to produce a (Japanese) staff big enough to reach as far down China's urban hierarchy as Standard Oil's (Western and Chinese) staff did. Compared to Mitsui, Naigai reached its limits in a more dramatic fashion. When it tried to replace Chinese Number Ones and their social networks with its own corporate hierarchy, it provoked the strikes of 1925–27 and was forced to retreat.

Similarly the Chinese-owned companies encountered and never fully overcame opposition from social networks of factory workers. Shenxin attacked and reduced the size of these networks more aggressively and successfully than China Match did, but neither Shenxin nor China Match ever eliminated from their factories all of the workers who were enmeshed in networks of Chinese Number Ones and gangsters.

By the same token, Chinese social networks had their limitations. Members of networks affiliated with foreign firms faced the ominous prospect that they and their jobs as intermediaries would become obsolete as soon as their foreign superiors learned about Chinese business practices, particularly in distribution and sales. As the case studies here show, some Chinese did suffer this fate, as evidenced by Standard Oil's dismissal of Ye Chengzhong, BAT's dismissal of Wu Tingsheng, and Mitsui's dismissal of Jin Yangsheng—not to mention the broader organizational shifts from commission agents to salaried staff members at Standard Oil and Mitsui and the ousters of Chinese Number Ones at Naigai and Shenxin.

Chinese social networks also were limited by internal dissension. To outsiders they gave the impression that their members were bound together in harmony based on family concord and native-place solidarity. But behind this facade were tensions that occasionally erupted in full-fledged disputes over business decisions. The most dramatic example cited here is Rong Zongjing's battle with his family and native-place associates over whether to invest outside their native place of Wuxi. As this case shows, a faction of a network might rebel against the network's established policies (as Rong Zongjing and his brother did by establishing Shenxin in Shanghai) and still work within the network for other purposes (as the Rong brothers did in staffing Shenxin with Wuxi natives).

Perhaps most fundamental of all for Chinese social networks were the limitations resulting from their particularism. These limitations were inherent in networks based on family ties and native-place connections even if "native place" was defined broadly and flexibly. And yet, as with all of these limitations, Chinese social networks found ways of overcoming particularism when tempted by irresistible opportunities or faced with dire threats from corporations.

The case of Zheng Bozhao, BAT's leading distributor, illustrates success in overcoming particularism in response to an opportunity presented by a corporation. As a Cantonese presiding over a network of members almost all from his native place of Xiangshan County in South China, Zheng was loath to elevate a non-Cantonese to a position of authority, and he never did so—until BAT offered him the chance to manage interregional marketing of its cigarettes throughout most of China. Only then did he recruit a non-Cantonese native, Feng Xifan, to serve as intermediary between Zheng's own network and networks from outside South China. In taking this step, Zheng showed that he could expand his particularistic network by circumventing the usual ban against members from outside his native place, and, as noted in chapter 3, he did so by bending rather than abandoning his particularistic principles, for he required Feng to serve a full apprenticeship and to acquire fluency in Cantonese before placing him in a position of authority.

In other cases networks overcame particularism in response to corporations' threats. At Naigai, as shown in chapter 5, networks of workers in factories did not overcome their particularism in the 1910s and early 1920s even though Number Ones were suffering from Naigai's erosion of their authority at that time. But in 1925, when these Number Ones' jobs were threatened by Naigai's policies, they set aside their subethnic differences and readily forged alliances with each other and with labor organizers from the Communist and Nationalist parties and the Green Gang.

These examples show that Chinese social networks were limited by particularism, but they also show that networks overcame their particularism in response to inducements or provocations from corporations. At key moments, even as corporations departed from their usual business practices to accommodate networks, so too did networks take extraordinary steps in dealing with corporations. In a word, the actions and interactions of hierarchies and social networks were contingent— contingent on each other and contingent on the social and economic context of their time.

HISTORICAL CONTINGENCIES AND FUTURE POSSIBILITIES

This historical interpretation of corporate hierarchies and social networks has implications for the future, because it shows their durability and raises the possibility that they persist even in the present. On the basis of these findings and other research, is it possible to predict the future of hierarchies and networks? Since others have ventured predictions for China and even worldwide, it seems appropriate to end by considering how to approach this question.

Scholars emphasizing differences among Western, Japanese, and Chinese ways of doing business have frequently left the impression that either hierarchies or networks represent evolutionary end-points of economic development. Alfred Chandler's and Japanese historians' favorable evaluations of Western and Japanese businesses' corporate hierarchies suggest that the strengths of these organizations in the past will enable them to prevail indefinitely in the West and Japan; and Gary Hamilton's and other sociologists' assertion that Chinese networks have followed "the same patterns of business relations" in the present as in the past provides a trajectory for East Asia reaching from the nineteenth century into the future. Imagining worldwide possibilities, Chandler has gone so far as to say that corporate hierarchies have "spread" from the "seedbed of managerial capitalism" in the United States to Europe and Asia in the twentieth century, and as might be expected, Hamilton has objected to this assertion, maintaining that Asian organizational forms have been distinctly Asian, not Western, from beginning to end.[4] This disagreement between Chandler and Hamilton is part of a broader debate over the "modernist thesis"—the contention that economic institutions will converge as societies industrialize, leaving a common form of organization in every society all over the world at some point in the future.

In today's China recent research provides little support for the modernist thesis. Since the death of Mao Zedong and the beginning of Deng Xiaoping's economic reforms in the late 1970s, China's market has attracted a wide variety of businesses (including, as noted earlier, the heirs of several corporations described in this book), and these businesses do not seem to be converging as institutions or giving rise to a single organizational form. On the contrary, as the economist and management specialist John Child has recently concluded, "If we leave aside the nonmarketized state sector, [we find at present a] diversity of successful business forms within China, each of them with unique features."[5]

Faced with this "diversity of successful business forms," it may be tempting to classify them according to the nationalities of their owners and to divide their practices into Western, Japanese, or Chinese ways of doing business in China. But if this book is any indication, then such a classification will provide no more than a convenient point of departure for understanding the present just as it provides no more than a convenient point of departure for understanding the past. To deepen our understanding of how business practices work, it is suggested here, we need to shift our focus from businesses' nationalities to their interactions with local society in China or any other country, and we need to trace these interactions over time. In this way we might rise to a challenge recently posed by the social theorist Walter W. Powell. "To make serious progress in understanding the diversity of organizational forms [anywhere in the world]," he has insisted, "we need arguments that are much more historically contingent and context dependent."[6]

Notes

ABBREVIATIONS

KMBK   Nihon keieishi kenkyujo (Japan Business History Institute), ed. *Kohon Mitsui Bussan kabushiki kaisha* (A Hundred-Year History of the Mitsui Trading Company), vol. 1. Tokyo, 1978.

LHS   Shanghai shehui kexue yuan jingji yanjiu suo (Shanghai Academy of Social Sciences Institute of Economics), comp. *Liu Hongsheng qiye shiliao* (Historical Materials on Liu Hongsheng's Enterprises). Shanghai: Shanghai renmin chubanshe, 1981.

MJS   *Mitsui jigyoshi* (A History of the Mitsui Enterprises), *honhen* (main part), vol. 3. Tokyo: Mitsui Bunko, 1980.

RJ   Shanghai shehui kexue yuan jingji yanjiu suo (Shanghai Academy of Social Sciences Institute of Economics), comp. *Rong jia qiye shiliao* (Historical Materials on the Rong Family Enterprises). Shanghai: Shanghai renmin chubanshe, 1980.

SJWS   Shanghai shehui kexue yuan jingji yanjiu suo (Shanghai Academy of Social Sciences Institute of Economics), comp. *Shanghai jindai wujin shangye shi* (A History of the Hardware Trade in Modern Shanghai). Shanghai: Shanghai shehui chubanshe, 1990.

Strikes and Lockouts Bureau of Social Affairs, City Government of Greater Shanghai, comp. *Strikes and Lockouts in Shanghai since 1918.* Bilingual edition, Chinese title: *Jin shiwunian lai Shanghai zhi bagong tingye* (Strikes and Lockouts in China during the Past Fifty Years). Shanghai: Zhonghua shuju, 1933.

YM Shanghai shehui kexue yuan jingji yanjiu suo (Shanghai Academy of Social Sciences Institute of Economics), comp. *Ying Mei yanjiu gongsi zai Hua qiye ziliao huibian* (Collected Materials on the Enterprises of the British-American Tobacco Company in China). 4 vols. Beijing: Zhonghua shuju, 1983.

ZMHG Qingdao gong shang xingzheng guanli zhu shiliao zhu (Committee on Historical Materials concerning the Administration and Management of Industry and Commerce in Qingdao), ed. *Zhongguo minzu huochai gongye* (China's National Match Industry). Beijing: Zhonghua shuju, 1963.

CHAPTER 1. INTRODUCTION: CORPORATIONS VERSUS NETWORKS

1. Walter W. Powell, "Neither Market nor Hierarchy: Network Forms of Organization," in Barry M. Staw and L. L. Cummings, eds., *Research in Organizational Behavior,* vol. 12 (Greenwich, Conn.: JAI Press, 1990), 303, 324.

2. Alfred D. Chandler, Jr., *Scale and Scope: The Dynamics of Industrial Capitalism* (Cambridge, Mass.: Harvard University Press, 1990), 261.

3. Alfred D. Chandler, Jr., *The Visible Hand: The Managerial Revolution in American Business* (Cambridge, Mass.: Harvard University Press, 1977), 484–500.

4. William D. Wray, "Afterword: The Writing of Japanese Business History," in William D. Wray, ed., *Managing Industrial Enterprise: Cases from Japan's Prewar Experience* (Cambridge, Mass.: Council on East Asian Studies, Harvard University, 1989), 325–26. Emphasis in original.

5. Kawabe Nobuo, "The Distribution Systems in Japan before World War II," *Business and Economic History,* 2d ser., no. 18 (1989): 42; Yui Tsunehiko, "Development, Organization, and International Competitiveness of Industrial Enterprises in Japan, 1880–1915," *Business and Economic History,* 2d ser., no. 17 (1988): 40.

6. Wong Siu-lun, "Chinese Entrepreneurs and Business Trust," in Gary G. Hamilton, ed., *Business Networks and Economic Development in East and Southeast Asia* (Hong Kong: Centre of Asian Studies, University of Hong Kong, 1991), 24.

7. Edward Chen and Gary G. Hamilton, "Introduction: Business Networks and Economic Development," in Hamilton, ed., *Business Networks,* 6; Gary G. Hamilton, "The Organizational Foundations of Western and Chinese Commerce: A Historical and Comparative Analysis," in Hamilton, ed., *Business Networks,* 48–65.

8. S. Gordon Redding, "Weak Organizations and Strong Linkages: Managerial Ideology and Chinese Family Business Networks," in Hamilton, ed., *Business Networks,* 45.

9. Chandler has not dealt historically with relations between American businesses and American local merchants in detail, but his suggestion that businesses set up their own marketing organizations and imposed their own direct distribution systems because of local merchants' "inadequacies" (Chandler, *The Visible Hand,* 287) has been challenged by Charles Perrow. In a heated exchange, Chandler and Perrow have clarified their respective interpretations of businesses' motives but have added nothing substantive on the nature of relations between businesses and local networks in American history. See Charles Perrow, "Markets, Hierarchies and Hegemony," in Thomas K. McCraw, ed., *The Essential Chandler: Essays toward a Historical Theory of Big Business* (Boston: Harvard Business School Press, 1988), 432–37; and Alfred D. Chandler, Jr., "Historical Determinants of Managerial Hierarchies: A Response to Perrow," in McCraw, ed., *The Essential Chandler,* 451–61.

10. On foremen's resistance in twentieth-century American history, see Sanford M. Jacoby, *Employing Bureaucracy: Managers, Unions and the Transformation of Work in American Industry, 1900–1945* (New York: Columbia University Press, 1985). On foremen's resistance in twentieth-century British history, see Craig R. Littler, *The Development of the Labour Process in Capitalist Societies: A Comparative Study of the Transformation of Work Organizations in Britain, Japan, and the U.S.A.* (London: Heinemann Educational, 1982). Chandler has acknowledged his decision to omit from his work "the effect of the broader cultural environment on the evolution of the modern industrial enterprise [and] the labor story." See his *Scale and Scope,* 13.

11. Yui, "Development," 35; Kawabe, "The Distribution System," 42; and W. Mark Fruin, *The Japanese Enterprise System: Competitive Strategies and Cooperative Structures* (Oxford: Clarendon Press, 1994), 148, 180–81.

12. Fruin, *The Japanese Enterprise System,* 135, 169–76. The quotation is from p. 169.

13. Solomon B. Levine, "Labor Markets and Collective Bargaining in Japan," in William W. Lockwood, ed., *The State and Economic Enterprise in Japan* (Princeton: Princeton University Press, 1965), 642–47; Andrew Gordon, *The Evolution of Labor Relations in Japan: Heavy Industries, 1853–1955* (Cambridge, Mass.: Council on East Asian Studies, Harvard University, 1988), 54–57.

14. Mira Wilkins, "The Impacts of American Multinational Enterprise on American-Chinese Economic Relations, 1786–1949," in Ernest R. May and John K. Fairbank, eds., *America's China Trade in Historical Perspective: The Chinese and American Performance* (Cambridge, Mass.: Council on East Asian

Studies, Harvard University, 1986), 264. See also Howard Cox, "Learning to Do Business in China: The Evolution of BAT's Cigarette Distributing Network, 1902–1941," *Business History* 39, no. 3 (1997): 54–55.

15. Wang Jingyu, *Shijiu shiji xifang ziben zhuyi dui Zhongguo de jingji qin-lue* (Western Capitalism's Economic Invasion of China during the Nineteenth Century) (Beijing: Renmin chubanshe, 1983), 106–13; Huang Yifeng, "Guanyu jiu Zhongguo maiban jieji de yanjiu" (A Study of the Comprador Class in Old China), *Lishi yanjiu* (Historical Research) 87, no. 3 (June 15, 1964): 89–116, republished in Fudan daxue lishi xi (Fudan University History Department) et al., eds., *Jindai Zhongguo zichan jieji yanjiu* (Studies of the Capitalist Class in Modern China) (Shanghai: Fudan daxue chubanshe, 1984), 251–58; Nie Baozhang, "Lun yanghang maiban de benzhi tezheng—Da Riben xuezhe Gui-tan Daozhao jianyu yanbian 'Zhongguo jindai jingji shi' xiansheng shangjue" (On the Essential Subordination of Compradors in Foreign Firms—A Reply to the Discussion by Japanese Scholar Miyata Michiaki and Other Contributors to "The History of China's Modern Economy"), *Jindai Zhongguo* (Modern China) 3 (May 1993): 1–16.

16. Rhoads Murphey, *The Outsiders: The Western Experience in India and China* (Ann Arbor: University of Michigan Press, 1977), 103; Rhoads Murphey, "The Treaty Ports and China's Modernization," in Mark Elvin and G. William Skinner, eds., *The Chinese City between Two Worlds* (Stanford: Stanford University Press, 1974), 30, 35. It should be noted that Murphey has considered kerosene and cigarettes (the products sold in China by Standard Oil Company and British-American Tobacco Company) to have been more appealing to Chinese consumers than other Western goods generally were, but he has not made Standard Oil Company, British-American Tobacco Company, or any other foreign business an exception to his conclusion that Chinese merchants retained control over marketing of all imported goods—kerosene and cigarettes along with the rest. See Murphey, "The Treaty Ports," 30.

17. Hao Yen-p'ing, *The Comprador in Nineteenth-Century China: Bridge between East and West* (Cambridge, Mass.: Harvard University Press, 1970), chaps. 5–7.

18. Dwight H. Perkins, "Introduction: The Persistence of the Past," in Dwight H. Perkins, ed., *China's Modern Economy in Historical Perspective* (Stanford: Stanford University Press, 1975), 6.

19. Peter Duus, "Zaikabo: Japanese Cotton Mills in China, 1895–1937," in Peter Duus, Ramon H. Meyers, and Mark R. Peattie, eds., *The Japanese Informal Empire in China, 1985–1937* (Princeton: Princeton University Press, 1989), 96–97.

20. Emily Honig, *Sisters and Strangers: Women in the Shanghai Cotton Mills, 1919–1949* (Stanford: Stanford University Press, 1986), 80, 82, 87, 123.

21. William T. Rowe, *Hankow: Commerce and Society in a Chinese City, 1796–1889* (Stanford: Stanford University Press, 1984), 10, 317.

22. William C. Kirby, "China Unincorporated: Company Law and Business Enterprise in Twentieth-Century China," *Journal of Asian Studies* 54, no. 1 (February 1995): 46, 51.

23. G. William Skinner, "Regional Urbanization in Nineteenth-Century

China," in G. William Skinner, ed., *The City in Late Imperial China* (Stanford: Stanford University Press, 1977), 211–49.

24. Frederic Wakeman, Jr., and Yeh Wen-hsin, eds., *Shanghai Sojourners* (Berkeley: Institute of East Asian Studies, University of California, 1992).

CHAPTER 2. STANDARD OIL COMPANY

1. Chandler, *The Visible Hand*, 422.

2. Chandler, *Scale and Scope*, 94.

3. Ralph W. Hidy and Muriel E. Hidy, *Pioneering in Big Business, 1882–1911* (New York: Harper, 1955), 144–54.

4. Huang Yifeng, Jiang Duo, Tang Quanshi, and Chen Jiang, *Jiu Zhongguo de maiban jieji* (The Comprador Class in Old China) (Shanghai: Shanghai renmin chubanshe, 1982).

5. Hao, *The Comprador*, 12.

6. In 1876 this store was renamed Old Shunji Imports (Lao shunji yanghuo hang). Ho Ping-ti, *The Ladder of Success in Imperial China: Aspects of Social Mobility, 1368–1911* (New York: Columbia University Press, 1962), 308–9; Wang Jingyu, comp., *Zhongguo jindai gongye shi ziliao, dier ji* (Historical Materials on Modern Chinese Industry, 2d coll.) (Beijing: Kexue chubanshe, 1957), vol. 2, 954–56; Arnold Wright, ed., *Twentieth-Century Impressions of Hong Kong, Shanghai, and Other Treaty Ports of China: Their History, People, Commerce, Industries and Resources* (London: Lloyds Greater Britain Publishing Company, 1908), 560; *SJWS*, 264–68.

7. Ho, *The Ladder*, 309; Fan Xintian, "Wo suozhidaode Meifu gongsi" (What I Know about Standard Oil Company) (1964), reprinted in *Gong shang jingji shiliao congkan* (Collected Historical Materials on Industry, Commerce, and the Economy), no. 4 (Beijing: Wenshi ziliao chubanshe, 1984), 55; Min Wen, "Ying Mei san da you hang qinru Tianjin gaishu" (A Brief Account of the Invasion of Tianjin by Three Big British and American Petroleum Companies), in *Tianjin wenshi ziliao xuanji* (Collected Literary and Historical Materials on Tianjin), no. 28 (Tianjin: Tianjin renmin chubanshe, 1984), 115; Hao Yen-p'ing, *The Commercial Revolution in Nineteenth-Century China: The Rise of Sino-Western Mercantile Capitalism* (Berkeley: University of California Press, 1986), 274; Miao Lihua, "Meifu shiyou gongsi" (Standard Oil Company), *Jiu Shanghaide wai shang yu maiban* (Foreign Merchants and Compradors in Old Shanghai), in *Shanghai wenshi ziliao xuanji* (Collected Literary and Historical Materials on Shanghai), no. 56 (Shanghai: Shanghai renmin chubanshe, 1987), 45; *SJWS*, 265–66; Huang, "Guanyu jiu Zhongguo," 97; *North China Herald and Supreme Court and Consular Gazette,* January 3, 1900.

8. *North China Herald and Supreme Court and Consular Gazette,* January 3, 1900; Huang, "Guanyu jiu Zhongguo," 97. In the 1880s Ye diversified, investing in industrial enterprises, banks, and real estate. He opened his first factory, Xiechang Match Mill, at Shanghai in 1890 and added branch mills at Hankou and Suzhou in 1897. Meanwhile, he also started the Lunhua Silk Mill in 1894. In the late 1890s he held investments in five native banks (*qianzhuang*) and one modern bank, and his real estate company owned more than 400 mu

of property in Hongkou district of Shanghai. *SJWS*, 266–67; Zhongguo renmin yinhang (People's Bank of China), comp., *Shanghai qianzhuang shiliao* (Historical Materials on Shanghai's Native Banks) (Shanghai: Shanghai renmin chubanshe, 1961), 743–44.

9. Shiba Yoshinobu, "Ningpo and Its Hinterland," in G. William Skinner, ed., *The City in Late Imperial China* (Stanford: Stanford University Press, 1977), 437; Rowe, *Hankow,* 231; Leung Yuen Sang, "Regional Rivalry in Mid-Nineteenth-Century Shanghai: Cantonese vs. Ningpo Men," *Ch'ing-shih wen-t'i* 4, no. 8 (December 1982): 29–50; Susan Mann Jones, "The Ningpo *Pang* and Financial Power at Shanghai," in Mark Elvin and G. William Skinner, eds., *The Chinese City between Two Worlds* (Stanford: Stanford University Press, 1974), 73–96.

10. Bryna Goodman, *Native Place, City, and Nation: Regional Networks and Identities in Shanghai, 1853–1937* (Berkeley: University of California Press, 1995), chap. 1.

11. Fan, "Wo suozhidaode Meifu gongsi," 39; Wang Zhizhou, "Wo jia sandai maiban jishi" (My Family's Record as Compradors for Three Generations), in *Tianjin de yanghang yu maiban* (The Foreign Firms and Compradors of Tianjin) (Tianjin: Tianjin renmin chubanshe, 1987), 206. In North China, Wang Minghuai, in turn, created his own network of family members and native-place associates from Ningbo, and later he formed an alliance with the region's most powerful political and military leader, Li Hongzhang. See Huang Yifeng et al., *Jiu Zhongguo,* 251–53.

12. Zhou Jidong and Huang Ziquan, "Hankou Meifu yanghang jilue" (An Account of the Foreign Firm Standard Oil in Hankou) (1963), reprinted in *Wuhan gong shang jingji shiliao* (Historical Materials on Industry, Commerce, and the Economy of Wuhan), no. 2 (Wuhan: Guogu Hubeisheng xinsheng yinduchang, 1984), 26–28.

13. Jones, "The Ningpo *Pang,*" 82.

14. Hao, *The Comprador,* 186, 189; *Zhenhai xianzhi* (Gazetteer of Zhenhai district, 1931) vol. 27, 40a–b; Wright, ed., *Twentieth-Century Impressions,* 560.

15. *Zhenhai xianzhi,* vol. 27, 40a–b; *North China Herald and Supreme Court and Consular Gazette,* January 3, 1900.

16. Ho, *The Ladder of Success,* 309.

17. Quoted in Edward LeFevour, *Western Enterprise in Late Ch'ing China: A Selective Survey of Jardine, Matheson & Company's Operations, 1842–1895* (Cambridge, Mass.: East Asian Research Center, Harvard University, 1968), 144.

18. LeFevour, *Western Enterprise,* 145.

19. LeFevour, *Western Enterprise,* 145. LeFevour has inferred that "Ching Chang," the romanized name mentioned in Jardine's correspondence, "possibly" referred to Zheng Guanying, but in light of Ye's role as Standard Oil's sole agent and his Western associates' romanization of his given name in other documents as "Ching Chang" or "Ching Chong," there is no doubt that Jardine's managers were referring to Ye. For romanization of Ye's name as "Ching Chong," see, for example, *North China Herald and Supreme Court Gazette,*

January 3, 1900; and Wright, ed., *Twentieth-Century Impressions*, 560. On Ye's use of "Ching Chong" as the romanized name for his business, see *SJWS*, 265.

20. *SJWS*, 265.

21. *SJWS*, 265.

22. *SJWS*, 265; Minjian Shanghai weiyuanhui Shanghaishi gong shang lian (Committee on the Reconstruction of Shanghai and the Shanghai Alliance of Industry and Commerce), "Diguozhuyi shiyou qin Hua jianshu" (A Brief Account of Petroleum's Imperialistic Penetration into China), in *Gong shang jingji shiliao congkan* (Collected Historical Materials on Industry, Commerce, and the Economy), no. 4 (Beijing: Wenshi ziliao chubanshe, 1984), 22–23. When Ye ceased to distribute for Standard Oil, he began to carry kerosene supplied by European companies that are described later in this chapter.

23. Quoted in LeFevour, *Western Enterprise*, 146.

24. LeFevour, *Western Enterprise*, 145–46.

25. "Mr. Everall Retires," *Mei Foo Shield* 5, no. 10 (January 1929): 2; Fan, "Wo suozhidaode Meifu gongsi," 39.

26. Hao, *The Comprador*, 173–74.

27. Minjian Shanghaishi weiyuanhui, "Diguozhuyi," 23; Miao, "Meifu shiyou gongsi," 45; Wright, ed., *Twentieth-Century Impressions*, 558; Hao, *The Comprador*, 142.

28. Zhang Yi, "Meifu huoyou gongsi Guangzhou fengongsi qinli ji jianwen" (Memoirs and Experiences with the Guangzhou Branch of the Standard Oil Company), *Guangzhou wenshi ziliao* (Literary and Historical Materials on Guangzhou) 16 (1965): 2, 8.

29. On Melchers, see William C. Kirby, *Germany and Republican China* (Stanford: Stanford University Press, 1984), 13–14.

30. On this tendering to German firms, see G. C. Allen and Audrey G. Donnithorne, *Western Enterprise in Far Eastern Economic Development* (London: Allen and Unwin, 1954), 44–45.

31. Zhou and Huang, "Hankou," 26–28; Fan, "Wo suozhidaode Meifu gongsi," 38–39.

32. Hidy and Hidy, *Pioneering*, 265.

33. Hidy and Hidy, *Pioneering*, 265.

34. John Martin Rosenthal, "The China Market, Myth or Reality? The Case of Standard Oil, 1875–1918" (M.A. thesis, Cornell University, 1980), 16–23.

35. Rosenthal, "The China Market," 27–28.

36. Henri Deterding, *An International Oilman* (London: Harper and Brothers, 1934), 48.

37. Quoted in Kendall Beaton, *Enterprise in Oil: A History of Shell in the United States* (New York: Appleton-Century-Crofts, 1957), 32.

38. Quoted in Hidy and Hidy, *Pioneering*, 264.

39. Hidy and Hidy, *Pioneering*, 549.

40. Hidy and Hidy, *Pioneering*, 549; Beaton, *Enterprise*, 46–50.

41. Minjian Shanghaishi weiyuanhui, "Diguozhuyi," 24; Liu Wenlin, "Ying shang Yaxiya huoyou gongsi" (The British Asiatic Petroleum Company) (1964), reprinted in *Wuhan gong shang jingji shiliao*, 36.

42. Cao Zengxiang, "Yaxiya huoyou gongsi gaikuang" (On the Asiatic Petroleum Company), in *Jiu Shanghai wenshi ziliao xuanji* (Collected Literary and Historical Materials on Shanghai) (Shanghai: Shanghai renmin chubanshe, 1987), 58.

43. Cao, "Yaxiya," 57.

44. Liu, "Ying shang," 39; Yin Xiyao, "Meifu shiyou gongsi dui dongbei shichang de longduan" (Standard Oil Company's Monopoly of the Market in the Northeast), *Liaoning wenshi ziliao xuanji* (Collected Literary and Historical Materials on Liaoning) 3 (1963): 31–32; Ying Ziduo and Peng Suiliang, "Ying shang Yaxiya huoyou gongsi zhengduo Chongqing xiaochang" (Seizure of Chongqing's Markets by British Merchants in the Asiatic Petroleum Company), in *Chongqing gong shang shiliao* (Historical Materials on the Industry and Commerce of Chongqing), no. 1 (Chongqing: Chongqing chubanshe, 1982), 83.

45. Hu Yufen, "Huiyi Guangzhou Yaxiya shiyou gongsi" (Recollections of the Asiatic Petroleum Company in Guangzhou), in *Gong shang jingji shiliao congkan* (Collected Historical Materials on Industry, Commerce, and the Economy), no. 4 (Beijing: Wenshi ziliao chubanshe, 1984), 85.

46. Minjian Shanghaishi weiyuanhai, "Diguozhuyi," 23; Min Wen, "Ying Mei san da youhang," 120. The Five Foreign Goods Shop continued to serve as China's most common distributors of these five consumer products throughout the first half of the twentieth century. See STAB, July 7, 1937, p. 7; and H. L. Beemer to the General Manager in Shanghai, July 27, 1948, Standard Oil Papers, Shanghai Municipal Archives, file 13902/6829.

47. Liu, "Ying shang," 39–40; Hu, "Huiyi," 85.

48. The company retained this policy right up to the 1940s. See Cao, "Yaxiya," 58–59; and Minjian Shanghaishi weiyuanhui, "Diguozhuyi," 25.

49. Hidy and Hidy, *Pioneering*, 267.

50. "The Standard Oil Company in China," *Petroleum Review*, March 7, 1914.

51. On the locations of Standard Oil's concrete containers, each having a capacity of about 1,500 tons of oil, see Min Wen, "Ying Mei," 116; and Zhou and Huang, "Hankou," 26.

52. Fan gives several examples and quotes a "lien form" in English. Fan, "Wo suozhidaode Meifu gongsi," 39–40, 55–58.

53. Miao, "Meifu," 50; Fan, "Wo suozhidaode Meifu gongsi," 41; Zhou and Huang, "Hankou," 25–26.

54. Quoted in the *New York Sun*, April 13, 1913. For a fictionalized portrait of an American whom Standard Oil trained in New York and employed in China, see Alice Tisdale Hobart, *Oil for the Lamps of China* (New York: Grosset and Dunlop, 1933).

55. On the generous raises given to one successful representative, Harold Sheridan, see H. J. Sheridan to F. C. Sheridan, July 8, 1917; March 26, 1918; January 3, 1922. According to his regular (monthly and at times weekly) correspondence with his mother, salaries did not level off or decline until the late 1920s and early 1930s. See H. J. Sheridan to F. C. Sheridan, March 19, 1928 and May 20, 1933. All of these letters are in the Sheridan Papers.

56. H. J. Sheridan to F. C. Sheridan, April 13, July 7, September 21, 1913, Sheridan Papers; Fan, "Wo suozhidaode Meifu gongsi," 45–46.

57. H. J. Sheridan to F. C. Sheridan, July 13, 1913, Sheridan Papers.

58. H. J. Sheridan to F. C. Sheridan, August 13, 1913, Sheridan Papers.

59. H. J. Sheridan to F. C. Sheridan, January 31, 1915, Sheridan Papers.

60. H. J. Sheridan to F. C. Sheridan, September 21, 1913, Sheridan Papers.

61. *Mei Foo Shield* 5, no. 10 (January 1929): 11; Fan, "Wo suozhidaode Meifu gongsi," 45.

62. Fan, "Wo suozhidaode Meifu gongsi," 41; *New York Sun,* April 13, 1913.

63. Fan, "Wo suozhidaode Meifu gongsi," 39–40, 42–43.

64. H. J. Sheridan to F. C. Sheridan, August 13, 1913, Sheridan Papers.

65. *Mei Foo Shield* 5, no. 10 (January 1929): 11.

66. This term "native staff," as used by Standard Oil, was regarded by Chinese staff members as demeaning; they associated it with uncivilized primitive people (*tu ren*). Later, in 1927, when Chiang Kai-shek's Northern Expedition unleashed a wave of nationalistic protests in Shanghai, Chinese at Standard Oil complained to the Western management about this term and had it changed to "Chinese staff." Fan, "Wo suozhidaode Meifu gongsi," 46.

67. Fan, "Wo suozhidaode Meifu gongsi," 40.

68. Fan, "Wo suozhidaode Meifu gongsi," 46.

69. Fan, "Wo suozhidaode Meifu gongsi," 46.

70. Fan, "Wo suozhidaode Meifu gongsi," 46–47; Zhang Yi, "Meifu," 4.

71. Fan, "Wo suozhidaode Meifu gongsi," 46–47; Zhang Yi, "Meifu," 5.

72. Fan, "Wo suozhidaode Meifu gongsi," 47–48.

73. For examples of Chinese employees, see Zhang Yi, "Meifu," 5; Min Wen, "Ying Mei," 119–20. For an example of a Western employee, see H. J. Sheridan to F. C. Sheridan, September 21, 1913, January 11, 1914, November 28, 1915, April 15, 1916, July 7, 1927, August 30, 1927; H. J. Sheridan to R. M. Sheridan, May 16, 1915, all in Sheridan Papers.

74. Cao, "Yaxiya," 57–58.

75. A former employee noted that the company probably preferred these options because it hoped to use the large funds of cash deposits as working capital, but its plan was frustrated by Chinese agents' continuing preference to keep their deposits in Chinese yuan, which could be withdrawn at a moment's notice whenever they wished to terminate their contracts. See Fan, "Wo suozhidaode Meifu gongsi," 48–50.

76. Fan, "Wo suozhidaode Meifu gongsi," 50.

77. Carl Crow, *Foreign Devils in the Flowery Kingdom* (New York: Harper and Brothers, 1940), 48; "The Standard Oil Company in China," 262.

78. Fan, "Wo suozhidaode Meifu gongsi," 50–51.

79. P. C. Gibbons, "Are you Getting China's Drug Dollars?" *Export Advertiser* 2, no. 4 (April 1930): 8.

80. On the Qing dynasty's law of "avoidance," see Ch'u Tung-tsu, *Local Government in China under the Ch'ing* (Cambridge, Mass.: Harvard University Press, 1962), 21–22.

81. Cao, "Yaxiya," 57.

82. Minjian Shanghaishi weiyuanhui, "Diguozhuyi," 26–27; Fan, "Wo suozhidaode Meifu gongsi," 51; G. William Skinner, "Marketing and Social Structure in Rural China," *Journal of Asian Studies* 24, no. 1 (November 1964): 20.

83. Julean H. Arnold et al., *China: A Commercial and Industrial Handbook,* U.S. Department of Commerce, Trade Promotion Series No. 38 (Washington, D.C.: Government Printing Office, 1926), 87; Albert Feuerwerker, *The Foreign Establishment in China in the Early Twentieth Century* (Ann Arbor: Center for Chinese Studies, University of Michigan, 1976), 84.

84. John King Fairbank, *The Great Chinese Revolution: 1800–1985* (New York: Harper and Row, 1986), 179.

85. Hidy and Hidy, *Pioneering,* 552.

86. Fan, "Wo suozhidaode Meifu gongsi," 50.

87. Min Wen, "Ying Mei," 115–16; Yin, "Meifu shiyou gongsi," 30; Fan, "Wo suozhidaode Meifu gongsi," 57; Huang, "Guanyu jiu Zhongguo," 99.

88. Fan, "Wo suozhidaode Meifu gongsi," 57.

89. Min Wen, "Ying Mei," 120.

90. "The Standard Oil Company in China," 262.

91. Rosenthal, "The China Market," 36–41; Cheng Chu-yuan, "The United States Petroleum Trade with China, 1876–1949," in Ernest R. May and John K. Fairbank, eds., *America's China Trade in Historical Perspective: The Chinese and American Performance* (Cambridge, Mass.: Council on East Asian Studies, Harvard University, 1986), 220–23. These figures should be interpreted in light of two qualifications. First, the company trading in China here designated as "Standard" underwent several changes in identity during this period: it was known first as the Standard Oil Company until broken up by the U.S. Supreme Court in 1911; then as Standard Oil of New York, 1911–33; then as the Standard-Vacuum Oil Company from 1931 to 1962. Second, these figures indicate the percentages of the market that Standard shared with Texaco; I have combined the two because even though Standard Oil and Texaco competed in China, Standard never owned less than 50 percent of the stock in Texaco during this period. From a global perspective, it is worth noting that behind the long and confusing list of names of Standard and other firms is a broader continuity in the history of the oil industry. The independents and Standard's subsidiaries that were all formed before 1911 have dominated the worldwide petroleum industry ever since. See Irvine H. Anderson, Jr., "Petroleum as a Strategic Commodity in American-East Asian Relations" (paper prepared for the Conference on American–East Asian Economic Relations, Mt. Kisco, New York, June 25–27, 1976), 203–6; and Chandler, *The Visible Hand,* 353.

92. Wilkins, "The Impacts," 266; Michael H. Hunt, "Americans in the China Market: Economic Opportunities and Economic Nationalism, 1890s-1931," *Business History Review* 51 (Autumn 1977): 282–83.

93. Miao, "Meifu," 48.

94. Between the end of World War II in 1945 and the eve of the Communist victory in 1949, Standard Oil brought its marketing operation back "under Company (including Agency) control" at 308 of its 405 prewar locations according to its own calculations. See the quarterly report from Standard-Vacuum Oil Company's Reclamation and War Claims Department, January 28, 1949,

file 14510/8182, Standard-Vacuum Oil Company's Papers. See also Cheng Chu-yuan, "The United States Petroleum Trade," 214–20.

CHAPTER 3. BRITISH-AMERICAN TOBACCO COMPANY

1. Chandler, *The Visible Hand,* 389, 390.

2. On Standard Oil's unsuccessful searches for oil in China, see Cheng, "The United States Petroleum Trade," 225–30; Noel H. Pugach, "Standard Oil and Petroleum Development in Early Republican China," *Business History Review* 45, no. 4 (Winter 1971): 452–73.

3. FO 228/2154, Jordan to the Ministry of Foreign Affairs, May 31, 1912; *YM,* vol. 2, 540–42.

4. James A. Thomas, *A Pioneer Tobacco Merchant in the Orient* (Durham, N.C.: Duke University Press, 1928), 85–86.

5. Cheng Renjie, "Ying Mei yan gongsi maiban Zheng Bozhao" (British-American Tobacco Company's Comprador Zheng Bozhao), in *Wenshi ziliao xuanji* (Collected Literary and Historical Materials), no. 1 (Shanghai: Shanghai renmin chubanshe, 1978), 136; Wu Sing Pang, interview with the author, September 16, 1988; Sherman Cochran, *Big Business in China: Sino-Foreign Rivalry in the Cigarette Industry, 1890–1930* (Cambridge, Mass.: Harvard University Press, 1980), 15, 17, 242 n. 30.

6. James Lafayette Hutchison, *China Hand* (Boston: Lothrop, Lee and Shepard, 1936), 221.

7. Lee Parker and Ruth Dorval Jones, *China and the Golden Weed* (Ahoskie, N.C.: Herald, 1976), 33.

8. Jesse Gregory Lutz, *China and the Christian College, 1850–1950* (Ithaca: Cornell University Press, 1971), 505; interviews with Yu Aofeng, January 1964; *YM,* vol. 2, 524–26.

9. *YM,* vol. 2, 526–28, 540–43, 679; Cheng Renjie, "Ying Mei," 132–33; Cobbs to Cheang (Zheng), May 16, 1919, Thomas Papers; Cochran, *Big Business,* 16–22, 27–35, 131, 98.

10. Cheng Renjie, "Ying Mei," 135; *YM,* vol. 2, 543.

11. Wright, *Twentieth-Century Impressions,* 544; Lutz, *China,* 111.

12. Miao Lihua, "Wu Tingsheng yu Ying Mei yan gongsi" (Wu Tingsheng and British-American Tobacco Company), in *Jiu Shanghai de wai shang yu maiban,* 145; Thomas, *A Pioneer,* 131.

13. Miao, "Wu," 145–48; Cheng Renjie, "Ying Mei," 133.

14. Wu Sing Pang, "Mr. Wu Recalls His Family's BAT Links of Pre-war Years," *B.A.T. News* (Spring 1988): 10.

15. Wu, "Mr. Wu," 10.

16. Cheng Renjie, "Ying Mei," 134; *YM,* vol. 2, 629.

17. Miao, "Wu," 147–48.

18. Cheng Renjie, "Ying Mei," 137.

19. Cheng Renjie, "Ying Mei," 130.

20. Oi Senzo, "Shina ni okeru Ei-Bei tabako torasuto keiei keitai, zai-Shi gaikoku kigyo no hatten to baiben soshiki no ichikosatsu" (The Form of Administration of British-American Tobacco Company in China: A Study of the

Development of Foreign Enterprises in China and of the Comprador System), *Toa kenkyu shoho* (Report of the East Asia Institute) 26 (February 1944): 12–13; Marie-Claire Bergère, *The Golden Age of the Chinese Bourgeoisie, 1911–1937*, translated from the French by Janet Lloyd (Cambridge: Cambridge University Press, 1989), 145.

21. Cheng Renjie, "Ying Mei," 135–36; *YM*, vol. 2, 629.

22. Cheng Renjie, "Ying Mei," 134.

23. Thomas to Flowers, March 5, 1928, Thomas Papers.

24. Liu Hongsheng to his sons, January 7, 1933, file 14–013, Liu Papers. For a similar assessment of Zheng's wealth and stinginess, see the transcription of the interviews with Chen Chuxiang, Cheng Renjie, et al., December 3, 1962, in the Center for Research in Chinese Business History, Shanghai Academy of Social Sciences, Shanghai.

25. Cox, "Learning," 36.

26. "Ying Mei yancao gongsi zai Hua qiye ziliao huibian" (Collected Materials on the Enterprises of British-American Tobacco Company in China), vol. 4, 9.

27. Cheng Renjie, "Ying Mei," 131, 134–35.

28. Cheng Renjie, "Ying Mei," 131, 134.

29. Miao, "Wu," 146; Cheng Renjie, "Ying Mei," 133.

30. Miao, "Wu," 147.

31. Wu, "Mr. Wu," 10–11; Cochran, *Big Business,* 44–45.

32. Miao, "Wu," 146–47.

33. Miao, "Wu," 148.

34. Rose to the Earl of Gosford, April 5, 1924, quoted in Zhang Zhongli (Chang Chung-li), "The Development of Foreign Enterprise in Old China and Its Characteristics: The Case of the British-American Tobacco Company" (paper presented at the University of Washington, July 15, 1982), 21.

35. Cheng Renjie, "Ying Mei," 131.

36. Cheng Renjie, "Ying Mei," 135, 141; *YM*, vol. 2, 629.

37. Cheng Renjie, "Ying Mei," 137–38, 140; *YM*, vol. 2, 514, 524–31, 566–67, 580–81; Xiao Zhuwen, "Tianjin Ying Mei yan gongsi de jingji lüe-duo" (British-American Tobacco Company's Economic Plunder of Tianjin), *Tianjin wenshi ziliao xuanji* (Collected Literary and Historical Materials on Tianjin) 3 (1979): 185–87; contract from Thomas to Cheang (Zheng), May 16, 1919, Thomas Papers.

38. *YM*, vol. 2, 447; Cochran, *Big Business,* 132.

39. *YM*, vol. 2, 622–24, 628.

40. Cheng Renjie, "Ying Mei," 133–34.

41. Cheng Renjie, "Ying Mei," 133–34, 138.

42. Chen Zengnian, "Ying Mei yan gongsi de xiaoshouwang" (British-American Tobacco Company's Marketing Network), *Xueshu yuekan* (Academic Monthly) 140 (January 1981): 19–20; Wang Xi, "Yige guoji tuolasi zai Zhongguo de lishi jilu—Ying Mei yan gongsi zai Hua huodong fenxi" (A Historical Record of an International Trust in China: An Analysis of British-American Tobacco Company's Activities in China), in Chen Hansheng, ed., *Diguozhuyi gongye ziben yu Zhongguo nongmin* (Imperialistic Industrial Capital and Chinese Peasants) (Shanghai: Fudan daxue chubanshe, 1984), 111; Cheng Renjie,

"Ying Mei," 130, 163; *YM*, vol. 2, 423–29, 444–50, 526–32; Cochran, *Big Business,* 131.

43. Cochran, *Big Business,* 198; Xiao, "Tianjin," 185–87.

44. *YM*, vol. 2, 540–43; Cobbs to Cheang (Zheng), May 16, 1919, Thomas Papers; Cochran, *Big Business,* 16–22, 27–35, 131, 198.

45. For the few documented cases of the company's punishment of commission agents, see *YM*, vol. 2, 528–29, 610–19, 635–43, 679–86.

46. *YM*, 733–46. On BAT's competition from its chief rival, Chinese-owned Nanyang Brothers Tobacco Company, see Cochran, *Big Business.*

47. Cochran, *Big Business,* 16, 22, 129, 132, 137, 140–45, 164, 199.

48. Charles Tatlow, "Report," OSJ/6/4 (1920), Unilever Historical Archives, Unilever House, Blackfriars, London.

49. *YM*, vol. 3, 1115–17.

50. Chang Kuo-t'ao (Zhang Guotao), *The Rise of the Chinese Communist Party, 1921–1927,* vol. 1 of *The Autobiography of Chang Kuo-t'ao* (Lawrence: University of Kansas Press, 1971), 172.

51. British-American Tobacco Company, Ltd., *The Record in China of the British-American Tobacco Company, Limited* (Shanghai, 1925?), 14–21; *YM*, vol. 1, 151; Lowe Chuan-hua, *Facing Labor Issues in China* (London: Allen and Unwin, 1934), 65–71.

52. Rose to Jiliemu (Gilliam?), February 21, 1923, *YM*, vol. 3, 1121.

53. Elizabeth J. Perry, *Shanghai on Strike: The Politics of Chinese Labor* (Stanford: Stanford University Press, 1993), 136.

54. Perry, *Shanghai,* 153–56.

55. *YM*, vol. 3, 1127–28.

56. *YM*, vol. 3, 1053, 1113–14.

57. *YM*, vol. 3, 1135.

58. Yip Hon-ming, "Merchant Capital, the Small Peasant Economy, and Foreign Capitalism: The Case of Weixian, 1900s–1937" (Ph.D. dissertation, University of California at Los Angeles, 1988), 205.

59. Yip, "Merchant Capital," 200–206, 222; Chen Han Seng, *Industrial Capital and Chinese Peasants: A Study of the Livelihood of Chinese Tobacco Cultivators* (Shanghai: Kelly and Walsh, 1939), 26.

60. Yip, "Merchant Capital," 211; Cochran, *Big Business,* 22, 141.

61. Hsu Yung-sui, "Tobacco Marketing in Eastern Shantung," in Institute of Pacific Relations, comp. and trans., *Agrarian China: Selected Source Materials from Chinese Authors* (London: Allen and Unwin, 1939), 173; Yip, "Merchant Capital," 231–32; Chen, *Industrial Capital,* 50.

62. Zhang Jiatuo, "Ludong zhongyanqu sangeyue de guangan" (Impressions of Three Months in the Tobacco Cultivating Region of Eastern Shandong), *Dongfang zazhi* (Eastern Miscellany) 33, no. 6 (June 1936): 32–35; Yip, "Merchant Capital," 205–6.

63. Chen, *Industrial Capital,* 11; Yip, "Merchant Capital," 286–87.

64. *YM*, vol. 3, 997–98; Yip, "Merchant Capital," 206–8; Chen, *Industrial Capital,* 27; Zhang, "Ludong," 29–35.

65. Yip, "Merchant Capital," 228.

66. Min Chi, "Foreign Industrial Capital and the Peasantry in Honan,"

in Institute of Pacific Relations, *Agrarian China,* 176; Zhang Youyi, comp., *Zhongguo jindai nongye shi ziliao dier ji, 1912–1927* (Historical Materials on Modern Chinese Agriculture, 2d ed., 1912–27) (Beijing: Sanlian shudian, 1957), 201.

67. Min Chi, "Foreign Industrial Capital," 176–77; Chen, *Industrial Capital,* 29.

68. Wu, "Mr. Wu," 11; Chen, *Industrial Capital,* 29.

69. Min Chi, "Foreign Industrial Capital," 178–79; Chen, *Industrial Capital,* 30–32.

70. Min Chi, "Foreign Industrial Capital," 178; Wu, "Mr. Wu," 11.

71. Mira Wilkins and Howard Cox have reached different conclusions. As noted in chapter 1, Wilkins attributed BAT's success to its use of Western-style direct distribution and its reliance on Western expertise. In her brief discussion of BAT in China, she did not evaluate its reliance on Western institutions in detail (partly because she focused on American-controlled multinational corporations and BAT came under British control in the mid-1920s). In his article Cox evaluated BAT's reliance on Western institutions and attributed its success to "systems of market intelligence, of dealer guarantees, and of financial accounting procedures [that] were the products of Western business enterprise" (Cox, "Learning," 54). He argued that BAT's Western business expertise enabled it to distribute "in the furthest reaches of China" and to make Zheng Bozhao conduct business "increasingly along Western lines" (Cox, "Learning," 56). I agree that BAT introduced its Western "systems" in China but believe that Cox exaggerated BAT's transformation of Chinese commission agents' business practices and underestimated the capabilities of Chinese commission agents' social networks. In the 1920s and 1930s, after the company dismissed Wu Tingsheng (an advocate of Western business practices) and shifted responsibility to Zheng Bozhao and other Chinese commission agents, it readily accommodated Zheng by granting him autonomy and overlooking his violations of its regulations. To make a case to the contrary, one would need to demonstrate not merely that BAT provided an example from which Zheng learned lessons (as Cox has asserted) but that the company exposed Zheng's violations of its regulations and forced him to modify his behavior. On Cox's point about BAT's distributing "in the furthest reaches of China," it would be a mistake to assume that only a Western company using a Western approach could do so. For examples of Chinese traders distributing nationwide in China without relying on Western businesses or Western systems, see Wang Yeh-chien, "Spatial and Temporal Patterns of Grain Prices in China, 1740–1910" (paper presented at the conference on Spatial and Temporal Trends and Cycles in Chinese Economic History, Bellagio, Italy, August 1984); Rowe, *Hankow,* 54–62; and Thomas G. Rawski, *Economic Growth in Prewar China* (Berkeley: University of California Press, 1989), 145–55.

CHAPTER 4. MITSUI TRADING COMPANY

1. *KMBK,* 207.

2. *KMBK,* 240–41.

3. Ralph M. Odell, *Cotton Goods in China,* U.S. Department of Commerce, Bureau of Foreign and Domestic Commerce, Special Agents Series No. 107 (Washington D.C.: Government Printing Office, 1916), 7.

4. Chao Kang, *The Development of Cotton Textile Production in China* (Cambridge, Mass.: East Asian Research Center, Harvard University, 1977), 96.

5. Yamamura Kan'ichi, ed., *Toa shintaisei no senku: Mori Kaku* (Forerunner of a New Order in Asia: Mori Kaku) (Tokyo: Mori Kaku denki hensankai, 1940), chaps. 2–4, esp. 104, 111, 172.

6. Togai Yoshio, *Mitsui Bussan kaisha no keiei shiteki kenkyu* (A Study in Economic History of Mitsui Trading Company) (Tokyo: Tokyo keizai shinposha, 1974), 55.

7. *Yamamoto Jotaro: Denki* (Tokyo: Denki hensankai, 1942), 117–18; William D. Wray, "Japan's Big-Three Service Enterprises in China, 1896–1936," in Peter Duus, Ramon H. Myers, and Mark R. Peattie, eds., *The Japanese Informal Empire in China, 1895–1937* (Princeton: Princeton University Press, 1989), 46.

8. *KMBK,* 215–16; Douglas R. Reynolds, "Japan Does It Better: Toa Dobun Shoin (1900–1945) and Its Mission," in Akira Iriye et al., *Essays in the History of the Chinese Republic* (Urbana: University of Illinois Center for Asian Studies, 1983), 32.

9. Pan Siyue, "Xiamen Riben sanjing yanghang chuzhangsuo" (Mitsui's Branch Office in Xiamen), *Xiamen wenshi ziliao xuanji* (Xiamen Literary and Historical Materials), no. 4 (July 1983): 16–20.

10. Pan, "Xiamen," 37.

11. Minutes of the meeting of branch managers, general affairs division of Mitsui Trading Company, April 1902, Mitsui Bunko, Bussan file 197–1, 9–11; *KMBK,* 208–9; *MJS,* 52; Douglas R. Reynolds, "Chinese Area Studies in Prewar China: Japan's Toa Dobun Shoin in Shanghai, 1900–1945," *Journal of Asian Studies* 45, no. 5 (1986): 957.

12. Takamura Naosuke, *Nihon bosekigyoshi josetsu* (An Introduction to the History of the Cotton Spinning Industry in Japan), vol. 1 (Tokyo: Hanawa shobo, 1971), 189–98; Kuwayama Mikio, "Sogo-shosha and the Economic Development of Pre-war Japan" (Ph.D. dissertation, University of Toronto, 1982), 171–94, 497–99.

13. *KMBK,* 208; Ishii Kanji, "Nisshin sengo keiei" (Business after the Sino-Japanese War), *Iwanami koza, Nihon rekishi,* vol. 16, *Kindai* 3 (Tokyo: Iwanami shoten, 1976), 68.

14. Quoted by Murakami Ichiro, *Manshu to Mitsui* (Manchuria and Mitsui) (April 1941), in Mitsui Bunko, file 475, 27–28.

15. *KMBK,* 281–82; *MJS,* 53; Takamura Naosuke, *Kindai Nihon mengyo to Chugoku* (The Modern Japanese Cotton Industry in China) (Tokyo: Tokyo daigaku shuppankai, 1982), 61; Kuwayama, "Sogo-shosha," 208.

16. *KMBK,* 282; *MJS,* 52–53; Murakami, *Manshu,* 28; W. A. Graham Clark, *Cotton Goods in Japan and Their Competition on the Manchurian Market,* U.S. Department of Commerce, Bureau of Foreign and Domestic Commerce, Special Agents Series No. 86 (Washington, D.C.: Government Printing Office, 1914), 256.

17. Quoted by Murakami, *Manshu*, 29–30.

18. *KMBK*, 282, 362. On the Yokohama Specie Bank's alignment with Mitsui and the Japanese government in support of this plan, see Hamashita Takeshi, "Studies on Modern Chinese Business History in Japan" (paper presented at the Workshop on Chinese Business History, University of Akron, Akron, Ohio, October 28, 1995), 28–35.

19. Takamura, *Kindai,* 61.

20. *MJS,* 51–54.

21. Chao, *The Development,* 119–20; Odell, *Cotton Goods,* 28, 51, 60–61, 116; *KMBK,* 282; Takamura, *Kindai,* 61; Clark, *Cotton Goods,* 256.

22. Quoted in *MJS,* 53.

23. Negishi Tadashi, *Baiben seido no kenkyu* (A Study of the Comprador System) (Tokyo: Nihon tosho kabushiki kaisha, 1948), 209–11.

24. Robert H. G. Lee, *The Manchurian Frontier in Ch'ing History* (Cambridge, Mass.: Harvard University Press, 1970), 98.

25. Odell, *Cotton Goods,* 111.

26. Quoted in Odell, *Cotton Goods,* 115.

27. Odell, *Cotton Goods,* 113.

28. Odell, *Cotton Goods,* 106–7, 111.

29. George E. Anderson, *Cotton-Goods Trade in China,* U.S. Department of Commerce and Labor, Bureau of Manufactures, Special Consular Report No. 44 (Washington, D.C.: Government Printing Office, 1911), 30–31.

30. Murakami, *Manshu,* 30–31.

31. Quoted in *KMBK,* 282–83.

32. *KMBK,* 282; Odell, *Cotton Goods,* 60, 113; Clark, *Cotton Goods,* 272.

33. Clark, *Cotton Goods,* 260; Odell, *Cotton Goods,* 107.

34. Anderson, *Cotton-Goods Trade,* 29.

35. Odell, *Cotton Goods,* 107.

36. Takamura, *Nihon,* vol. 1, 199; Takamura, *Kindai,* 57–58; *MJS,* 81–85; *KMBK,* 241; Matsumoto Hiroshi, "Nihon shihonshugi kakuritsuki ni okeru Mitsui Bussan kaisha no hatten" (The Development of Mitsui Trading Company during the Formative Period of Japanese Capitalism), *Mitsui Bunko ronso* 7 (1973): 171–90.

37. *KMBK,* 357–59, 362–63; *MJS,* 78–83.

38. Anderson, *Cotton-Goods Trade,* 30.

39. Anderson, *Cotton-Goods Trade,* 30–31.

40. *MJS,* 88.

41. Cochran, *Big Business,* 16–22.

42. Clark, *Cotton Goods,* 264–65, 271–72.

43. Quoted in Odell, *Cotton Goods,* 115.

44. Clark, *Cotton Goods,* 272.

45. *KMBK,* 283, 362; China, Inspectorate General of Customs, *Decennial Reports, 1902–1911* (Shanghai, 1913), 72, 114, 135.

46. Odell, *Cotton Goods,* 58–59.

47. Pan, "Xiamen," 37.

48. Based on thorough research, the American diplomatic historian Michael

Hunt has concluded that for Standard Oil in China during the late nineteenth and early twentieth century "direct [American] government support was marginal to long-term success and to the solution of daily problems" (Hunt, "Americans," 297). My research on BAT shows that in China it sought and received help from officials representing the British and American governments during Chinese antiforeign boycotts and strikes, but by contrast with Mitsui, BAT did not gain exclusive access to any of China's regional markets as a result of intervention by its home government (Cochran, *Big Business,* 205 passim).

49. Thomas F. Millard, *America and the Far Eastern Question* (New York: Moffat, Yard, 1909), 227.

50. Paul A. Varg, *The Making of a Myth: The United States and China, 1897–1912* (East Lansing: Michigan State University Press, 1968), 139–46; Akira Iriye, *Pacific Estrangement: Japanese and American Expansion* (Cambridge, Mass.: Harvard University Press, 1972), 185–94; Michael H. Hunt, *Frontier Defense and the Open Door: Manchuria in Chinese-American Relations, 1985–1911* (New Haven: Yale University Press, 1973), 108–13.

51. Chao, *The Development,* chap. 9; Chao Kang, "The Chinese-American Cotton-Textile Trade," in May and Fairbank, eds., *America's China Trade,* 123–27; Bruce L. Reynolds, "The East Asian 'Textile Cluster' Trade, 1868–1973: A Comparative-Advantage Interpretation," in May and Fairbank, eds., *America's China Trade,* 131–33.

52. Marius B. Jansen, *The Japanese and Sun Yat-sen* (Cambridge, Mass.: Harvard University Press, 1954), 146–47, 161, 165–66, 185.

53. Scott J. Moss, *An Economic Theory of Business Strategy: An Essay in Dynamics without Equilibrium* (New York: Wiley, 1981), 110–11.

CHAPTER 5. NAIGAI COTTON COMPANY

1. This decision-making process has been ably analyzed by Kuwahara Tetsuya on the basis of painstaking research in archival sources. See Kuwahara, *Kigyo kokusaika no shiteki bunseki: senzenki Nihon boseki kigyo no Chugoku toshi* (An Analytic History of the Internationalization of Enterprises: Prewar Japanese Cotton Textiles Enterprises' Investments in China) (Tokyo: Moriyama shoten, 1990).

2. E. Patricia Tsurumi, *Factory Girls: Women in the Thread Mills of Meiji Japan* (Princeton: Princeton University Press, 1990), 194.

3. *Naigai wata kabushiki kaisha 50-nen shi* (A Fifty-Year History of the Naigai Cotton Company) (Osaka: Naigai wata kabushiki kaisha, 1937), 57; Takamura, *Kindai,* 119, table 7; Chao, *The Development,* 301, table 40; Jean Chesneaux, *The Chinese Labor Movement, 1919–1927,* translated from the French by H. M. Wright (Stanford: Stanford University Press, 1968), 84; Kuwahara Tetsuya, "The Establishment of Oligopoly in the Japanese Cotton-Spinning Industry and the Business Strategies of Latecomers: The Case of Naigaiwata & Co., Ltd.," in Nakagawa Keiichiro and Morikawa Hidemasa, eds., *Japanese Yearbook on Business History: 1986* (Tokyo: Japan Business History Institute, 1986), 124, 133–34 n. 43. Naigai rose from Japan's fortieth largest firm in 1918

(with assets of 15,612,000 yen) to Japan's twenty-sixth largest in 1930 (with assets of 46,548,000 yen). See Fruin, *The Japanese Enterprise System*, appendix, tables A.1–A.2.

4. Naigai was given its name in 1887. It was previously known as the Osaka Cotton Trading Company, which had operated in China between 1877 and 1887. *Naigai*, 6.

5. Kuwahara, "The Establishment," 107–8; *Naigai*, 34.

6. Kuwahara, "The Establishment," 105–6; Kuwahara, *Kigyo*, 76–77.

7. Kuwahara, "The Establishment," 124, 131 n. 29; Kuwahara, *Kigyo*, 97–100; Takamura, *Kindai*, 90; *Naigai*, 36–37; B. Y. Lee, "Japanese Influence in China's Cotton Industry," *China Weekly Review* 31, no. 6 (January 10, 1925): 159.

8. Quoted in Kuwahara, "The Establishment," 124.

9. Nishikawa Kiichi, *Chushi rodosha no genjo* (Present Conditions of Chinese Laborers) (Tokyo, 1925), 101–2, 180.

10. Lee, "Japanese Influence;" Tang Hai, *Zhongguo laodong wenti* (China's Labor Problems) (Shanghai, 1926), 97–98; Arno S. Pearse, *Cotton Industry of Japan and China* (Manchester: Taylor, Garnett, Evans, 1929), 161, 172.

11. B. Y. Lee, "Real Causes behind Japanese Mill Strikes," *China Weekly Review* 31, no. 13 (February 28, 1925): 363.

12. Lee, "Real Causes," 363.

13. Takamura, *Kindai*, 176.

14. Lee, "Real Causes," 363.

15. Udaka Yasushi, *Shina rodo mondai* (Labor Problems in China) (Shanghai: Kokusai bunka kenkyukai, 1926), 695.

16. Nishikawa, *Chushi*, 140; Takamura, *Kindai*, 176–77. See also Ono Kazuko, *Chinese Women in a Century of Revolution, 1850–1950* (Stanford: Stanford University Press, 1989), 118–19.

17. Takamura, *Kindai*, 179.

18. Honig, *Sisters*, 179, table 6.

19. Nishikawa, *Chushi*, 140; Udaka, *Shina*, 216.

20. Robin Porter, *Industrial Reformers in Republican China* (Armonk, N.Y.: M. E. Sharpe, 1994), 37.

21. Quoted in Porter, *Industrial Reformers*, 37; Udaka, *Shina*, 343; Nishikawa, *Chushi*, 140–41; H. D. Lamson, "The Problem of Housing for Workers in China," *Chinese Economic Journal* 11, no. 2 (1932): 139–62.

22. Nishikawa, *Chushi*, 140; Udaka, *Shina*, 344. Other Japanese cotton mills, notably Kanegafuchi Cotton Spinning Company and Shanghai Cotton Spinning Company (Shanghai boseki kabushiki kaisha), supplied similar housing for workers. See Nishikawa, *Chushi*, 133–35; Pearse, *Cotton Industry*, 165–69. The Japanese-owned South Manchuria Railway and the Sino-British Kailuan Mines also provided housing for Chinese workers in China at the time. See Lowe, *Facing Labor Issues*, 132; and Tim Wright, *Coal Mining in China's Economy and Society, 1895–1937* (Cambridge: Cambridge University Press, 1984), 179–80.

23. In Shanghai smaller Japanese cotton mills such as Toyo Boseki also had

company welfare programs, albeit less comprehensive ones. Nishikawa, *Chushi,* 138–44; Udaka, *Shina,* 139, 346; *Naigai,* 137–45; Kuwahara, *Kigyo,* 287.

24. Chesneaux, *The Chinese Labor Movement,* 214–17; and see chap. 6 below.

25. Rose to Jiliemu (Gilliam?), February 21, 1923, *Ying Mei,* vol. 3, 1121.

26. *Strikes and Lockouts,* appendix 1:1, 3, 4, 6, 8, 10, 11, 13; Takamura, *Kindai,* 100.

27. Liu Guanzhi, "Guanyu 1924–1925 nian Shanghai gongren yudong de huiyi" (Memoirs Concerning the Shanghai Labor Movement, 1924–1925) *Zhongguo gongyun shiliao* (Historical Materials on China's Labor Movement), no. 1 (1960): 96; *Jiu Zhongguo de zibenzhuyi shengchan guanxi* (Capitalist Relations of Production in Old China) (Beijing: Renmin chubanshe, 1977), 165–68.

28. Ono, *Chinese Women,* 131.

29. Quoted in Honig, *Sisters,* 51.

30. Honig, *Sisters,* 51.

31. Liu, "Guanyu 1924–1925 nian," 96.

32. Quoted in Martin W. Frazier, "Mobilizing a Movement: Cotton Mill Foremen in the Shanghai Strikes of 1925," *Republican China* 20, no. 1 (November 1994): 15. See also his table 2 on p. 14.

33. Liu, "Guanyu 1924–1925 nian," 109; Frazier, "Mobilizing a Movement," 12; Perry, *Shanghai,* 78.

34. Chang, *The Rise,* vol. 1, 414.

35. Liu, "Guanyu 1924–1925 nian," 104, 111–12; *Jiu Zhongguo,* 55.

36. Quoted in Honig, *Sisters,* 205.

37. The standard account of these events in English has long been Chesneaux, *The Chinese Labor Movement,* chap. 11. For a recent revisionist interpretation based on contemporary accounts by British police and a Japanese manager from Naigai, see Frazier, "Mobilizing a Movement," 20–23. For Naigai's published version, see *Naigai,* 70–74.

38. Quoted in Frazier, "Mobilizing a Movement," 29.

39. Liu, "Guanyu 1924–1925 nian," 114–16; Zhang Weizhen, "Zhang Weizhen tongzhi tan Shanghai wusa yundong" (Comrade Zhang Weizhen Talks about Shanghai's May Thirtieth Movement), *Dangshi yanjiu ziliao* (Research Materials on the Party History), no. 1 (Chengdu: Sichuan renmin chubanshe, 1982), 308.

40. These complaints were not exaggerations. See Frazier, "Mobilizing a Movement," 17–18; and Perry, *Shanghai,* 57 n.

41. Frazier, "Mobilizing a Movement," 23, 28–29; Liu, "Guanyu 1924–1925 nian," 134. The strikes continued against British-owned enterprises until September 30, 1925.

42. Quoted in *North China Herald,* July 3, 1926.

43. Quoted in *Jiu Zhongguo,* 165–68. Zhang Peide, "Luelun ershiniandai Shanghai de laozi guanxi" (On the Relations between Capital and Labor in Shanghai during the Twenties), in *Shanghai: Tongwang shijie zhiqiao* (Shanghai: Gateway to the World) (Shanghai: Shanghai shehui kexue yuan chubanshe,

1989), 26–27; "Strikes in Shanghai," *Chinese Economic Monthly* 3, no. 10 (October 1926): 463, 466.

44. Harold Isaacs, *The Tragedy of the Chinese Revolution*, 2d rev. ed. (Stanford: Stanford University Press, 1961), chaps. 10–11.

45. Perry, *Shanghai*, 88–103.

46. *Strikes and Lockouts*, appendix 1:65, 73; Zhu Bangxing, Hu Linge, and Xu Sheng, eds., *Shanghai chanye yu Shanghai zhigong* (Shanghai Industry and Shanghai Workers) (Hong Kong: Yuandong chubanshe, 1939), 110.

47. *Jiu Zhongguo*, 169; Xia Yan, *Baoshengong* (Contract Labor) (Beijing: Gongren chubanshe, 1959), 4.

48. Honig, *Sisters*, 119, 130; *Jiu Zhongguo*, 172–77; Zhu et al., eds., *Shanghai chanye*, 83. Kuwahara has noted that more than half of the Japanese-owned cotton mills in Shanghai used contract labor as of 1937. See his *Kigyo*, 281.

49. Honig, *Sisters*, 130.

50. Pearse, *Cotton Industry*, 149.

51. Kuwahara, *Kigyo*, 268; Zhu et al., eds., *Shanghai chanye*, 29; Kuwahara Tetsuya, pers. com., 1988.

52. Ono, *Chinese Women*, 118, table 4.

53. Ito Chu shoji kabushiki kaisha (C. Itoh Trading Company), *Ito Chu shoji hyakunenshi* (A Hundred-Year History of C. Itoh Trading Company) (Osaka: Ito Chu shoji kabushiki kaisha, 1969), 102–4, 120.

54. Naigai, 107–10; Ito, *Ito Chu*, 104, on Naigai in the Northeast. For descriptions of Japanese China specialists who fanned out from Qingdao to buy raw cotton and sell yarn and cloth in North China, see, on Shandong province in general, Philip C. C. Huang, *The Peasant Economy and Social Change in North China* (Stanford: Stanford University Press, 1985), 129–32; on eastern Shandong province, Yip, "Merchant Capital," chaps. 7–8, esp. 371, 385–98, 462–85; and, on western Shandong province, Kenneth Pomeranz, *The Making of a Hinterland: State, Society, and Economy in Inland North China, 1853–1937* (Berkeley: University of California Press, 1993), 72–73.

CHAPTER 6. SHENXIN COTTON MILLS

1. *RJ*, 281; Lai Chuen-yan David, "The Cotton Spinning and Weaving Industry in China: A Study in Industrial Geography" (Ph.D. dissertation, University of London, 1967), 116, table 31, 398–401, appendix 3.

2. Qian Zhonghan, "Minzu zibenjia: Rong Zongjing, Rong Desheng" (National Capitalists: Rong Zongjing and Rong Desheng), *Nanjing wenshi ziliao xuanji* (Collected Literary and Historical Materials on Nanjing) 2 (1963): 115; Wang Shaoguang, "Failure of Charisma: The Cultural Revolution in Wuhan" (Ph.D. dissertation, Cornell University, 1990), 132–33.

3. *RJ*, 54–56; Xu Weiyong and Huang Hanmin, *Rongjia qiye fazhan shi* (A History of the Rong Family's Enterprises) (Beijing: Renmin chubanshe, 1985), 33.

4. G. William Skinner, "Chinese Peasants and the Closed Community: An Open and Shut Case," *Comparative Studies in Society and History* 13 (1971): 277.

5. G. William Skinner, "Mobility Strategies in Late Imperial China: A Regional Systems Analysis," in Carol A. Smith, ed., *Regional Analysis*, vol. 1, *Economic Systems* (New York: Academic Press, 1976), 335–36.

6. Xu and Huang, *Rongjia*, 2. Earlier, at the tender age of seven, Rong had been sent for the first time to Shanghai to do an apprenticeship, but, still a small boy, he had become ill and soon returned to Wuxi. See *RJ*, 3.

7. *RJ*, 8; Xu and Huang, *Rongjia*, 5. On the Xue family's "empire of filatures and cocoons," see Lillian M. Li, *China's Silk Trade: Traditional Industry in the Modern World, 1842–1937* (Cambridge, Mass.: Council on East Asian Studies, Harvard University, 1981), 192–93. On the subsequent career of Rong Zongjing's son-in-law, Xue Shouxuan, see Lynda S. Bell, "From Comprador to County Magnate: Bourgeois Practice in the Wuxi County Silk Industry," in Joseph W. Esherick and Mary Backus Rankin, eds., *Chinese Local Elites and Patterns of Dominance* (Berkeley: University of California Press, 1990), 133–38.

8. *RJ*, 17–26; Xu and Huang, *Rongjia*, 12–13, 24.

9. Rong Desheng, *Lenong ziding xingnian jishi* (Autobiography of Rong Desheng) (n.p., 1943), 37b–38a, 40a.

10. Qian Zhonghan, "Wuxi de wuge zhuyao chanye ziben xitong de xingsheng yu fazhan" (The Formation and Development of Five Major Networks of Industrial Capital in Wuxi), *Wenshi ziliao xuanji* (Collected Literary and Historical Materials) 24 (1961): 138–42; "Wuxi Rongshi qiye jiazu jiqi qijia de mianfenye" (The Foundation for the Fortune of the Rong Family and the Flour Industry in Wuxi), *Xin shijie* (New World) (November 1944): 19; Gui Jirui, "Wuxi zai ershi niandai xingcheng jingji zhongxin de yuanyin jiqi zhineng" (Origins and Professional Capabilities behind Wuxi's Emergence as an Economic Center during the 1920s), *Lishi dang'an* (Historical Archives) 4 (1985): 107–12.

11. *RJ*, 51–52; Xu and Huang, *Rongjia*, 24.

12. Besides Rong Ruixing, other Wuxi sojourners who had invested in Rong Zongjing's enterprises included Zhu Zhongbu, a tax official assigned to a post in Guangdong province, and Zhu Dachun (Zhu Lanfang), a comprador at Jardine, Matheson and Company, who had moved from Wuxi to Shanghai in 1872 (one year before Rong Zongjing) and had become by the early twentieth century one of China's leading investors in industrial enterprises. See *RJ*, 13, 17–26; Xu and Huang, *Rongjia*, 7, 12–13, 24; Qian Zhonghan, "Minzu zibenjia," 115; Qian Zhonghan, "Wuxi," 110; Wellington K. K. Chan, *Merchants, Mandarins, and Modern Enterprise in Late Ch'ing China* (Cambridge, Mass.: Council on East Asian Studies, Harvard University, 1977), 148–52; Hao, *The Comprador*, 100–101, 134–36; Wang, *Zhongguo*, vol. 3, 959.

13. *RJ*, 48–49, 60–61; Zhang Tan, "The Origin and Early Development of the Jung Family Business (1896–1922)" (seminar paper, Michigan State University, 1985), 29.

14. *RJ*, 54–56; Xu and Huang, *Rongjia*, 32–33.

15. *RJ*, 59, 86–87; Xu and Huang, *Rongjia*, 26. For a revealing insight into the relationship between bold Rong Zongjing and prudent Rong Desheng by a

banker who knew them personally, see Yao Songlin, *Zhang hang fuwuji* (My Work at the Bank of China) (Taibei: Zhuanji wenxue zazhishe, 1968), 20.

16. Xu and Huang, *Rongjia,* 30.

17. *RJ,* 95.

18. *RJ,* 95–97, 410–11; Xu and Huang, *Rongjia,* 31–34.

19. *RJ,* 90–94; Zhou Zhengang, "Wuhan de Rongjia qiye" (The Rong Family Enterprises in Wuhan), *Dang'an yu lishi* (Archives and History) 5 (1986): 76.

20. One of these factories, Shenxin Mill No. 6, was originally opened in Changzhou in 1925, but it was moved to Shanghai in 1930. See *RJ,* 283.

21. *RJ,* 461–62.

22. *RJ,* 100.

23. Rong Zongjing's purchasing agents dealt with food guilds (*liang hang*), paying a 1–1.5 percent commission; food guilds, in turn, dealt with rural township guilds (*xiang hang*), paying a 1 percent commission; and rural township guilds bought grain from peasants, exacting a 2 percent commission from them. *RJ,* 82–83, 101–2; Wuxishi zhengxie wenshi ziliao yanjiu weiyuanhui (Wuxi People's Consultative Conference Committee on Literary and Historical Materials), "Minzu zibenjia Rongshi fazhan jianshi gao" (A Brief History of the Development of the Rong Family as National Capitalists), *Wuxi wenshi ziliao* (Literary and Historical Materials on Wuxi), pt. 1 (May 19, 1980): 65.

24. *RJ,* 553.

25. Xu and Huang, *Rongjia,* 86–87.

26. Yao, *Zhong hang,* 19.

27. *Strikes and Lockouts,* appendix 1.

28. *RJ,* 320–34.

29. As Perry has pointed out, I proposed in an earlier study the hypothesis that nationalism caused Chinese workers to go on strike more often against foreign-owned companies than against Chinese-owned ones. In light of her recent research and my own (as presented in this chapter and chaps. 3 and 5), I am now persuaded that Chinese workers did not go on strike primarily because of nationalism. See Perry, *Shanghai,* 163–64; Cochran, *Big Business,* 207–8.

30. Perry, *Shanghai,* 164 n., 248–53.

31. *RJ,* 288.

32. Wuxishi, "Minzu zibenjia Rongshi," pt. 3, 78; *RJ,* 287–88; Qian, "Minzu zibenjia," 117.

33. *Maoxin Fuxin Shenxin zong gongsi sazhounian jiniance 1898–1928* (Thirtieth Anniversary Volume Commemorating the Maoxin and Fuxin Flour Mills, the Shenxin Cotton Mills, and the General Corporation) (Shanghai: Maoxin Fuyin Shenxin zong gongsi, 1929), 1–22; Wuxishi, "Minzu zibenjia Rongshi," pt. 2, 78; *RJ,* 287–89.

34. Xu and Huang, *Rongjia,* 39.

35. Li Guowei, "Rongjia jingying fangzhi he zhifen qiye liushinian gaishu" (Sixty Years of the Rong Family Business in the Management of Textile and Flour Industries), *Wenshi ziliao xuanji* (Collected Literary and Historical Materials) 7 (1980): 31.

36. Xu and Huang, *Rongjia,* 39; *RJ,* 222; Rong, *Lenong,* 25–26.

37. *RJ,* 222; Xu and Huang, *Rongjia,* 79, 243–44; Wuxishi, "Minzu ziben-jia Rongshi," pt. 2, 76.

38. Earlier the Rongs had sent family members abroad on buying trips. On Rong Yuequan's trip in 1919, see *RJ,* 69. On the prominence of the Lowell Tex-tile School, see Melvin Thomas Copeland, *The Cotton Manufacturing Industry of the United States* (Cambridge, Mass.: Harvard University Press, 1912), 136; and Arthur L. Eno, Jr., "Minds among the Spindles: A Cultural History," in Arthur L. Eno, ed., *Cotton Was King: A History of Lowell, Massachusetts* (Lowell: Massachusetts Historical Society, 1976), 238.

39. Rong, *Lenong,* 61; Wuxishi, "Minzu zibenjia Rongshi," pt. 3, 78; "Wuxi Rongshi," 25; Xu and Huang, *Rongjia,* 243–44; Qian Mu, *Bashi yi shuangqin: Shiyou zayi* (Reminiscences at the Age of Eighty about My Parents: Memories of Teachers and Friends) (Changsha: Yulu shushe, 1987), 230–32; Jerry Dennerline, *Qian Mu and the World of Seven Mansions* (New Haven: Yale University Press, 1988), 67, and, for photographs, 34.

40. *RJ,* 137.

41. *RJ,* 155–59; Xu and Huang, *Rongjia,* 76–78.

42. *RJ,* 159–63; Xu and Huang, *Rongjia,* 76–78; Kong Lingren et al., eds., *Zhongguo jindai qiye de kaituo zhe* (Pioneers in Modern Chinese Enterprises) (Jinan: Shandong renmin chubanshe, 1991), vol. 2, 140.

43. *RJ,* 155–56, 584–86; Xu and Huang, *Rongjia,* 115–19; Xue Mingjian, "Banli Shenxin san chang laogong shiye de jingyan" (My Experiences Handling Welfare for Workers in Shenxin's No. 3 Factory), *Jiaoyu yu zhiye* (Education and Vocations) 165 (1935): pt. 2, 411–12.

44. *RJ,* 163, 581–82; Xue, "Banli Shenxin," pt. 1, 336–38, pt. 2, 413; Xu and Huang, *Rongjia,* 76–78.

45. Kong et al., eds., *Zhongguo,* vol. 2, 291–300; Xu and Huang, *Rongjia,* 243.

46. *RJ,* 583–84.

47. *RJ,* 583–84; Xu and Huang, *Rongjia,* 115–17.

48. *RJ,* 284.

49. Zhu et al., *Shanghai chanye,* 25–60, esp. 30.

50. Honig, *Sisters,* 114, 179–80; Lai, "The Cotton Spinning and Weaving Industry," 399.

51. *RJ,* 211–12; Mei Zhengshao, *Haishang wenren Du Yuesheng* (The Coastal Celebrity Du Yuesheng) (Zhengzhou: Henan renmin chubanshe, 1987), 105–7.

52. Perry, *Shanghai,* 98–99. On Du's influence in Shanghai, see also Frederic Wakeman, Jr., *Policing Shanghai, 1927–1937* (Berkeley: University of Califor-nia Press, 1995); and Brian G. Martin, *The Shanghai Green Gang: Politics and Organized Crime, 1919–1937* (Berkeley: University of California Press, 1996).

53. Honig, *Sisters,* 123.

54. Shen Feide et al., eds., *Jiu Shanghai de yan du chang* (Old Shanghai's Opium, Gambling, and Prostitution) (Shanghai: Baijia chubanshe, 1988), 234.

55. *RJ,* 195–97. This passage includes minutes of the meetings of the Asso-ciation of Chinese Cotton Mill Owners for May 2, 4, and 16, 1927, which pro-

vide more precise details than have been previously available on this case. This evidence shows that the members of the association bought shares of the government's bonds according to the number of spindles in their factories at Shanghai, Wuxi, and Changzhou. Under this arrangement, Rong Zongjing and Rong Desheng, as Shenxin's owners, had to buy bonds valued at approximately 100,000 yuan. This figure confirms the estimate of 100,000 yuan made by Rong Yiren (Rong Desheng's son) in 1956 and cuts down to size overestimates that have ranged from 250,000 yuan to as high as 1,000,000 yuan. For overestimates by historians and by journalists (as cited by historians), see Parks M. Coble, Jr., *The Shanghai Capitalists and the Nationalist Government, 1927–1937* (Cambridge, Mass.: Council on East Asian Studies, Harvard University, 1980), 35; and Richard C. Bush, *The Politics of Cotton Textiles in Kuomintang China, 1927–1937* (New York: Garland, 1982), 113.

56. Bush, *The Politics of Cotton Textiles,* 110–12.

57. *RJ,* 196–98; Bush, *The Politics of Cotton Textiles,* 111–13.

58. *RJ,* 202. For an interpretation of business-government relations along these official lines, see Coble, *The Shanghai Capitalists,* chaps. 3–5.

59. Bush, *The Politics of Cotton Textiles,* 214–15.

60. Quoted in Bush, *The Politics of Cotton Textiles,* 215–16.

61. Quoted in Bush, *The Politics of Cotton Textiles,* 218.

62. *RJ,* 262, 370, 388, 391–94, 549; Bush, *The Politics of Cotton Textiles,* 220–25; Coble, *The Shanghai Capitalists,* 136–39; Parks M. Coble, Jr., *Facing Japan: Chinese Politics and Japanese Imperialism, 1931–1937* (Cambridge, Mass.: Council on East Asian Studies, Harvard University, 1991), 158–59.

63. Bush, *The Politics of Cotton Textiles,* 223–24; Coble, *The Shanghai Capitalists,* 129–32.

64. Bush, *The Politics of Cotton Textiles,* 226, 230.

65. *RJ,* 411–13. On the Political Study Clique as a group held together by "strong personal ties," see Tien Hung-mao, *Government and Politics in Kuomintang China, 1927–1937* (Stanford: Stanford University Press, 1972), 65–71.

66. Qian, "Wuxi," 115–16. Perhaps because he was Rong Zongjing's heir apparent, Rong Hongyuan seems to have been a prime target for criticism. In particular, he was accused of bad judgment in buying North American wheat, which resulted in heavy losses for Fuxin. See *RJ,* 380, 408.

67. *RJ,* 414–26; Xu and Huang, *Rongjia,* 96–101; Bush, *The Politics of Cotton Textiles,* 233–43.

68. *RJ,* 432–33.

69. *RJ,* 466–67; Bush, *The Politics of Cotton Textiles,* 244–46.

70. *RJ,* 464–65.

71. Bush has also described related events (including the proposed auction of one of Shenxin's mills and the role of Japanese in the transaction) that precipitated Rong Zongjing's struggle with officials in the Nationalist government. See Bush, *The Politics of Cotton Textiles,* chap. 5.

72. Rong was not alone in using native-place connections to defend himself against the Nationalist government in the 1930s. For other examples, see Goodman, *Native Place,* 286.

73. Kirby, "China Unincorporated," 51.

74. For other examples of hierarchical and authoritarian Chinese networks, see chap. 4 above; and Perry, *Shanghai*, 50–52.

CHAPTER 7. CHINA MATCH COMPANY

1. Håkan Lindgren, *Corporate Growth: The Swedish Match Industry in Its Global Setting* (Stockholm: Liber Forlag, 1979), pt. 3 and 352–57, tables 20–22; Håkan Lindgren, "The Kreuger Crash of 1932: In Memory of a Financial Genius, or Was He a Simple Swindler?" *Scandinavian Economic History Review* 30, no. 3 (1982): 202.

2. Wang, "Failure of Charisma," 132–33.

3. Rong did play a leading role in one large bureaucratic organization, the Association of Chinese Cotton Mill Owners, but he tried to subordinate it to his own network. On his "selfish" efforts and failures at leadership of the association, see Bush, *The Politics of Cotton Textiles*, 329 passim.

4. Liu's Hongsheng Mills were valued at 579,245 yuan, one partner's Yingchang Match Mills at 716,811 yuan, and the other partner's Zhonghua Match Mills at 300,062 yuan. *ZMHG*, 60.

5. Yeh Wen-hsin, *The Alienated Academy: Culture and Politics in Republican China, 1919–1937* (Cambridge, Mass.: Council on East Asian Studies, Harvard University, 1990), 75.

6. Liu Nianzhi, *Shiyejia Liu Hongsheng chuanlü—huiyi wode fuqin* (A Biography of the Industrialist Liu Hongsheng—Reminiscences of My Father) (Beijing: Wenshi ziliao chubanshe, 1982), 2–3; *LHS*, 3.

7. *LHS*, vol. 1, 311; Yeh, *The Alienated Academy*, 323 n. 73; *Men of Shanghai and North China* (Shanghai: University Press, 1935), 341.

8. *LHS*, vol. 1, 295, 311.

9. Hu Shigui, "Wo suozhidao de Liu Hongsheng xiansheng" (What I Know about Mr. Liu Hongsheng), in *Tongzhan gongzuo shiliao xuanji: Shanghai wenshi ziliao* (Collected Materials on the Work of the United Front: Collected Literary and Historical Materials on Shanghai), no. 8 (Shanghai: Shanghai renmin chubanshe, 1989), 176–77.

10. Ellsworth C. Carlson, *The Kaiping Mines (1877–1912)* (Cambridge, Mass.: East Asian Research Center, Harvard University, 1957), 82, 146; Liu, *Shiyejia Liu Hongsheng*, 7–8.

11. Liu, *Shiyejia Liu Hongsheng*, 6–13; *ZMHG*, 56–57; *LHS*, vol. 1, 21; Carlson, *The Kaiping Mines*, 82, 146.

12. Liu, *Shiyejia Liu Hongsheng*, 6–13; Wright, *Coal Mining*, 100; *ZMHG*, 56–57; *LHS*, 283–84, 324–30; Zhang Meizhi, "Zhongguo xindai qiye de jingying xintai: Yi Liu Hongsheng qiye weili de ge'an yanjiu (1911–1949)" (Management of China's Modern Enterprises: A Case Study of Liu Hongsheng's Enterprises [1911–1949], M.A. thesis, National Taiwan University, 1987), 175.

13. Dong Qijun, "Ningbo luhu tongxianghui" (The Association of Ningbo Sojourners in Shanghai), *Zhejiang wenshi ziliao xuanji* (Collected Literary and Historical Materials on Zhejiang) 39 (March 1989): 48.

14. Liu, *Shiyejia Liu Hongsheng,* 4–5, 14–15; *LHS,* vol. 2, 18, 81–82.

15. See Jones, "The Ningpo *Pang,*" 82–83.

16. *LHS,* vol. 1, 6, 18, 23, 33, 58, 72, 76, 159.

17. Lu Zhilian, "'Qiye dawang' Liu Hongsheng" (King of the Entrepreneurs Liu Hongsheng), *Zhejiang wenshi ziliao xuanji* (Collected Literary and Historical Materials on Zhejiang) 39 (March 1989): 153.

18. Hu, "Wo suozhidaode Liu Hongsheng xiansheng," 167–69; Liu, *Shiyejia Liu Hongsheng,* 32, 34; *LHS,* vol. 2, 316–19.

19. "Shanghai Woolen Textile Factories," *Chinese Economic Journal* 11, no. 6 (December 1932): 443.

20. Liu, *Shiyejia Liu Hongsheng,* 30.

21. *LHS,* 315.

22. Liu, *Shiyejia Liu Hongsheng,* 58.

23. Liu, *Shiyejia Liu Hongsheng,* 54, 58, 74–75; *LHS,* 315.

24. *ZMHG,* 82; *LHS,* 79–80, 323.

25. Sandren to Lieu [Liu], February 4, 1926, file 02–003, Liu Papers; *LHS,* vol. 1, 28, 60.

26. *LHS,* vol. 1, 137–38. Shao Erkang's home county in Ningbo prefecture was Zhenhai. See *Chuka zenkoku chu nichi jitsugyoka koshinroku (Shanghai no bu),* 239.

27. *LHS,* vol. 1, 133–34.

28. *ZMHG,* 60–65; *LHS,* vol. 1, 137, 146–49.

29. *LHS,* vol. 1, 349–54; *ZMHG,* 82.

30. *ZMHG,* 71–73.

31. *ZMHG,* 78–81.

32. Eurén to Fr. Ljungberg, March 3, 1934, *China Manschuriet 1934,* Swedish Match Archives. For details on Swedish Match's operations in China, see Sherman Cochran, "Losing Money Abroad: The Swedish Match Company in China during the 1930s," *Business and Economic History,* 2d ser., 16 (1987): 83–91; and Sherman Cochran, "Three Roads into Shanghai's Market: Japanese, Western, and Chinese Companies in the Match Trade, 1895–1937," in Wakeman and Yeh, eds., *Shanghai Sojourners,* 46–56.

33. *LHS,* vol. 1, 147; vol. 2, 171.

34. Liu to his sons, April 23, 1932, file 14–042, Liu Papers.

35. Fr. Ljungberg to Eurén, July 13, 1934, *China Manschuriet 1934,* Swedish Match Archives.

36. Eurén to Swedish Match, March 20, 1933, *STAB Korr China 1933,* Swedish Match Archives.

37. *LHS,* vol. 2, 153–54; *ZMHG,* 76.

38. *LHS,* vol. 2, 149–50.

39. Li Zheng, "Zhengda huochai chang" (Zhengda Match Mill), *Ningbo wenshi ziliao* (Literary and Historical Materials on Ningbo) 6 (October 1987): 30–31, 33–34.

40. Eurén to Swedish Match, May 20 and November 24, 1933, *STAB Korr China 1933,* Swedish Match Archives.

41. Eurén to Swedish Match, November 24, 1933, *STAB Korr China 1933,* Swedish Match Archives.

42. Eurén to Swedish Match, March 2, 1934, *China Manschuriet 1934*, Swedish Match Archives.

43. *ZMHG*, 101; *LHS*, vol. 2, 177–81, 187. A copy of the cartel agreement appears in *LHS*, vol. 2, 177–82.

44. Eurén to Lieu [Liu], February 27, 1934, *China Manschuriet 1934*, Swedish Match Archives.

45. A copy of the agreement between the Joint Sales Office and Swedish Match dated July 27, 1935, appears in *Ing. F. Dahl, Kina Div Avtal 1935–39*, Swedish Match Archives; and *LHS*, vol. 2, 189–194.

46. *ZMHG*, 106–7; Zhang Qifu and Wei Heng, *Huochai dawang Liu Hongsheng* (Liu Hongsheng the Match King) (Xinxiang, Henan: Henan renmin chubanshe, 1990), 119–21; "Memorandum on Limitation of Production of Match Factories," May 25, 1934, *China Manschuriet 1934*; *LHS*, vol. 2, 196–97, 201, 204–6.

47. Agreement dated July 27, 1935, in *Ing F. Dahl, Kina Div. Avtal 1935–39*, vol. 10, no. 47, Swedish Match Archives.

48. *ZMHG*, 104–5.

49. Handwritten addendum to memo of January 28, 1936, *Ing F. Dahl, Kina Div. Avtal 1935–39*, vol. 10, no. 47.

50. *ZMHG*, 100.

51. Coble, *The Shanghai Capitalists*, 240–50; Bergère, *The Golden Age*, 288–93; Kirby, *Germany*, 90–101, 262–64.

52. *ZMHG*, 41, 59–60, 96–98.

53. Number Two Archives, file 825/293 on the match industry; *ZMHG*, 96–99; *LHS*, vol. 2, 96–99, 172–73.

54. *LHS*, vol. 2, 207, 211–13.

55. Memo, January 28, 1936, *Ing F. Dahl, Kina Div. Avtal 1935–39*, vol. 10, no. 4; *ZMHG*, 109–110.

56. *LHS*, vol. 1, 303; vol. 2, 26, 173, 211; *ZMHG*, 99–100; Zhang and Wei, *Huochai dawang*, 121–22; Hu, "Wo suozhidaode Liu Hongsheng xiansheng," 176–77.

57. *LHS*, vol. 2, 211; Huai Shu, *Zhongguo jingji neimo* (Behind the Scenes in the Chinese Economy) (Hong Kong: Xinmin ju chubanshe, 1948), 85–86.

58. Liu to Wu, March 13, 1936, Liu Papers, compiled under "Zhongguo xiandai zhengzhi shi ziliao huigao" (Collection of Materials on Modern China's Political History), vol. 2, no. 23, 5219.

59. Wu Dingchang, "Zhonghua quanguo huochai chan xiao lianyingshe de shewu yu lianying jiufen, 1936–1937 nian" (Business Affairs and Disputes of China's National Match Union, 1936–1937), Liu Hongsheng Papers.

60. *ZMHG*, 119–20.

61. Quotations from memo, January 28, 1936, and Eurén to Swedish Match, February 19, 1937, both in *Ing F. Dahl, Kina Div. Avtal 1935–39*; and from the enclosure in the letter from Amfeaco (the China branch of Swedish Match) to Swedish Match, July 24, 1937, *STAB Statistical Department, Marknadsanalyser* (1935), all in Swedish Match Archives.

62. *ZMHG*, 106, 120–21; Eurén to Swedish Match, February 19, 1937, *Ing F. Dahl, Kina Div. Avtal 1935–39*, vol. 10, no. 47.

63. *ZMHG*, 88–91, 105, 110–16, 118; *LHS*, vol. 2, 230–42.

64. Memorandum Regarding Consolidation Excise Tax on Matches in China, *STAB Statistical Department Marknadsanalyser* (1935).

65. Coble, *The Shanghai Capitalists*, 240–50; Bergère, *The Golden Age*, 288–93; Kirby, *Germany*, 90–101, 262–64.

66. For a parallel case, see Lynda Bell's account of Xue Shouxuan's "merger strategy" in forming the Xingye Silk Company at Wuxi in 1936 and Xue's success at developing it by working "in tandem" with the Nationalist government. Lynda S. Bell, "One Industry, Two Chinas: Silk Filatures and Peasant-Family Production in Wuxi County, 1865–1937" (unpublished manuscript), 252–63.

67. Liu, *Shiyejia Liu Hongsheng*, 69–70.

68. In 1936 Liu's eldest son, Liu Nianren, questioned the reliability of Liu Hongsheng's most trusted associate, Hua Runchuan, and conducted a reaudit of Hua's account books dating back to 1932. In the same year Liu Nianren and one of his brothers replaced Hua as the only managers authorized to sign checks on behalf of Liu Hongsheng See Chan Kai Yiu, "The Management of Modern Business in Republican China: The Case of Liu Hongsheng and His Enterprises, 1920–1937" (paper presented at the conference the Rise of Business Corporations in China from Ming to Present, University of Hong Kong, July 12–13, 1996). During the next few years, Liu occasionally intervened and overruled his sons, but by 1941 he seemed to have given them responsibility for managing virtually all of the family's assets. Lieu [Liu] to his sons, June 25, 1939, and Lieu [Liu] to Franklin and other boys and girls, October 14, 1941, both in file 14–041, Liu Papers.

CHAPTER 8. CONCLUSION: CORPORATIONS AND NETWORKS

1. Irvine H. Anderson, Jr., *The Standard-Vacuum Oil Company and United States East Asian Policy, 1933–1941* (Princeton: Princeton University Press, 1975); Marie-Claire Bergère, "Shanghai Capitalists and the Transition from Nationalist to Communist Regime (1948–1952)," in Lee Yung-san and Liu Ts'ui-jung, eds., *China's Market Economy in Transition* (Taipei: Academia Sinica, 1990); Sherman Cochran, "Businesses, Governments, and War in China, 1931–1949," in Akira Iriye and Warren Cohen, eds., *American, Chinese, and Japanese Perspectives on Wartime Asia, 1931–1949* (Wilmington, Del.: Scholarly Resources, 1990); Parks M. Coble, "Chinese Capitalism in the Lower Yangzi Area during the Sino-Japanese War, 1937–1945" (paper presented at the annual meeting of the Association of Asian Studies for the Midwest Region, University of Western Illinois, September 24, 1994).

2. Chandler, *The Visible Hand*, 350–53; Cochran, *Big Business*, 270; Yamazaki Hiroaki, "The Logic of the Formation of General Trading Companies in Japan," in Yonekawa Shin'chi and Yoshihara Hideki, eds., *Business History of General Trading Companies, the International Conference on Business History 13, Proceedings of the Fuji Conference* (Tokyo: University of Tokyo Press, 1987); Ozawa Terutomo, *Multinationalism, Japanese Style: The Political Economy of Outward Dependency* (Princeton: Princeton University Press, 1979);

Bergère, "Shanghai Capitalists"; *ZMHG*, 142–52, 224; Jasper Becker, "Hardship in Shanghai as Spindles Stop," *South China Morning Post,* Hong Kong, December 21, 1996, 20.

3. On this subject the literature is rich. On American history, see David Montgomery, *The Fall of the House of Labor: The Workplace, the State, and American Labor Activism* (Cambridge: Cambridge University Press, 1987); Daniel Nelson, *Managers and Workers: Origins of the New Factory System in the United States, 1880–1920* (Madison: University of Wisconsin Press, 1975); Tamara Hareven, *Family Time and Industrial Time* (Cambridge: Cambridge University Press, 1982); and Jacoby, *Employing Bureaucracy.* On British history, see Reinhard Bendix, *Work and Authority: Ideologies of Management in the Course of Industrialization* (New York: Wiley, 1956); E. J. Hobsbawm, *Labouring Men: Studies in the History of Labour* (Garden City, N.Y.: Doubleday, 1964); and Littler, *The Development.* On Japanese history, see Levine, "Labor Markets"; Gordon, *The Evolution.*

4. Chandler, *The Visible Hand,* 498, 500; Gary G. Hamilton and Nicole Woolsey Biggart, "Market, Culture, and Authority: A Comparative Analysis of Management and Organization in the Far East," *American Journal of Sociology,* 94 Suppl. (1988): S68, S83.

5. John Child, *Management in China during the Age of Reform* (Cambridge: Cambridge University Press, 1994), 307.

6. Powell, "Neither Market nor Hierarchy," 323.

Glossary

ba da tonghang　八大同行
bai lao touzi　拜老頭子
banghui　幫會
banzhuang　辦莊
bao jia　保甲
bao laoban　包老板
baogong tou　包工頭
baoshengong　包身工
Baoxing　保興
baozheng zhidu　保證制度
baozhengshu　保證書
baozhuang bu　包裝部
boekijin　貿易人
bu　部
buhao　布號

Cai Yuanpei　蔡元培
can hang　蠶行
cesuo pai　廁所牌
Chaoyang mazi　潮陽麻子
Chen Bofan　陳伯藩
Chen Gongbo　陳公博
Chen Guangfu　陳光甫
Chen Shutang　陳樹棠
Chen Yichi　陳亦墀
Cheng Renjie　程仁杰
chengwang chengba　稱王稱霸
chengxiong daodi　稱兄道弟
Chengzhong xuetang　澄衷學堂

chiang deng　牆燈
Chiang Kai-shek　蔣介石
chou laofei　酬勞費
chuan hu　傳呼
Chusheng　楚勝
chuzhongsheng　初中生
Cui Zunsan　崔尊三
cun　村

da chengshi　大城市
da jiang yuan　大醬園
da jingli　大經理
Da Shanghai gong'anju　大上海公安局
Da Ying pai　大英牌
Da Zhongguo huochai gongsi　大中國火柴公司
Da Zhonghua huochai gongsi　大中華火柴公司
da zhudian　大主點
daban　大班
dahui　大會
Dai Nippon　大日本
daili chu　代理處
daili shang　代理商
Daiyu congyou, guanli congyan　待遇從優, 管理從嚴
dao zhang　倒帳
daxie　大寫

217

Deng Xiaoping 鄧小平
dengji 登記
dai zhen 待征
diaocha yuan 調查員
Ding Shen'an 丁慎安
Dinghai nuzi zhongxue 定海女子中學
Dinghai zhongxue 定海中學
Doko 同興
Du Jiakun 杜家坤
Du Yuesheng 杜月笙
duan 段
Dutian dahui 都天大會
duxiao 獨銷

er mutou 二木頭
erban 二班
er wu kujuan 二五庫卷

Fanhuang du julebu 梵皇渡俱樂部
fen hang 分行
fen zhuang 分莊
feng shui 風水
Feng Xifan 馮錫藩
Feng Yuxiang 馮玉祥
fengzi 瘋子
fu li 副理
Fu Shaoting 符紹庭
fu zuren 副主任
Fuji godo 富士合同
Fujino Kamenosuke 藤野龜之助
Fukui Kikusaburo 福井菊三郎
fukutsu no toshi 不屈の鬥志
fuli sheshi 福利設施
fupi 復辟
Fuzhou hua 福州話

gaozhongsheng 高中生
Ge Zhuxuan 戈竹軒
Gong Hexuan 龔和軒
Gong xin hao 公信號
Gong yi 公益
gongchang 工廠
gongcheng shi 工程師
gonghui 工會
Gongren zizhi fating 工人自治法庭
Gongshang pai 工商派

gongtou 工頭
Gongyi gongshang zhongxue 公益工商中學
Gongyi hang 公益行
Gu Haijian 谷海鑒
Gu Xueqiao 顧雪橋
Gu Zhenghong 顧正紅
gua hua 掛畫
Guan Yu 關羽
Guandi hui 關帝會
Guangsheng 廣生
guanli 管理
guanli yuan 管理員
gudong 股東
Guo Yunge 郭雲閣
Guochan huochai zhizao tongye lianhe banshichu 國產火柴製造同業聯合辦事處
Guomindang 國民黨
Guowu yuan 國務院

Han Fuju 韓復榘
Han shunji 漢順記
Hangzhou jiazhong gongye xuexiao 杭州甲種工業學校
Hengchangyuan 恒昌源
hetong 合同
Hongsheng 鴻生
Hongyuan 鴻源
houbu dao 後補道
Huaide tang 懷德堂
Huang Jinrong 黃金榮
Huang Yicong 黃以聰
Huang Yifeng 黃逸峰
Huang Zhaotang 黃兆棠
Huashang shachang lianhe hui 華商紗廠聯合會
huibi 迴避
huigongke 惠工科
hyo 俵

Inoue Taizo 井上泰三
Ito chu shoji kabushiki kaisha 伊藤忠商事株式會社
jianchayuan 檢查員
jiandu 監督
Jiangnan 江南

jianshi 監事
jianxiao dian 兼銷店
jiazhang 家長
jin qu 近區
Jin Shunji 津順記
Jin Yangsheng 金仰生
jianglijin 獎勵金
Jing hua 競化
jingli 經理
jingxiao shang 經銷商
Jingxiao tongye lianhe hui 經銷同
　業聯合會
jixiao 寄銷
jue suan 決算
julebu 俱樂部

Kailuan 開灤
Kan Angui 闞安貴
Kanegafuchi 鐘淵
Kanekin 金井
kan shi nin 監視人
kao gong ke 考工科
kao gong yuan 考工員
ke shang 客商
keiretsu 系列
H. H. Kong (Kong Xiangxi) 孔祥熙
kongzhi 控制
kuaiji 會計

lao gongren 老工人
Lao shunji 老順記
Laogong zizhiqu 勞工自治區
Laogongmao 老公茂
Li Guowei 李國偉
lianxisheng 練習生
lilong 里弄
lingshou dian 零售店
lingshou shang 零售商
Liu chang gongren lianhe weiyuanhui
　六廠工人聯合委員會
Liu Hongsheng 劉鴻生
Liu Jisheng 劉吉生
Lu Yongxiang 盧永祥
Lunchuan zhaoshang ju 輪船招商局

mai dian 賣店
Mao Zedong 毛澤東

Maoxin 茂新
Masuda Takashi 益田孝
mei 美
mei zhan 煤棧
Mei'an 美安
Meichuan 美川
Meifu 美孚
meihao 煤號
Meilu 美瀘
Meiping 美平
Meitan 美灘
Meiying 美鷹
Meiyun 美雲
Meixia 美峽
Mie 三重
Minsheng 民生
Mitsui bussan kabushiki kaisha
　三井物產株式會社
Mori Kaku 森恪
mune wari nagaya 棟割長屋

Naigai wata kabushiki kaisha 內外
　綿株式會社
Nan shunji 南順記
neidi 內地
nian hua 年畫
Nie Baozhang 聶寶璋
Nihon menka 日本綿花
Nihon menpu yushutsu kumiai
　日本綿布輸出組合
Nikka 日華
Nishikawa Kiichi 西川喜一

Okayama 岡山
Osaka Godo 大阪合同

Pan Gongzhan 潘公展
pao xiang jian 跑鄉間
paojie 跑街
pu bao 鋪保

Qi Jiguang 戚繼光
qian baiwan fuweng 千百萬富翁
qianke 揝客
qianzhuang 錢莊
qinqi 親戚
qiong xiang pi rang 窮鄉僻壤

qu 區
qu hang 區行
qu jingxiao shang 區經銷商
qu zhang 區長
Quanguo jingji weiyuanhui 全國經
　濟委員會
Quanshe 拳社

Ren Bozhong 任伯重
Rong Binggen 榮炳根
Rong Desheng 榮德生
Rong Erren 榮爾仁
Rong Hongyuan 榮鴻元
Rong Ruixing 榮瑞馨
Rong Weiren 榮偉仁
Rong Xitai 榮熙泰
Rong Yiren 榮毅仁
Rong Zongjing 榮宗敬
Rongshi jiashu 榮氏家塾
Ruiji 瑞記

sanban 三班
Sen tai rong 森泰蓉
Shanghai mianfen ye gonghui 上海
　麵粉業工會
Shanghai shachang gonghui 上海紗
　廠工會
shangren 商人
Shanhai 上海
Shanhai seizo 上海製造
Shantou hua 汕頭話
Shao Erkang 邵爾康
Shen Baozhen 沈葆楨
Shen Kunshan 沈崑山
shen shang 紳商
Shenxin shachang 申新紗廠
Shina shugyosei 支那修業生
shinkoku shogyo minaraisei 清國商
　業見習生
shiyong ren 試用人
shouzhi yuan 收支員
Shuiyue 水月
Shuiyue shachang 水月紗廠
Shunji yanghuo hao 順記洋貨號
si xiao 私銷
Siming gongsuo 四明公所
Siming yinhang 四明銀行

sogo shosha 總合商社
Song Hanzhang 宋漢章
S. L. Soong (Song Ziliang) 宋子良
T. V. Soong (Song Ziwen) 宋子文
Sun Chuanfang 孫傳芳
Sun Yat-sen 孫逸仙

Takahashi Korekiyo 高橋是清
Takamura Naosuke 高村直助
tangguan 堂倌
Tangshan 唐山
Tao Bingjun 陶秉鈞
Tao Jingxuan 陶靜軒
Tao Tingyao 陶庭瑤
Tenman 天滿
Tian Junchuan 田俊川
Toa 東亞
Toa dobun shoin 東亞同文書院
Toka 東華
Tongyi 同益
Tongyihe 同益和
Toyota 豐田
tudi 徒弟
tuhao lieshen 土豪劣紳
tuixiao yuan 推銷員

waibu 外埠
waibu fenxiao paojie 外埠分銷
　跑街
Wang Abao 王阿寶
Wang Guanshi 王冠時
Wang Jingwei 汪精衛
Wang Jingyu 汪敬虞
Wang Minghuai 王銘槐
Wang Yuqing 王禹卿
Wei Wenpu 韋文圃
wenren 聞人
Wing Tai 永泰
Wu Caiqin 鄔采芹
Wu Dingchang 吳鼎昌
wu jin 五金
wu teshu shigu 無特殊事故
Wu Tingsheng 鄔挺生
Wu Zhihui 吳稚輝
Wuxi xian shangmin xiehui 無錫縣
　商民協會
wuyang zihao 五洋字號

Xiamen hua 廈門話
xian cheng 縣城
xiangzhang 鄉長
xiangzhen shangdian 鄉鎮商店
xiao dongyang 小東洋
xiao jingli 小經理
xiao pifa shang 小批發商
xiao zhaoya 小爪牙
xiao zhudian 小主點
xiaofei hezuo she 銷費合作社
Xiaohuo jiangli zhidu 銷貨獎勵
   制度
Xiehe maoyi gongsi 協和貿易公司
xieli 協理
xin zhiyuan 新職員
xingshang 行商
xingzheng weiyuan hui 行政委員會
Xu Jinsen 徐金森
Xuchang 許昌
Xue Baorun 薛寶潤
Xue Mingjian 薛明劍
Xue Nanming 薛南溟
Xue Shouxuan 薛壽宣
xuesheng zhi 學生制

Yamamoto Jotaro 山本條太郎
yan hang 煙行
Yan Xishan 閻錫山
yang fen 洋粉
yang sha 洋紗
yangchenggong 養成工
Yangshupu 楊樹浦
Yanjing 燕京
yanye bu 煙葉部
Ye Chengzhong 葉澄衷
Ye Suzhen 葉素貞
ye wu 業務
yexinjia 野心家
Yihe 怡和
Yingchang 癸昌
yingye ke 營業科
yingye renyuan 營業人員
yingye yuan 營業員
Yitaixing 義泰興
Yokohama 橫濱
Yong'an 永安
Yong'an tang 永安堂

yongjin 佣金
Yongtaihe 永泰和
Yongtaizhan 永泰棧
you mianzi 有面子
yu suan 預算
Yu yuan 豫源
yuan qu 遠區
Yuan sheng hao 源盛號
Yu da xiang shanghao 裕大祥商號
Yue Fei 岳飛
Yuho 裕豐
Yui Tsunehiko 由井常彦
yunshu bu 運輸部
yunshubu zhuren 運輸部主任

za huo 雜貨
zhanfang 棧房
Zhang Guotao 張國燾
Zhanghua 章華
Zhang Jia'ao 張嘉敖
Zhang Renjie 張人傑
Zhang Xiaofang 張筱舫
Zhang Xiaolin 張嘯林
Zhang Zuolin 張作霖
Zhao Zhongtao 趙仲陶
Zheng Bozhao 鄭伯昭
Zheng Guanzhu 鄭觀柱
Zheng Zhongwei 鄭仲威
Zhengda 正大
zhengli 整理
zhengshi gongren 正式工人
Zhenxing 振興
zhidao yuan 指導員
Zhide 至德
Zhigong yangchengsuo 職工養成所
zhihang 支行
zhiyuan 職員
zhiyuan huahong 職員花紅
zhiyuan techou 職員特酬
zhong xiao chengshi 中小城市
Zhong xiao tang 忠孝堂
Zhonghua matou gufen youxian
   gongsi 中華碼頭股份有限公司
Zhonghua quanguo huochai chan-
   xiao lianying she 中華全國火
   柴產銷聯營社
Zhongnan 中南

zhongxia ceng tuixiao shang　中下
　　層推銷商
Zhou Yangshan　周仰山
Zhu Dachun　祝大椿
zhuang piao　莊票
zhuanyan bu　裝煙部
Zhunxian tang　尊賢堂
zhuyao shangbiao　主要商標

Zijin shan　紫金山
ziyi　咨議
Zong gongsi　總公司
zong guanli chu　總管理處
zong jingli　總經理
zong shiwusuo　總事務所
zong wu　總務

Bibliography

ARCHIVAL SOURCES

Center for Research in Chinese Business History, Institute of Economics, Shanghai Academy of Social Sciences, Shanghai.

Liu Hongsheng. Papers. Center for Research in Chinese Business History, Institute of Economics, Shanghai Academy of Social Sciences, Shanghai.

Mitsui Bunko (Mitsui Archives), Tokyo.

National Archives of the United States, Washington, D.C.

Number Two Archives, Nanjing.

Sheridan, Harold Joseph. Papers. These papers are contained within and cataloged under the Marion Campbell Sheridan Papers, New Haven Colony Historical Society, New Haven, Connecticut.

Standard Oil Company. Papers. Shanghai City Archives, Shanghai.

Swedish Match Central Archives, Vadstena Landsarchiv (Regional Archives, Vadstena), Sweden.

Thomas, James A. Papers. Manuscript Department, William R. Perkins Library, Duke University, Durham, N.C.

Unilever Historical Archives, Unilever House, Blackfriars, London.

"Ying Mei yancao gongsi zai Hua qiye ziliao huibian" (Collected Materials on the Enterprises of the British-American Tobacco Company in China). Center for Research in Chinese Business History, Shanghai Academy of Social Sciences, Shanghai. This unpublished set of records differs from the book that has been published under the same title (cited below) mainly in that it contains English-language documents that were translated into Chinese in the published version.

PUBLISHED SOURCES

Allen, G. C., and Audrey G. Donnithorne. *Western Enterprise in Far Eastern Economic Development*. London: Allen and Unwin, 1954.

Anderson, George E. *Cotton-Goods Trade in China*. U.S. Department of Commerce and Labor, Bureau of Manufactures, Special Consular Report No. 44. Washington, D.C.: Government Printing Office, 1911.

Anderson, Irvine H., Jr. "Petroleum as a Strategic Commodity in American-East Asian Relations." Paper prepared for the conference on American–East Asian Economic Relations, Mt. Kisco, New York, June 25–27, 1976.

———. *The Standard-Vacuum Oil Company and United States East Asian Policy, 1933–1941*. Princeton: Princeton University Press, 1975.

Arnold, Julean H., et al. *China: A Commercial and Industrial Handbook*. U.S. Department of Commerce, Trade Promotion Series No. 38. Washington, D.C.: Government Printing Office, 1926.

Beaton, Kendall. *Enterprise in Oil: A History of Shell in the United States*. New York: Appleton-Century-Crofts, 1957.

Becker, Jasper. "Hardship in Shanghai as Spindles Stop." *South China Morning Post*, Hong Kong, December 21, 1996, 20.

Bell, Lynda S. "From Comprador to County Magnate: Bourgeois Practice in the Wuxi County Silk Industry." In Joseph W. Esherick and Mary Backus Rankin, eds., *Chinese Local Elites and Patterns of Dominance*. Berkeley: University of California Press, 1990. Pp. 113–39.

———. "One Industry, Two Chinas: Silk Filatures and Peasant-Family Production in Wuxi County, 1865–1937." Unpublished manuscript, 1995.

Bendix, Reinhard. *Work and Authority: Ideologies of Management in the Course of Industrialization*. New York: Wiley, 1956.

Bergère, Marie-Claire. *The Golden Age of the Chinese Bourgeoisie, 1911–1937*. Translated from the French by Janet Lloyd. Cambridge: Cambridge University Press, 1989.

———. "Shanghai Capitalists and the Transition from Nationalist to Communist Regime (1948–1952)." In Lee Yung-san and Liu Ts'ui-jung, eds., *China's Market Economy in Transition*. Taipei: Academica Sinica, 1990. Pp. 515–36.

British-American Tobacco Company, Ltd. *The Record in China of the British-American Tobacco Company, Limited*. Shanghai, 1925 (?).

Bureau of Social Affairs, City Government of Greater Shanghai. *Strikes and Lockouts in Shanghai since 1918*. Bilingual edition with Chinese title, *Jinshi wunianlai Shanghai zhi bagong tingye* (Strikes and Lockouts in Shanghai during the Past Fifty Years). Shanghai: Zhonghua shuju, 1933.

Bush, Richard C. *The Politics of Cotton Textiles in Kuomintang China, 1927–1937*. New York: Garland, 1982.

Cao Zengxiang. "Yaxiya huoyou gongsi gaiguang" (On the Asiatic Petroleum Company). In *Jiu Shanghaide wai shang yu maiban* (Foreign Merchants and Compradors in Old Shanghai). *Shanghai wenshi ziliao xuanji* (Collected Literary and Historical Materials on Shanghai). Shanghai: Shanghai renmin chubanshe, 1987. Pp. 53–59.

Carlson, Ellsworth C. *The Kaiping Mines (1877–1912)*. Cambridge, Mass.: East Asian Research Center, Harvard University, 1957.

Chan Kai Yiu. "The Management of Modern Business in Republican China: The Case of Liu Hongsheng and His Enterprises, 1920–1937." Paper presented at the conference on the Rise of Business Corporations in China from Ming to Present, University of Hong Kong, July 12–13, 1996.

Chan, Wellington K. K. *Merchants, Mandarins, and Modern Enterprise in Late Ch'ing China.* Cambridge, Mass.: Council on East Asian Studies, Harvard University, 1977.

Chandler, Alfred D., Jr. "Historical Determinants of Managerial Hierarchies: A Response to Perrow." In Thomas K. McCraw, ed., *The Essential Chandler: Essays toward a Historical Theory of Big Business*. Boston: Harvard Business School Press, 1988. Pp. 451–61.

———. *Scale and Scope: The Dynamics of Industrial Capitalism*. Cambridge, Mass.: Harvard University Press, 1990.

———. *The Visible Hand: The Managerial Revolution in American Business*. Cambridge, Mass.: Harvard University Press, 1977.

Chang Kuo-t'ao (Zhang Guotao). *The Rise of the Chinese Communist Party, 1921–1927*. Vol. 1 of *The Autobiography of Chang Kuo-t'ao*. Lawrence: University of Kansas Press, 1971.

Chao Kang. "The Chinese-American Cotton-Textile Trade." In Ernest R. May and John K. Fairbank, eds., *America's China Trade in Historical Perspective: The Chinese and American Performance*. Cambridge, Mass.: Council on East Asian Studies, Harvard University, 1986. Pp. 103–27.

———. *The Development of Cotton Textile Production in China*. Cambridge, Mass.: East Asian Research Center, Harvard University, 1977.

Chen Chuxiang, Cheng Renjie, et al. Transcripts of interviews of December 3, 1962. Center for Research Chinese Business History, Shanghai Academy of Social Sciences, Shanghai.

Chen, Edward, and Gary G. Hamilton. "Introduction: Business Networks and Economic Development." In Gary G. Hamilton, ed., *Business Networks and Economic Development in East and Southeast Asia*. Hong Kong: Centre of Asian Studies, University of Hong Kong, 1991. Pp. 3–10.

Chen Han Seng. *Industrial Capital and Chinese Peasants: A Study of the Livelihood of Chinese Tobacco Cultivators*. Shanghai: Kelly and Walsh, 1939.

Chen Zengnian. "Ying Mei yan gongsi de xiaoshouwang" (British-American Tobacco Company's Marketing Network). *Xueshu yuekan* (Academic Monthly) 140 (January 1981): 16–21.

Cheng Chu-yuan. "The United States Petroleum Trade with China, 1876–1949." In Ernest R. May and John K. Fairbank, eds., *America's China Trade in Historical Perspective: The Chinese and American Performance*. Cambridge, Mass.: Council on East Asian Studies, Harvard University, 1986. Pp. 205–33.

Cheng Renjie. "Ying Mei yan gongsi maiban Zheng Bozhao" (British-American Tobacco Company's Comprador Zheng Bozhao). In *Wenshi ziliao xuanji* (Collected Literary and Historical Materials), no. 1. Shanghai: Shanghai renmin chubanshe, 1978. Pp. 130–54.

Chesneaux, Jean. *The Chinese Labor Movement, 1919–1927.* Translated from the French by H. M. Wright. Stanford: Stanford University Press, 1968.

Child, John. *Management in China during the Age of Reform.* Cambridge: Cambridge University Press, 1994.

China, Inspectorate General of Customs. *Decennial Reports, 1902–1911.* Shanghai, 1913.

Ch'u T'ung-tsu. *Local Government in China under the Ch'ing.* Cambridge, Mass.: Harvard University Press, 1962.

Chuka zenkoku chu nichi jitsugyoka koshinroku (Shanhai no bu) (A Roster of China's Chinese and Japanese Entrepreneurs) (Shanghai Section). 1936.

Clark, W. A. Graham. *Cotton Goods in Japan and Their Competition on the Manchurian Market.* U.S. Department of Commerce, Bureau of Foreign and Domestic Commerce, Special Agents Series No. 86. Washington, D.C.: Government Printing Office, 1914.

Coble, Parks M., Jr. "Chinese Capitalism in the Lower Yangzi Area during the Sino-Japanese War, 1937–1945." Paper presented at the annual meeting of the Association of Asian Studies for the Midwest Region, University of Western Illinois, September 24, 1994.

———. *Facing Japan: Chinese Politics and Japanese Imperialism, 1931–1937.* Cambridge, Mass.: Council on East Asian Studies, Harvard University, 1991.

———. *The Shanghai Capitalists and the Nationalist Government, 1927–1937.* Cambridge, Mass.: Council on East Asian Studies, Harvard University, 1980.

Cochran, Sherman. *Big Business in China: Sino-Foreign Rivalry in the Cigarette Industry, 1890–1930.* Cambridge, Mass.: Harvard University Press, 1980.

———. "Businesses, Governments, and War in China, 1931–1949." In Akira Iriye and Warren Cohen, eds., *American, Chinese, and Japanese Perspectives on Wartime Asia 1931–1949.* Wilmington, Del.: Scholarly Resources, 1990. Pp. 117–45.

———. "Losing Money Abroad: The Swedish Match Company in China during the 1930s." *Business and Economic History,* 2d ser., 16 (1987): 83–91.

———. "Three Roads into Shanghai's Market: Japanese, Western, and Chinese Companies in the Match Trade, 1895–1937." In Frederic Wakeman, Jr., and Yeh Wen-hsin, eds., *Shanghai Sojourners.* Berkeley: Institute of East Asian Studies, University of California, 1992. Pp. 35–75.

Copeland, Melvin Thomas. *The Cotton Manufacturing Industry of the United States.* Cambridge, Mass.: Harvard University Press, 1912.

Cox, Howard. "Learning to Do Business in China: The Evolution of BAT's Cigarette Distributing Network, 1902–1941." *Business History* 39, no. 3 (1997): 30–64.

Crow, Carl. *Foreign Devils in the Flowery Kingdom.* New York: Harper and Brothers, 1940.

Dennerline, Jerry. *Qian Mu and the World of Seven Mansions.* New Haven: Yale University Press, 1988.

Deterding, Henri. *An International Oilman.* London: Harper and Brothers, 1934.

Dong Qijun. "Ningbo luhu tongxianghui" (The Association of Ningbo Sojourners in Shanghai). *Zhejiang wenshi ziliao xuanji* (Collected Literary and Historical Materials on Zhejiang) 39 (March 1989): 40–49.

Du Xuncheng. *Riben zai jiu Zhongguo de touzi* (Japanese Investment in Old China). Shanghai: Shanghai shehui kexue yuan chubanshe, 1986.

Duus, Peter. "Zaikabo: Japanese Cotton Mills in China, 1895–1937." In Peter Duus, Ramon H. Myers, and Mark R. Peattie, eds., *The Japanese Informal Empire in China, 1895–1937*. Princeton: Princeton University Press, 1989. Pp. 65–100.

Eno, Arthur L., Jr., "Minds among the Spindles: A Cultural History." In Arthur L. Eno, Jr., ed., *Cotton Was King: A History of Lowell, Massachusetts*. Lowell: Massachusetts Historical Society, 1976.

Fairbank, John King. *The Great Chinese Revolution: 1800–1985*. New York: Harper and Row, 1986.

Fan Xintian. "Wo suozhidaode Meifu gongsi" (What I Know about Standard Oil Company) (1964). Reprinted in *Gong shang jingji shiliao congkan* (Collected Historical Materials on Industry, Commerce, and the Economy), no. 4. Beijing: Wenshi ziliao chubanshe, 1984. Pp. 37–59.

Feuerwerker, Albert. *The Foreign Establishment in China in the Early Twentieth Century*. Ann Arbor: Center for Chinese Studies, University of Michigan, 1976.

Frazier, Martin W. "Mobilizing a Movement: Cotton Mill Foremen in the Shanghai Strikes of 1925." *Republican China* 20, no. 1 (November 1994): 1–45.

Fruin, W. Mark. *The Japanese Enterprise System: Competitive Strategies and Cooperative Structures*. Oxford: Clarendon Press, 1994.

Gibbons, P. C. "Are You Getting China's Drug Dollars?" *Export Advertiser* 2, no. 4 (April 1930): 7–9, 24–26, 28, 30.

Goodman, Bryna. *Native Place, City, and Nation: Regional Networks and Identities in Shanghai, 1853–1937*. Berkeley: University of California Press, 1995.

Gordon, Andrew. *The Evolution of Labor Relations in Japan: Heavy Industries, 1853–1955*. Cambridge, Mass.: Council on East Asian Studies, Harvard University, 1988.

Gui Jirui. "Wuxi zai ershi niandai xingcheng jingji zhongxin de yuanyin jiqi zhineng" (Origins and Professional Capabilities behind Wuxi's Emergence as an Economic Center during the 1920s). *Lishi dang'an* (Historical Archives) 4 (1985): 107–12. Beijing.

Hamashita Takeshi. "Studies on Modern Chinese Business History in Japan." Paper presented at the Workshop on Chinese Business History, University of Akron, Akron, Ohio, October 28, 1995.

Hamilton, Gary G., ed. *Business Networks and Economic Development in East and Southeast Asia*. Hong Kong: Centre of Asian Studies, University of Hong Kong, 1991.

———. "The Organizational Foundations of Western and Chinese Commerce: A Historical and Comparative Analysis." In Gary G. Hamilton, ed., *Business*

Networks and Economic Development in East and Southeast Asia. Hong Kong: Centre of Asian Studies, University of Hong Kong. Pp. 48–65.

Hamilton, Gary G., and Nicole Woolsey Biggart. "Market, Culture, and Authority: A Comparative Analysis of Management and Organization in the Far East." *American Journal of Sociology,* 94 Suppl. (1988): S52–S94.

Hao Yen-p'ing. *The Commercial Revolution in Nineteenth-Century China: The Rise of Sino-Western Mercantile Capitalism.* Berkeley: University of California Press, 1986.

———. *The Comprador in Nineteenth-Century China: Bridge between East and West.* Cambridge, Mass.: Harvard University Press, 1970.

Hareven, Tamara. *Family Time and Industrial Time.* Cambridge: Cambridge University Press, 1982.

Hatano Yoshihiro. *Chugoku kindai kogyoshi no kenkyu* (A Historical Study of Modern Chinese Industry). Kyoto: Toyoshi kenkyukai, 1961.

Hidy, Ralph W., and Muriel E. Hidy. *Pioneering in Big Business, 1882–1911.* New York: Harper and Brothers, 1955.

Hitchcock, Frank H. *Our Trade with Japan, China, and Hong Kong, 1889–1899.* Washington, D.C.: Government Printing Office, 1900.

Ho Ping-ti. *The Ladder of Success in Imperial China: Aspects of Social Mobility, 1368–1911.* New York: Columbia University Press, 1962.

Hobart, Alice Tisdale. *Oil for the Lamps of China.* New York: Grosset and Dunlop, 1933.

Hobsbawn, E. J. *Labouring Men: Studies in the History of Labour.* Garden City, N.Y.: Doubleday, 1964.

Honig, Emily. *Sisters and Strangers: Women in the Shanghai Cotton Mills, 1919–1949.* Stanford: Stanford University Press, 1986.

Hsu Yung-sui. "Tobacco Marketing in Eastern Shantung" (1937). In Institute of Pacific Relations, comp. and trans., *Agrarian China: Selected Source Materials from Chinese Authors.* London: Allen and Unwin, 1939. Pp. 171–75.

Hu Shigui. "Wo suozhidao de Liu Hongsheng xiansheng" (What I Know about Mr. Liu Hongsheng). In *Tongzhan gongzuo shiliao xuanji: Shanghai wenshi ziliao* (Collected Materials on the Work of the United Front: Collected Literary and Historical Materials on Shanghai), no. 8. Shanghai: Shanghai renmin chubanshe, 1989. Pp. 167–81.

Hu Yufen. "Huiyi Guangzhou Yaxiya shiyou gongsi" (Recollections of the Asiatic Petroleum Company in Guangzhou). In *Gong shang jingji shiliao congkan* (Collected Historical Materials on Industry, Commerce, and the Economy), no. 4. Beijing: Wenshi ziliao chubanshe, 1984. Pp. 79–97.

Huai Shu. *Zhongguo jingji neimo* (Behind the Scenes in the Chinese Economy). Hong Kong: Xinmin ju chubanshe, 1948.

Huang, Philip C. C. *The Peasant Economy and Social Change in North China.* Stanford: Stanford University Press, 1985.

Huang Yifeng. "Guanyu jiu Zhongguo maiban jieji de yanjiu" (A Study of the Comprador Class in Old China). *Lishi yanjiu* (Historical Research) 87, no. 3 (June 15, 1964): 89–116. Republished in Fudan daxue lishi xi (Fudan University History Department) et al., eds., *Jindai Zhongguo zichan jieji yanjiu*

(Studies of the Capitalist Class in Modern China). Shanghai: Fudan daxue chubanshe, 1984. Pp. 250–90.

Huang Yifeng, Jiang Duo, Tang Quanshi, and Chen Jiang. *Jiu Zhongguo de maiban jieji* (The Comprador Class in Old China). Shanghai: Shanghai renmin chubanshe, 1982.

Hunt, Michael H. "Americans in the China Market: Economic Opportunities and Economic Nationalism, 1890s–1931." *Business History Review* 51 (Autumn 1977): 277–307.

———. *Frontier Defense and the Open Door: Manchuria in Chinese-American Relations, 1895–1911.* New Haven: Yale University Press, 1973.

Hutchison, James Lafayette. *China Hand.* Boston: Lothrop, Lee and Shepard, 1936.

Iriye, Akira. *Pacific Estrangement: Japanese and American Expansion.* Cambridge, Mass: Harvard University Press, 1972.

Isaacs, Harold. *The Tragedy of the Chinese Revolution.* 2d rev. ed. Stanford: Stanford University Press, 1961.

Ishii Kanji. "Nisshin sengo keiei" (Business after the Sino-Japanese War). *Iwanami koza, Nihon rekishi,* vol. 16, *Kindai* 3. Tokyo: Iwanami shoten, 1976. Pp. 47–94.

Ito Chu shoji kabushiki kaisha (C. Itoh Trading Company). *Ito Chu shoji hyakunenshi* (A Hundred-Year History of C. Itoh Trading Company). Osaka: Ito Chu shoji kabushiki kaisha, 1969.

Jacoby, Sanford M. *Employing Bureaucracy: Managers, Unions, and the Transformation of Work in American Industry, 1900–1945.* New York: Columbia University Press, 1985.

Jansen, Marius B. *The Japanese and Sun Yat-sen.* Cambridge, Mass.: Harvard University Press, 1954.

Jiu Zhongguo de zibenzhuyi shengchan guanxi (Capitalist Relations of Production in Old China). Beijing: Renmin chubanshe, 1977.

Jones, Susan Mann. "The Ningpo *Pang* and Financial Power at Shanghai." In Mark Elvin and G. William Skinner, eds., *The Chinese City between Two Worlds.* Stanford: Stanford University Press, 1974. Pp. 73–96.

Kawabe Nobuo. "The Distribution Systems in Japan before World War II." *Business and Economic History,* 2d ser., 18 (1989): 33–44.

Kirby, William C. "China Unincorporated: Company Law and Business Enterprise in Twentieth-Century China." *Journal of Asian Studies* 54, no. 1 (February 1995): 43–63.

———. *Germany and Republican China.* Stanford: Stanford University Press, 1984.

Kong Lingren et al., eds. *Zhongguo jindai qiye de kaituo zhe* (Pioneers in Modern Chinese Enterprises). 2 vols. Jinan: Shandong renmin chubanshe, 1991.

Kuwahara Tetsuya. "The Establishment of Oligopoly in the Japanese Cotton-spinning Industry and the Business Strategies of Latecomers: The Case of Naigaiwata & Co., Ltd." In Nakagawa Keiichiro and Morikawa Hidemasa, eds., *Japanese Yearbook on Business History: 1986.* Tokyo: Japan Business History Institute, 1986.

————. *Kigyo kokusaika no shiteki bunseki: Senzenki Nihon boseki kigyo no Chugoku toshi* (An Analytic History of the Internationalization of Enterprises: Prewar Japanese Cotton Textiles Enterprises and Their Investments in China). Tokyo: Moriyama shoten, 1990.

Kuwayama Mikio. "Sogo-shosha and the Economic Development of Pre-War Japan." Ph.D. dissertation, University of Toronto, 1982.

Lai, Chuen-yan David. "The Cotton Spinning and Weaving Industry in China: A Study in Industrial Geography." Ph.D. dissertation, University of London, 1967.

Lamson, H. D. "The Problem of Housing for Workers in China." *Chinese Economic Journal* 11, no. 2 (1932): 139–62.

Lee, B. Y. "Japanese Influence in China's Cotton Industry." *China Weekly Review* 31, no. 6 (January 10, 1925): 159–62.

————. "Real Causes behind Japanese Mill Strikes." *China Weekly Review* 31, no. 13 (February 28, 1925): 363, 380.

Lee, Robert H. G. *The Manchurian Frontier in Ch'ing History.* Cambridge, Mass.: Harvard University Press, 1970.

LeFevour, Edward. *Western Enterprise in Late Ch'ing China: A Selective Survey of Jardine, Matheson & Company's Operations, 1842–1895.* Cambridge, Mass.: East Asian Research Center, Harvard University, 1968.

Leung Yuen Sang. "Regional Rivalry in Mid-Nineteenth-Century Shanghai: Cantonese vs. Ningpo Men." *Ch'ing-shih wen-t'i* 4, no. 8 (December 1982): 29–50.

Levine, Solomon B. "Labor Markets and Collective Bargaining in Japan." In William W. Lockwood, ed., *The State and Economic Enterprise in Japan.* Princeton: Princeton University Press, 1965.

Li Guowei. "Rongjia jingying fangzhi he zhifen qiye liushinian gaishu" (Sixty Years of the Rong Family Business in the Management of Textile and Flour Industries). *Wenshi ziliao xuanji* (Collected Literary and Historical Materials) 7 (1980): 30–45. Shanghai.

Li, Lillian M. *China's Silk Trade: Traditional Industry in the Modern World, 1842–1937.* Cambridge, Mass.: Council on East Asian Studies, Harvard University, 1981.

Li Zheng. "Zhengda huochai chang" (Zhengda Match Mill). *Ningbo wenshi ziliao* (Literary and Historical Materials on Ningbo) 6 (October 1987): 30–37.

Lindgren, Håkan. *Corporate Growth: The Swedish Match Industry in Its Global Setting.* Stockholm: Liber Forlag, 1979.

————. "The Kreuger Crash of 1932: In Memory of a Financial Genius, or Was He a Simple Swindler?" *Scandinavian Economic History Review* 30, no. 3 (1982): 189–206.

Littler, Craig R. *The Development of the Labour Process in Capitalist Societies: A Comparative Study of the Transformation of Work Organization in Britain, Japan, and the U.S.A.* London: Heinemann Educational, 1982.

Liu Guanzhi. "Guanyu 1924–1925 nian Shanghai gongren yundong de huiyi" (Memoirs Concerning the Shanghai Labor Movement, 1924–1925). *Zhong-*

guo gongyun shiliao (Historical Materials on China's Labor Movement) 1 (1960): 34–82.

Liu Nianzhi. *Shiyejia Liu Hongsheng chuanlü—huiyi wode fuqin* (A Biography of the Industrialist Liu Hongsheng—Reminiscences of My Father). Beijing: Wenshi ziliao chubanshe, 1982.

Liu Wenlin. "Ying shang Yaxiya huoyou gongsi" (The British Asiatic Petroleum Company) (1964). Reprinted in *Wuhan gong shang jingji shiliao* (Historical Materials on Industry, Commerce, and the Economy of Wuhan), no. 2. Wuhan: Guogu Hubeisheng xinsheng yinduchang, 1984. Pp. 36–43.

Lowe Chuan-hua. *Facing Labor Issues in China*. London: Allen and Unwin, 1934.

Lu Zhilian. "'Qiye dawang' Liu Hongsheng" (King of the Entrepeneurs Liu Hongsheng). *Zhejiang wenshi ziliao xuanji* (Collected Literary and Historical Materials on Zhejiang) 39 (March 1989): 132–56.

Lutz, Jesse Gregory. *China and the Christian College, 1850–1950*. Ithaca: Cornell University Press, 1971.

Maoxin Fuxin Shenxin zong gongsi sazhounian jiniance 1898–1928 (Thirtieth Anniversary Volume Commemorating the Maoxin and Fuxin Flour Mills, the Shenxin Cotton Mills, and the General Corporation). Shanghai: Maoxin Fuxin Shenxin zong gongsi, 1929.

Martin, Brian G. *The Shanghai Green Gang: Politics and Organized Crime, 1919–1937*. Berkeley: University of California Press, 1996.

Matsumoto Hiroshi. *Mitsui zaibatsu no kenkyu* (A Study of the Mitsui Zaibatsu). Tokyo: Yoshikawa kobunkan, 1979.

———. "Nihon shihonhugi kakuritsuki ni okeru Mitsui Bussan kaisha no hatten" (The Development of Mitsui Trading Company during the Formative Period of Japanese Capitalism). *Mitsui Bunko ronso* 7 (1973): 107–99.

Mei Zhengshao. *Haishang wenren Du Yuesheng* (The Coastal Celebrity Du Yuesheng). Zhengzhou: Henan renmin chubanshe, 1987.

Men of Shanghai and North China. Shanghai: University Press, 1935.

Miao Lihua. "Meifu shiyou gongsi" (Standard Oil Company). *Jiu Shanghaide wai shang yu maiban* (Foreign Merchants and Compradors in Old Shanghai). In *Shanghai wenshi ziliao xuanji* (Collected Literary and Historical Materials on Shanghai), no. 56. Shanghai: Shanghai renmin chubanshe, 1987. Pp. 44–52.

———. "Wu Tingsheng yu Ying Mei yan gongsi" (Wu Tingsheng and British-American Tobacco Company). *Jiu Shanghai de wai shang yu maiban* (Foreign Merchants and Compradors in Old Shanghai). In *Shanghai wenshi ziliao xuanji* (Collected Literary and Historical Materials on Shanghai), no. 56. Shanghai: Shanghai renmin chubanshe, 1987. Pp. 145–55.

Millard, Thomas F. *America and the Far Eastern Question*. New York: Moffat, Yard, 1909.

Min Chi. "Foreign Industrial Capital and the Peasantry in Honan" (1936). In Institute of Pacific Relations, comp. and trans., *Agrarian China: Selected Source Materials from Chinese Authors*. London: Allen and Unwin, 1939. Pp. 175–79.

Min Wen. "Ying Mei san da you hang qinru Tianjin gaishu" (A Brief Account of the Invasion of Tianjin by the Three Big British and American Petroleum Companies). In *Tianjin wenshi ziliao xuanji* (Collected Literary and Historical Materials on Tianjin), no. 28. Tianjin: Tianjin renmin chubanshe, 1984. Pp. 113–27.

Minjian Shanghaishi weiyuanhui Shanghaishi gong shang lian (Committee on the Reconstruction of Shanghai and the Shanghai Alliance of Industry and Commerce). "Diguozhuyi shiyou qin Hua jianshu" (A Brief Account of Petroleum's Imperialistic Penetration into China). In *Gong shang jingji shiliao congkan* (Collection of Historical Materials on Industry, Commerce, and the Economy), no. 4. Beijing: Wenshi ziliao chubanshe, 1984. Pp. 19–36.

Mitsui jigyoshi (A History of the Mitsui Enterprises), *honken* (main part). Vol. 3, sec. 1. Tokyo: Mitsui Bunko, 1980.

Montgomery, David. *The Fall of the House of Labor: The Workplace, the State, and American Labor Activism.* Cambridge: Cambridge University Press, 1987.

Moss, Scott J. *An Economic Theory of Business Strategy: An Essay in Dynamics without Equilibrium.* New York: Wiley, 1981.

"Mr. Everall Retires." *Mei Foo Shield* 5, no. 10 (January 1929): 2.

Murakami Ichiro. *Manshu to Mitsui* (Manchuria and Mitsui) (April 1941). In Mitsui Bunko, file 475.

Murphey, Rhoads. *The Outsiders: The Western Experience in India and China.* Ann Arbor: University of Michigan Press, 1977.

———. "Treaty Ports and China's Modernization." In Mark Elvin and G. William Skinner, eds., *The Chinese City between Two Worlds.* Stanford: Stanford University Press, 1974. Pp. 17–71.

Naigai wata kabushiki kaisha 50-nen shi (A Fifty-Year History of Naigai Cotton Company). Osaka: Naigai wata kabushiki kaisha, 1937.

Negishi Tadashi. *Baiben seido no kenkyu* (A Study of the Comprador System). Tokyo: Nihon tosho kabushiki kaisha, 1948.

Nelson, Daniel. *Managers and Workers: Origins of the New Factory System in the United States, 1880–1920.* Madison: University of Wisconsin Press, 1975.

New York Sun, April 13, 1913.

Nie Baozhang. "Lun yanghang maiban de benzhi tezheng—Da Riben xuezhe Gutian Daozhao jianyu yanbian 'Zhongguo jindai jingji shi' xiansheng shangjue" (On the Essential Subordination of Compradors in Foreign Firms —A Reply to the Discussion by Japanese Scholar Miyata Michiaki and Other Contributors to "The History of China's Modern Economy"). *Jindai Zhongguo* (Modern China) 3 (May 1993): 1–16.

Nihon keieishi kenkyujo (Japan Business History Institute), ed. *Kohon Mitsui Bussan kabushiki kaisha* (A Hundred-Year History of Mitsui Trading Company). Vol. 1. Tokyo, 1978.

Nishikawa Kiichi. *Chushi rodosha no genjo* (Present Conditions of Chinese Laborers). Tokyo, 1925.

Odell, Ralph M. *Cotton Goods in China.* U.S. Department of Commerce, Bureau of Foreign and Domestic Commerce, Special Agents Series No. 107. Washington, D.C.: Government Printing Office, 1916.

Oi Senzo. "Shina ni okeru Ei-Bei tabako torasuto no keiei keitai, zai-Shi gaikoku kigyo no hatten to baiben soshiki no ichikosatsu" (The Form of Administration of the British-American Tobacco Company in China: A Study of the Development of Foreign Enterprises in China and of the Comprador System). *Toa kenkyu shoho* (Report of the East Asia Institute) 26 (February 1944): 1–47.

Ono Kazuko. *Chinese Women in a Century of Revolution, 1850–1950.* Stanford: Stanford University Press, 1989.

Ozawa Terutomo. *Multinationalism, Japanese Style: The Political Economy of Outward Dependency.* Princeton: Princeton University Press, 1979.

Pan Siyue. "Xiamen Riben sanjing yanghang chuzhangsuo" (Mitsui's Branch Office in Xiamen). *Xiamen wenshi ziliao xuanji* (Collected Literary and Historical Materials on Xiamen), no. 4 (July 1983): 15–38.

Parker, Lee, and Ruth Dorval Jones. *China and the Golden Weed.* Ahoskie, N.C.: Herald, 1976.

Pearse, Arno S. *Cotton Industry of Japan and China.* Manchester: Taylor, Garnett, Evans, 1929.

Perkins, Dwight H. "Introduction: The Persistence of the Past." In Dwight H. Perkins, ed., *China's Modern Economy in Historical Perspective.* Stanford: Stanford University Press, 1975.

Perrow, Charles. "Markets, Hierarchies and Hegemony." In Thomas K. McCraw, ed., *The Essential Chandler: Essays toward a Historical Theory of Big Business.* Boston: Harvard Business School Press, 1988. Pp. 432–47.

Perry, Elizabeth J. *Shanghai on Strike: The Politics of Chinese Labor.* Stanford: Stanford University Press, 1993.

Pomeranz, Kenneth. *The Making of a Hinterland: State, Society, and Economy in Inland North China, 1853–1937.* Berkeley: University of California Press, 1993.

Porter, Robin. *Industrial Reformers in Republican China.* Armonk, N.Y.: M. E. Sharpe, 1994.

Powell, Walter W. "Neither Market nor Hierarchy: Network Forms of Organization." In Barry M. Staw and L. L. Cummings, eds., *Research in Organizational Behavior,* vol. 12. Greenwich, Conn.: JAI Press, 1990. Pp. 295–336.

Pugach, Noel H. "Standard Oil and Petroleum Development in Early Republican China." *Business History Review* 45, no. 4 (Winter 1971): 452–73.

Qian Mu. *Bashi yi shuangqin: Shiyou zayi* (Reminiscences at the Age of Eighty about My Parents: Memories of Teachers and Friends). Changsha: Yulu shushe, 1987.

Qian Zhonghan. "Minzu zibenjia: Rong Zongjing, Rong Desheng" (National Capitalists: Rong Zongjing and Rong Desheng). *Nanjing wenshi ziliao xuanji* (Collected Literary and Historical Materials on Nanjing) 2 (1963): 115–21.

———. "Wuxi de wuge zhuyao chanye ziben xitong de xingcheng yu fazhan" (The Formation and Development of Five Major Networks of Industrial

Capital in Wuxi). *Wenshi ziliao xuanji* (Collected Literary and Historical Materials) 24 (1961): 98–153. Beijing.

Qingdao gong shang xingzheng guanli zhu shiliao zhu (Committee on Historical Materials concerning the Administration and Management of Industry and Commerce in Qingdao), ed. *Zhongguo minzu huochai gongye* (China's National Match Industry). Beijing: Zhonghua shuju, 1963.

Rawski, Thomas G. *Economic Growth in Prewar China.* Berkeley: University of California Press, 1989.

Redding, S. Gordon. "Weak Organizations and Strong Linkages: Managerial Ideology and Chinese Family Business Networks." In Gary G. Hamilton, ed., *Business Networks and Economic Development in East and Southeast Asia.* Hong Kong: Centre of Asian Studies, University of Hong Kong. Pp. 30–47.

Reynolds, Bruce L. "The East Asian 'Textile Cluster' Trade, 1868–1973: A Comparative-Advantage Interpretation." In Ernest R. May and John K. Fairbank, eds., *America's China Trade in Historical Perspective: The Chinese and American Performance.* Cambridge, Mass.: Council on East Asian Studies, Harvard University, 1986. Pp. 129–50.

Reynolds, Douglas R. "Chinese Area Studies in Prewar China: Japan's Toa Dobun Shoin in Shanghai, 1900–1945." *Journal of Asian Studies* 45, no. 5 (1986): 945–70.

———. "Japan Does It Better: Toa Dobun Shoin (1900–1945) and Its Mission." In Akira Iriye et al., *Essays in the History of the Chinese Republic.* Urbana: University of Illinois Center for Asian Studies, 1983. Pp. 30–37.

Rong Desheng. *Lenong ziding xingnian jishi* (Autobiography of Rong Desheng). N.p., 1943.

Rosenthal, John Martin. "The China Market, Myth or Reality? The Case of Standard Oil, 1875–1918." M.A. thesis, Cornell University, 1980.

Rowe, William T. *Hankow: Commerce and Society in a Chinese City, 1796–1889.* Stanford: Stanford University Press, 1984.

Saxonhouse, Gary R. "Country Girls and Communication among Competitors in the Japanese Cotton-Spinning Industry." In Hugh Patrick, ed., *Japanese Industrialization and Its Social Consequences.* Berkeley: University of California Press, 1976. Pp. 97–125.

Shanghai shehui kexue yuan jingji yanjiu suo (Shanghai Academy of Social Sciences Institute of Economics), comp. *Liu Hongsheng qiye shiliao* (Historical Materials on Liu Hongsheng's Enterprises). Shanghai: Shanghai renmin chubanshe, 1981.

———. *Rongjia qiye shiliao* (Historical Materials on the Rong Family Enterprises). Shanghai: Shanghai renmin chubanshe, 1980.

———. *Shanghai jindai wujin shangye shi* (A History of the Hardware Trade in Modern Shanghai). Shanghai: Shanghai shehui chubanshe, 1990.

———. *Ying Mei yanjiu gongsi zai Hua qiye ziliao huibian* (Collected Materials on the Enterprises of the British-American Tobacco Company in China). 4 vols. Beijing: Zhonghua shuju, 1983.

"Shanghai Woolen Textile Factories." *Chinese Economic Journal* 11, no. 6 (December 1932): 443.

Shen Feide et al., eds. *Jiu Shanghai de yan du chang* (Old Shanghai's Opium, Gambling, and Prostitution). Shanghai: Baijia chubanshe, 1988.

Shiba Yoshinobu. "Ningpo and Its Hinterland." In G. William Skinner, ed., *The City in Late Imperial China*. Stanford: Stanford University Press, 1977. Pp. 391–439.

Skinner, G. William. "Chinese Peasants and the Closed Community: An Open and Shut Case." *Comparative Studies in Society and History* 13 (1971): 270–81.

———. "Cities and the Hierarchy of Local Systems." In G. William Skinner, ed., *The City in Late Imperial China*. Stanford: Stanford University Press, 1977. Pp. 275–351.

———. "Marketing and Social Structure in Rural China." *Journal of Asian Studies* 24, no. 1 (November 1964): 3–43.

———. "Mobility Strategies in Late Imperial China: A Regional Systems Analysis." In Carol A. Smith, ed., *Regional Analysis,* vol. 1, *Economic Systems.* New York: Academic Press, 1976. Pp. 327–64.

———. "Regional Urbanization in Nineteenth-Century China." In G. William Skinner, ed., *The City in Late Imperial China*. Stanford: Stanford University Press, 1977. Pp. 211–49.

"The Standard Oil Company in China." *Petroleum Review,* March 7, 1914.

"Strikes in Shanghai." *Chinese Economic Monthly* 3, no. 10 (October 1926): 444–73.

Takamura Naosuke. *Kindai Nihon mengyo to Chugoku* (The Modern Japanese Cotton Industry in China). Tokyo: Tokyo daigaku shuppankai, 1982.

———. *Nihon bosekigyoshi josetsu* (An Introduction to the History of the Cotton Spinning Industry in Japan), vol. 1. Tokyo: Hanawa shobo, 1971.

Tang Hai. *Zhongguo laodong wenti* (China's Labor Problems). Shanghai, 1926.

Tatlow, Charles. "Report," OSJ/6/4 (1920). Unilever Archives, Unilever House, Blackfriars, London.

Thomas, James A. *A Pioneer Tobacco Merchant in the Orient.* Durham, N.C.: Duke University Press, 1928.

———. "Selling and Civilization." *Asia* 23, no. 12 (December 1923): 896–99, 948–50.

Tien Hung-mao. *Government and Politics in Kuomintang China, 1927–1937.* Stanford: Stanford University Press, 1972.

Togai Yoshio. *Mitsui Bussan kaisha no keiei shiteki kenkyu* (A Study in the Economic History of Mitsui Trading Company). Tokyo: Tokyo keizai shinposha, 1974.

Tsurumi, E. Patricia. *Factory Girls: Women in the Thread Mills of Meiji Japan.* Princeton: Princeton University Press, 1990.

Udaka Yasushi. *Shina rodo mondai* (Labor Problems in China). Shanghai: Kokusai bunka kenkyukai, 1926.

U.S. Department of Commerce and Labor, Bureau of Statistics. *Monthly Summary of Commerce and Finance of the United States* (title varies). Various dates.

Varg, Paul A. *The Making of a Myth: The United States and China, 1897–1912.* East Lansing: Michigan State University Press, 1968.

Wakeman, Frederic, Jr. *Policing Shanghai, 1927–1937*. Berkeley: University of California Press, 1995.

Wakeman, Frederic, Jr., and Yeh Wen-hsin, eds. *Shanghai Sojourners*. Berkeley: Institute of East Asian Studies, University of California, 1992.

Wang Jingyu, comp. *Zhongguo jindai gongye shi ziliao, dier ji* (Historical Materials on Modern Chinese Industry, 2d coll.). 2 vols. Beijing: Kexue chubanshe, 1957.

———. *Shijiu shiji xifang ziben zhuyi dui Zhingguo de jingji qinlue* (Western Capitalism's Economic Invasion of China during the Nineteenth Century). Beijing: Renmin chubanshe, 1983.

Wang Shaoguang. "Failure of Charisma: The Cultural Revolution in Wuhan." Ph.D. dissertation, Cornell University, 1990.

Wang Xi. "Yige guoji tuolasi zai Zhongguo de lishi jilu—Ying Mei yan gongsi zai Hua huodong fenxi" (A Historical Record of an International Trust in China: An Analysis of British-American Tobacco Company's Activities in China). In Chen Hansheng, *Diguozhuyi gongye ziben yu Zhongguo nongmin* (Imperialistic Industrial Capital and Chinese Peasants). Shanghai: Fudan daxue chubanshe, 1984. Pp. 94–140.

Wang Yeh-chien. "Spatial and Temporal Patterns of Grain Prices in China, 1740–1910." Paper presented at the conference on Spatial and Temporal Trends and Cycles in Chinese Economic History, Bellagio, Italy, August, 1984.

Wang Zhizhou. "Wo jia san dai maiban jishi" (My Family's Record as Compradors for Three Generations). In *Tianjin de yanghang yu maiban* (The Foreign Firms and Compradors of Tianjin). Tianjin: Tianjin renmin chubanshe, 1987. Pp. 206–14.

Who's Who in China. Shanghai: China Weekly Review, 1925.

Wilkins, Mira. "The Impacts of American Multinational Enterprise on American-Chinese Economic Relations, 1786–1949." In Ernest R. May and John K. Fairbank, eds., *America's China Trade in Historical Perspective: The Chinese and American Performance*. Cambridge, Mass.: Council on East Asian Studies, Harvard University, 1986. Pp. 259–92.

Williamson, Harold F., and Arnold R. Daum. *The American Petroleum Industry: The Age of Illumination, 1859–1899*. Evanston: Northwestern University Press, 1959.

Wong Siu-lun. "Chinese Entrepreneurs and Business Trust." In Gary G. Hamilton, ed., *Business Networks and Economic Development in East and Southeast Asia*. Hong Kong: Centre of Asian Studies, University of Hong Kong, 1991. Pp. 13–29.

Wray, William D. "Afterword: The Writing of Japanese Business History." In William D. Wray, ed., *Managing Industrial Enterprise: Cases from Japan's Prewar Experience*. Cambridge, Mass.: Council on East Asian Studies, Harvard University, 1989. Pp. 317–74.

———. "Japan's Big-Three Service Enterprises in China, 1896–1936." In Peter Duus, Ramon H. Myers, and Mark R. Peattie, eds., *The Japanese Informal Empire in China, 1895–1937*. Princeton: Princeton University Press, 1989. Pp. 31–64.

Wright, Arnold, ed. *Twentieth-Century Impressions of Hong Kong, Shanghai, and Other Treaty Ports of China: Their History, People, Commerce, Industries and Resources.* 3 vols. London: Lloyd's Greater Britain Publishing Company, 1908.

Wright, Tim. *Coal Mining in China's Economy and Society, 1895–1937.* Cambridge: Cambridge University Press, 1984.

Wu Dingchang. "Zhonghua quanguo huochai chan xiao lianyingshe de shewu yu lianying jiufen, 1936–1937 nian" (Business Affairs and Disputes of China's National Match Union, 1936–1937). Liu Hongsheng Papers. Center for Research in Chinese Business History, Institute of Economics, Shanghai Academy of Social Sciences.

Wu Sing Pang. "Mr. Wu Recalls His Family's BAT Links of Pre-war Years." *B.A.T. News* (Spring 1988): 10–13.

Wusa yundong bianxie zubian (Editorial Committee on the May Thirtieth Movement). *Wusa yundong* (May Thirtieth Movement). Shanghai: Shanghai renmin chubanshe, 1976.

"Wuxi Rongshi qiye jiazu jiqi qijia de mianfenye" (The Foundation for the Fortune of the Rong Family and the Flour Industry in Wuxi). *Xin shijie* (New World) (November 1944): 19–25. Chongqing.

Wuxishi zhengxie wenshi ziliao yanjiu weiyuanhui (Wuxi People's Consultative Conference Committee on Literary and Historical Materials). "Minzu zibenjia Rongshi fazhan jianshi gao" (A Brief History of the Development of the Rong Family as National Capitalists). *Wuxi wenshi ziliao* (Literary and Historical Materials on Wuxi), pt. 1 (May 19, 1980): 53–91; pt. 2 (March 21, 1981): 71–96; pt. 3 (August 30, 1981): 70–91.

Xia Yan. *Baoshengong* (Contract Labor). Beijing: Gongren chubanshe, 1959.

Xiao Zhuwen. "Tianjin Ying Mei yan gongsi de jingji lüeduo" (British-American Tobacco Company's Economic Plunder of Tianjin). *Tianjin wenshi ziliao xuanji* (Collected Literary and Historical Materials on Tianjin) 3 (1979): 166–94.

Xu Weiyong and Huang Hanmin. *Rongjia qiye fazhan shi* (A History of the Rong Family's Enterprises). Beijing: Renmin chubanshe, 1985.

Xue Mingjian. "Banli Shenxin san chang laogong shiye de jingyan" (My Experiences Handling Welfare for Workers in Shenxin's No. 3 Factory). *Jiaoyu yu zhiye* (Education and Vocations) 165 (1935): 333–39; 166 (1935): 411–20.

Yamamoto Jotaro: Denki. Tokyo: Denki hensankai, 1942.

Yamamura Kan'ichi, ed. *Toa shintaisei no senku: Mori Kaku* (Forerunner of a New Order in Asia: Mori Kaku). Tokyo: Mori Kaku denki hensankai, 1940.

Yamazaki Hiroaki. "The Logic of the Formation of General Trading Companies in Japan." In Yonekawa Shin'chi and Yoshihara Hideki, eds., *Business History of General Trading Companies, the International Conference on Business History 13, Proceedings of the Fuji Conference.* Tokyo: University of Tokyo Press, 1987.

Yao Songling. *Zhong hang fuwuji* (My Work at the Bank of China). Taibei: Zhuanji wenxue zazhishe, 1968.

Yeh Wen-hsin. *The Alienated Academy: Culture and Politics in Republican*

China, 1919–1937. Cambridge, Mass.: Council on East Asian Studies, Harvard University, 1990.

Yin Xiyao. "Meifu shiyou gongsi dui dongbei shichang de longduan" (Standard Oil Company's Monopoly of the Market in the Northeast). *Liaoning wenshi ziliao xuanji* (Collected Literary and Historical Materials on Liaoning) 3 (1963): 30–39.

Ying Ziduo and Peng Suiliang. "Ying shang Yaxiya huoyou gongsi zhengduo Chongqing xiaochang" (Seizure of Chongqing's Markets by British Merchants in the Asiatic Petroleum Company). In *Chongqing gong shang shiliao* (Historical Materials on the Industry and Commerce of Chongqing), no. 1. Chongqing: Chongqing chubanshe, 1982. Pp. 140–53.

Yip Hon-ming. "Merchant Capital, the Small Peasant Economy, and Foreign Capitalism: The Case of Weixian, 1900s–1937." Ph.D. dissertation, University of California at Los Angeles, 1988.

Yonekawa Shin'ichi. "University Graduates in Japanese Enterprises before the Second World War." *Business History* 26, no. 2 (July 1984): 193–218.

Yui Tsunehiko. "Development, Organization, and International Competitiveness of Industrial Enterprises in Japan, 1880–1915," *Business and Economic History,* 2d ser., no. 17 (1988): 31–48.

Zhang Jiatuo. "Ludong zhongyanqu sangeyue de guangan" (Impressions of Three Months in the Tobacco Cultivating Region of Eastern Shandong). *Dongfang zazhi* (Eastern Miscellany) 33, no. 6 (June 1936): 109–13.

Zhang Meizhi. "Zhongguo xiandai qiye de jingying xingtai: Yi Liu Hongsheng qiye weili de ge'an yanjiu (1911–1949)" (Management of China's Modern Enterprises: A Case Study of Liu Hongsheng's Enterprises [1911–1949]). M.A. thesis, National Taiwan University, 1987.

Zhang Peide. "Luelun ershiniandai Shanghai de laozi guanxi" (On the Relations between Capital and Labor in Shanghai during the Twenties). In *Shanghai: Tongwang shijie ziqiao* (Shanghai: Gateway to the World), vol. 2. Shanghai: Shanghai shehui kexue chubanshe, 1989. Pp. 18–37.

Zhang Qifu and Wei Heng. *Huochai dawang Liu Hongsheng* (Liu Hongsheng the Match King). Xinxiang, Henan: Henan renmin chubanshe, 1990.

Zhang Tan. "The Origin and Early Development of the Jung Family Business (1896–1922)." Seminar paper, Michigan State University, 1985.

Zhang Weizhen. "Zhang Weizhen tongzhi tan Shanghai wusa yundong" (Comrade Zhang Weizhen Talks about Shanghai's May Thirtieth Movement). *Dangshi yanjiu ziliao* (Research Materials on the Contemporary Period), no. 1. Chengdu: Sichuan renmin chubanshe, 1982.

Zhang Yi. "Meifu huoyou gongsi Guangzhou fengongsi qinli ji jianwen" (Memoirs and Experiences with the Guangzhou Branch of the Standard Oil Company). *Guangzhou wenshi ziliao* (Literary and Historical Materials on Guangzhou) 16 (1965): 1–19.

Zhang Youyi, comp. *Zhongguo jindai nongye shi ziliao dier ji, 1912–1927* (Historical Materials on Modern Chinese Agriculture, second collection, 1912–1927). Beijing: Sanlian shudian, 1957.

Zhang Zhongli (Chang Chungli). "The Development of Foreign Enterprise in

Old China and Its Characteristics: The Case of the British-American Tobacco Company." Paper presented at the University of Washington, July 15, 1982.

Zhenhai xianzhi (Gazetteer of Zhenhai District). 1931.

Zhongguo renmin yinhang (People's Bank of China), comp. *Shanghai qianzhuang shiliao* (Historical Materials on Shanghai's Native Banks). Shanghai: Shanghai renmin chubanshe, 1961.

Zhou Jidong and Huang Ziquan. "Hankou Meifu yanghang jilue" (An Account of the Foreign Firm Standard Oil in Hankou) (1963). Reprinted in *Wuhan gong shang jingji shiliao* (Historical Materials on Industry, Commerce, and the Economy of Wuhan), no. 2. Wuhan: Guogu Hubeisheng xinsheng yinduchang, 1984. Pp. 23–35.

Zhou Zhengang. "Wuhan de Rongjia qiye" (The Rong Family Enterprises in Wuhan). *Dang'an yu lishi* (Archives and History) 5 (1986): 75–80.

Zhu Bangxing, Hu Linge, and Xu Sheng, eds. *Shanghai chanye yu Shanghai zhigong* (Industry and Labor in Shanghai). Hong Kong: Yuandong chubanshe, 1939.

Index

Text:	10/13 Sabon
Display:	Sabon
Composition:	G & S Typesetters, Inc.
Printing and binding:	Edwards Brothers